Jacky Newbrook with Richard Acklam and Araminta Crace

going for Gold

Intermediate

teacher's book

Longman

www.longman.com

Pearson Education Limited
Edinburgh Gate
Harlow
Essex CM20 2JE
England
and Associated Companies throughout the World.

www.longman.com/exams

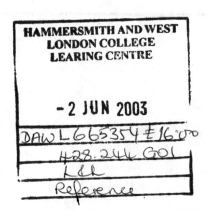

First published 2003

ISBN 0 582 518091

Set in Frutiger 10/13pt

Printed in Spain by Graficas Estella

Acknowledgements
We are grateful to the following for permission to reproduce copyright material:

BBC Worldwide Limited for an extract adapted from *The Human Face* by Brian Bates with John Cleese © Brian Bates and John Cleese 2001; Music Sales Limited and other music publishing companies for the lyrics to "Don't say you love me" recorded by The Corrs, "When you say nothing at all" recorded by Ronan Keating, and "Feelin' so good" recorded by Jennifer Lopez; and Origin Publishing for an extract adapted from "The original female eco-warrior" by Robert Matthews published in *Focus* November 2000.

Illustrated by David Mostyn, Chris Rothero, Harry Venning
Designed by Oxford Designers & Illustrators
Project Managed by Helena Gomm

Contents

Introduction

Profile of an Intermediate student

The students with whom you will be using *Going for Gold Intermediate* will have studied English for around 300 hours. They may have taken or be planning to take the Preliminary English Test (PET) or one or more Certificates in English Language Skills (CELS) at Preliminary level. These exams are based on the Council of Europe Threshold level, or the Common European Framework level B1. Your students may also be intending to take the Cambridge First Certificate in English (FCE) exam after another year or two years of study.

According to the Threshold specifications, Intermediate-level speakers:

- should be able to cope in a range of everyday situations which require a largely predictable use of language.
- should be able to deal with authentic materials, such as public notices, guides and magazine articles.
- should be able to get necessary information from information centres, understand a commentary and ask questions to get more information when travelling abroad.
- should not be expected to deal with technical language.
- if working, can describe their own job area, exchange factual information, receive instructions and deal with telephone messages.
- can write personal letters within a standard format.
- should be able to understand more than just facts from reading and listening texts.

Although success in the Preliminary English Test is a good indicator of later success at FCE, your students may not be interested in taking international exams at this stage, but in improving their English for study or personal reasons.

Intermediate-level students will have met many of the basic **grammatical** areas before, but they may still make fairly basic errors and may have difficulty in using the structures naturally. They will need to revise and practise such familiar grammatical areas as verb tenses, reported speech, etc. and to work on eliminating any errors they may make with basic structures, such as direct questions. It will be necessary to introduce them to some more complex structures such as conditionals.

They may feel that they lack **vocabulary** and they will want to increase the number of words they can recognise and use easily. Basic lexical sets will need to be revised and extended, and they will need to expand their knowledge of word formation and phrasal verbs. They will need help and advice in developing strategies to extend their usable vocabulary, including use of a dictionary and outside reading.

When **speaking**, they will probably have an idea of some of the communicative functions of English, but they may not use them naturally. They may feel that they need a lot of speaking practice to increase their confidence in their own communicative ability. Their pronunciation needs to be clear and comprehensible, although not necessarily perfect! They will be able to manage basic **listening** tasks, such as listening for factual information, but they may have some difficulty with more abstract texts. When they are **reading**, they should be able to extract specific information, but they will need help in handling more complex tasks such as identifying the structure of a text, identifying reference and inferring meaning from context.

They will have had practice in **writing** various text types, such as letters, but they may need help in editing and identifying errors so that they can improve the accuracy of their work. They will also need to work on a greater variety of writing task types, such as memos, notes and articles.

An Intermediate course should consolidate, refine and extend what students already know, provide them with techniques for continuing to learn and provide help with specific techniques required by any exams they may choose to take. During an Intermediate course, students should be developing their own study skills and strategies for improving their own language ability. They should be thinking about ways of recording vocabulary that suit their own learning style, doing further grammar work to build on what is done in the

Coursebook, and identifying other ways of continuing to learn after the course.

The table below gives a general overview of the Common European Framework levels and the Cambridge main suite and CELS exams, and where the *Going for Gold* and *Gold* series fits into this.

Common European Framework level	Guided Learning Hours from beginner	Cambridge ESOL Main suite exams	Cambridge ESOL Certificates in English Language Skills (CELS)	Gold series
A2	Approx. 180–200	KET (Key English Test)		
B1	Approx. 350–400	PET (Preliminary English Test)	CELS Preliminary	Going for Gold Intermediate
B2	Approx. 500–600	FCE (First Certificate in English)	CELS Vantage	Going for Gold Upper Intermediate / First Certificate Gold
C1	Approx. 700–800	CAE (Certificate in Advanced English)	CELS Higher	Advanced Gold
C2	Approx. 1,000–2,000	CPE (Certificate of Proficiency in English		NEW Proficiency Gold

Features of the *Going for Gold* course

Going for Gold is a two-level Intermediate and Upper Intermediate course designed to develop students' language skills and provide a gradual introduction to the requirements of the Cambridge PET and FCE exams. *Going for Gold Intermediate* is suitable for PET preparation, particularly if used with the *PET Gold Exam Maximiser*. *Going for Gold Upper-Intermediate* is the perfect lead-in to *First Certificate Gold*. *Going for Gold* may also be used with students wishing to sit the Cambridge Certificates in English Language Skills.

The components of the *Going for Gold Intermediate* course include: *Going for Gold Intermediate Coursebook*, class cassettes and CDs; *Going for Gold Intermediate Language Maximiser*, cassettes or audio CDs, and this *Teacher's Book*.

Also available is the *PET Gold Exam Maximiser*, which may be used as well as or instead of the *Going for Gold Intermediate Language Maximiser* with students planning to take PET. In full colour, the *PET Gold Exam*

Maximiser provides comprehensive exam training for the PET as well as revision and practice of key grammar and vocabulary tested in the exam. It may also be used on its own as an intensive short course for the PET.

Going for Gold Intermediate Coursebook

Organisation of the Coursebook

The *Going for Gold Intermediate Coursebook* progressively develops students' competence in all areas of language through 15 graded units. At the same time, graded tasks of the type found in the Cambridge PET and FCE exams provide students with a gradual introduction to the requirements of the exams. Units 1–7 contain PET style tasks, while Units 8–15 move on to include tasks in FCE format. The different task types are labelled in the Teacher's Book.

Units 3, 6, 9 and 12 are each followed by a *Progress check*, which reviews students' knowledge of the language presented in the previous units. The Progress checks include exercises in graded PET and FCE exam format.

Each unit in the *Going for Gold Intermediate Coursebook* provides an integrated package containing the presentation and practice of grammar and vocabulary as well as the four skills, all linked to a theme.

In addition to the units themselves, at the back of the *Going for Gold Intermediate Coursebook* you will find a unit by unit *Grammar reference*, a *Writing reference* and *Communication activities*. The Grammar reference summarises and gives examples of the grammar points presented in each unit. The Writing reference is divided into two sections. Section A provides help with the basics of writing, including how to construct accurate sentences, paragraphing, spelling and punctuation. Section B provides model answers for all the types of writing taught in the course (informal letters, stories, compositions, reports, articles) together with Dos and Don'ts and useful language.

Grammar

Various different approaches are used for the presentation and practice of grammar points. Structures to be presented are often taken from authentic texts used previously in the unit, and then presented through analysis of errors or matching rules to examples. This is followed by a number of controlled practice activities, both spoken and written, and freer practice activities where students can use the target structure for themselves in writing or speaking. The Teacher's Book provides notes and suggestions for procedures for dealing with the grammar sections and there are cross-references in the Coursebook to the relevant sections of the Grammar reference.

Vocabulary

A variety of presentation and practice techniques is used in *Going for Gold*. The vocabulary work puts words into a context, and often links them to lexical sets which give the students key topic vocabulary. There is also work on word formation.

The practice activities provide students with techniques for organising vocabulary in different ways as well as giving them the chance to use the words they have learned in speaking or writing. There is an emphasis on dictionary work, and on ways of recording vocabulary.

Reading

This symbol ⚡ highlights general ways of dealing with particular types of reading tasks.

Authentic texts used in the Coursebook are taken from a range of sources (newspapers, magazines, etc.) and many texts have photographs or illustrations, which can be used as a way of getting students interested in the topic of the text or predicting the content. A wide variety of real-life reading skills are presented and practised, including guessing unknown words through context. Where the skills are tested in an international exam, this is highlighted in the Teacher's Book and suggestions are made for helping students deal with this exam task.

There are often discussion tasks following the reading texts to allow students to discuss the topic further and to enable them to use and remember key vocabulary from the text.

Listening

The listening texts are taken from a range of sources, and the recordings present students with a variety of (mild) accents. Key vocabulary is often presented before students listen, and there are activities providing practice in the key skills areas of listening for specific information, listening for gist and inferring meaning. The ⚡ symbol highlights general ways of dealing with particular types of listening tasks.

There are also some songs, which provide further skills practice as well as the opportunity for students to listen for pleasure.

Writing

Writing activities reflect real-life tasks, including some of those expected in the international exams. There is support for students in completing the tasks, including vocabulary, planning and editing. The Writing reference at the back of the Coursebook also provides help in all these areas, including models and exercises. Students are encouraged to work together to help each other to correct their work, to enable them to develop their editing skills. There is a marking scheme suggested in the Teaching procedures section on page 10 which will also encourage students to develop their editing skills.

Speaking

The grammar, vocabulary, reading, listening and writing sections all provide opportunities for speaking practice through pair and group work. This may be controlled or free practice. There are also specific speaking practice activities in each unit, and further speaking practice in some of the photocopiable activities. The teacher's notes also suggest some further speaking practice where appropriate.

There is an emphasis on communicative language and strategies, and students are encouraged to respond to what is said to them so that their conversations sound natural.

Watch Out! boxes

These are designed to pick up on mistakes that are commonly made by Intermediate students. They are often language points that have already been taught at lower levels, but which students continue to find difficult. The boxes also identify possible problem areas with new structures so that students are less likely to have difficulty with them. The boxes are interactive, making it easier for students to remember the point.

Grammar reference

Students are referred to the Grammar reference throughout *Going for Gold Intermediate Coursebook*. They should use it for revision and for checking when they are not clear on a grammatical point. They should be encouraged to develop the habit of checking for themselves, as this will foster independence and make it easier for them to continue learning after the course.

Writing reference

The writing reference is an important component of the course.

Section A provides help with basic writing skills. Short tasks check students' understanding of these skills, so the section can be used for teaching as well as reference.

Section B provides model answers for each of the text types in the course, and students can refer to these for guidance when they meet a new text type.

Going for Gold Intermediate Language Maximiser

The other major component of *Going for Gold Intermediate* is the *Going for Gold Language Maximiser*. Working through the exercises in the Language Maximiser will help students consolidate and extend the language and skills presented in the Coursebook. The Language Maximiser is available in two versions, with or without key. The key contains answers to all the exercises, and tapescripts for speaking and listening tasks. Cassettes or audio CDs are available, containing all the listening material.

Organisation of the Language Maximiser

The Language Maximiser consists of 15 units which correspond thematically to the Coursebook. Each unit provides extensive consolidation and extension of grammar and vocabulary covered in the Coursebook unit. There is also further practice of writing to support the relevant section in each Coursebook unit. Speaking sections consolidate and practise functions presented in the Coursebook, such as expressing opinions, negotiating and coming to a decision.

In addition, the Language Maximiser provides eight further topic-related reading tasks and eight listening tasks.

Using the Language Maximiser

The Language Maximiser can be used in class as a means of providing immediate follow-up work for grammar and vocabulary or writing. Alternatively, students can do the appropriate exercises for homework. The additional reading, listening and speaking practice can also be done in class or for additional practice at home.

Going for Gold Intermediate Teacher's Book

This Teacher's Book provides guidance on how to use the material in the Coursebook effectively. The section on *Teaching procedures and advice* (p. 8) suggests general approaches to the different sections of the course and ways to deal with the different skills components.

The general aims of each unit section are explained at the start, to facilitate lesson planning. Exam information boxes indicate when activities and tasks provide relevant training and practice for PET, FCE or CELS. Teaching tips show how approaches to exam-type tasks in the classroom can also help students with improving their general language ability.

Answers to all exercises in the Coursebook are found at the end of each section of notes. Explanations of right/wrong answers are often provided, where helpful. The recording scripts for all the listening tasks in the units are at the back of the Teacher's Book so that they can be photocopied easily if you want to use them with your students.

At the back of the Teacher's Book you will also find a section of photocopiable activities, which provide extra communicative practice in key skills areas. These are linked to the units and provide extra practice of an important area presented in the unit. Detailed teaching notes state the aims and rationale of each photocopiable activity, and provide a step-by-step procedure for using them in class.

You will also find a bank of 15 photocopiable tests, including 10 Unit tests and five Progress tests. The Progress tests are to be used after your students have completed Units 3, 6, 9, 12 and 15. These revise and test the material covered in the previous three units. The Unit tests consist of exercises which test the material covered in a single unit. They are easy to administer and should take no more than 30 minutes for students to complete. The Progress tests should take about one hour to complete. Answer keys to the tests are provided and students can correct their own work if you prefer.

Teaching procedures and advice

General approach

The *Going for Gold Intermediate Coursebook* aims to develop students' overall language knowledge and ability to cope in general situations. Described below are suggested procedures for dealing with grammar, vocabulary and skills. The unit-by-unit notes contain further specific suggestions for activities where appropriate, together with suggestions as to when to use the photocopiable activities at the end of this Teacher's Book. The Coursebook also aims to train the skills and techniques required by the PET, FCE and CELS exams, and there are exercises in exam format and exam hints.

Checking answers

When checking answers to work done in any section of the Coursebook, it is a good idea to follow the same approach.

- Encourage students to work in pairs wherever possible so that they have to justify and explain their answers to each other. This makes them refer back to the reading text, listening text or grammar explanation, and may often help them to see whether they have made a mistake.
- If students have been working alone, then allow them to compare their answers before checking them with the whole class so that they have to explain and justify their answers.
- When checking answers with the class, always discuss wrong answers as this helps students to see how to find the correct answer.

General procedures for reading

Useful real-life reading skills developed in *Going for Gold Intermediate Coursebook* include:

- understanding main ideas and details
- inferring writer's attitude or opinion
- identifying the purpose of a text

- guessing the meaning of unknown words and phrases through context
- understanding text organisation.

These are also key skills areas for the PET, FCE and CELS exams.

Students should be encouraged to use what they know – layout, style, headings, title – to help them to deal with any unknown parts of a text **before** they start to read. To help them do this, it is a good idea to start by getting an overall impression of a text before looking at different parts of it in detail. The Coursebook provides pre-reading activities to train students to approach texts in this way.

Some possible ways of approaching a reading text include:

- introducing the topic of the text in a general discussion before students open their books. This will arouse their interest in the text, and may elicit some of the key vocabulary and ideas so that the text will be easier for them to read.
- encouraging students to notice the layout and to use the title of any text to get an idea of the text type and to predict the content.
- telling students to skim through the text to check their predictions and to get a general idea of content, purpose and how the text is organised.

Make sure that students understand the task and what they have to do. Explain that the reading skills used are different for each different exercise, and encourage them to talk about the approach they could take to each reading task.

When you are reading a text in class, it is a good idea to set a time limit. This will make it easier to deal with the task in class, and it will also start to develop students' confidence in dealing with a variety of reading tasks in a limited time, as in exams.

Decide whether you want to allow students to use dictionaries in class. Learning to use a dictionary correctly is a valuable skill and enables the students to work on other texts outside class without the help of a teacher. (If the task includes working out the meaning of words from context, then obviously dictionaries should not be used.)

General procedures for vocabulary development

Students at this level often feel that they need more vocabulary work, and the Coursebook has many sections providing key topic vocabulary. Words are always given a context, so that students can see how they are actually used.

Encourage students to work out the meaning of words for themselves wherever possible, and to recognise and work out contextualised clues. They will gain confidence if they realise that they do not need to understand every single word in a text, and that they can often work out the meaning of the important key items for themselves.

Encourage students to use a monolingual dictionary rather than a bilingual dictionary, as this will help them to avoid direct translation. They should use a good monolingual dictionary such as the *Longman WordWise Dictionary*, which gives information not only about meaning but also about grammar and pronunciation, and provides examples of possible contexts.

Encourage students to think about the best ways of recording vocabulary. Remind them that it is better not to write down single words, but to link them to phrases or put them in sentences. They could:
- use index cards, with example sentences.
- use a notebook and record vocabulary under topics, e.g. words connected with travel. This is especially useful for exam work: the PET exam has a clear topic list.
- use a spidergram to give a visual picture of how words fit together. This may help them to remember the words more easily.

Some suggestions for reviewing vocabulary in class
- Develop a routine of starting each lesson by asking students to recall five new words or phrases they learned in the previous lesson. If they do this in small groups, this will increase the number of words discussed and remembered. Each group could then report their words back to the class.
- Write some words from an earlier unit on the board and ask students to write a two-line dialogue or short story using these words in a natural way. They could read their dialogues to the class or to another pair.

- Write some key words on pieces of paper and put these into a box. Ask individual students (or pairs of students) to pick out a word and then use that word in a sentence. The class can say if the word was used correctly or not.

General procedures for listening

Pre-listening tasks in the Coursebook help students to predict the content of what they will hear. As with reading activities, it is easier if students have an idea of what the task is about.
- Introduce the topic of the text in a general discussion before students listen, to arouse their interest. The discussion may also elicit some key vocabulary and ideas that will make the listening task easier for them.
- Remind students to read through the task before they listen, to help them predict what they might hear.
- After playing the recording once, encourage students to compare their answers. This will help them to understand and explain what they've heard, and will also reinforce skills they need for exams.
- Use the tapescripts if students have real difficulty with the listening, but only as a follow-up activity. If you do allow students to read the tapescript, then play the recording while they follow it (stopping at any points where they had particular difficulty). Then finish the lesson by taking the tapescript away and playing the recording again to reinforce the target listening skill.
- After completing any listening tasks, ask follow-up discussion questions so that students can react to the topic and give their opinions. There are suggestions in the Coursebook for these questions.

General procedures for presenting and practising grammar

In the Coursebook, grammar is always presented in a context. There are tasks which activate students' understanding of the rules for using the target structure, and opportunities for further practice. Ask students to check their answers with each other before you go through them with the whole class, and encourage them to use the Grammar reference for themselves. This will make them more independent of the teacher and help them to develop their own strategies for continued learning.

General procedures for writing

Encourage students to use the Writing reference section in the Coursebook, as this provides help with key writing skills, such as spelling and text organisation as well as model answers for different types of writing.

Students should be encouraged to follow the following procedure whenever they do any written task:

- Read the question or task and highlight any key words and instructions on what to include.
- Think about the topic and make notes. Make a plan.
- Expand the notes into the full writing task.
- Read the finished writing through to check that it makes sense and is clear. Check carefully for spelling, punctuation and other mistakes.

Encourage students to exchange their writing for other students to check – this will help them to develop their own editing skills. When students write in class, encourage them to work in pairs for the same reason.

When you mark students' written work, it will encourage them to edit and evaluate their own work if you use the correction code that follows. Underline the part of the sentence where the mistake is and write the appropriate code at the end of the line. Go through the code at the beginning of the course and make sure that the students understand what it means. After that they should be able to correct their own work.

Correction code

Vf = verb form, e.g. My father always <u>play</u> football on Saturdays.

Vt = verb tense, e.g. Last year I <u>have visited</u> France.

Ww = wrong word, e.g. We arrived <u>to</u> the meeting five minutes early.

Wo = word order, e.g. I <u>do usually</u> my homework in the evening.

G = grammar, e.g. Why <u>you not tell</u> me you were Italian?

Sp = spelling, e.g. I like going out with my <u>freinds</u>.

P = punctuation, e.g. Do you like tea<u>!</u>

? = meaning or handwriting not clear, e.g. I went to London next week.

^ = missing word, e.g. I wrote an <u>email my</u> friend yesterday.

General procedures for speaking

The fluency activities in the Coursebook are a very important part of the course, and students should be given time to complete them. There are three ways of dealing with these speaking activities:

- as a whole class
- in pairs
- in groups.

The teaching notes for individual units provide suggestions on the best approach to take with different speaking tasks. When the task mirrors an exam task then it is a good idea to do it in pairs, as in the exam.

There are also short speaking sections at the end of many listening or reading tasks, where students are asked for their opinions on what they have heard or read. These provide an ideal opportunity for students to use new vocabulary in a meaningful and productive way.

Encourage students to respond to what others say, and teach strategies for moving conversations along. There is help in the Coursebook with this, and there are also suggested activities in the teaching notes for individual units and extra photocopiable activities.

Try not to 'assess' students when they are doing a speaking activity. Instead, monitor their mistakes and go through the mistakes with the whole class, either immediately after the activity or in a later lesson. Don't say who made the errors. Alternatively, you could write a worksheet with sentences containing the errors and use it as a class diagnostic activity or short test later.

There is pronunciation work in the Coursebook and some extra practice in the photocopiable activities. When you write new words on the board, you could encourage students to mark the stress on the words, to develop their awareness of the importance of this aspect of pronunciation.

Overview of the PET, FCE and CELS exams

The PET exam

The PET exam tests the use of language in real-life situations in Reading, Writing, Listening and Speaking. The exam is based on the Council of Europe Threshold Level (Common European Framework B1, ALTE Level 2), and is approximately two-thirds of the way towards the First Certificate in English.

Aims of PET

PET reflects the use of language in real life. It corresponds closely to an active and communicative approach to learning English, while still placing importance on clarity and accuracy. The successful PET candidate should be able to communicate satisfactorily in most everyday situations with both native and non-native speakers of English. This aim corresponds to the recommendations of the Council of Europe's Threshold Specification (Common European Framework B1).

Assessment and marking

In the exam the four skills are tested in three papers. Each component carries 25% of the final mark. The actual scores are weighted to achieve this balance. There is no minimum pass mark for individual papers. There are two passing grades, Pass with Merit (approximately 85% of the total mark) and Pass (approximately 70% of the total mark). There are also two failing grades, Narrow Fail (within 5% of Pass mark) and Fail.

Paper 1 Reading and Writing 1 hour 30 mins

The *Reading* paper has five parts. There are 35 questions and each question has one mark. The student score is then converted to a final mark out of 25.

Part 1	Multiple-choice questions	5 questions	Students read notices, signs or messages and decide what they mean.
Part 2	Matching descriptions to texts	5 questions	Students read descriptions of people and match them to appropriate holidays, books, etc.
Part 3	True/false	10 questions	Students read a factual text and decide if statements are true or false.
Part 4	Multiple-choice questions	5 questions	Students choose the best answer to questions with four options.
Part 5	Multiple-choice cloze	10 questions	Students choose the best word to fill a gap in a text from four options.

The *Writing* paper has three parts.
Part 1 has 5 questions and 5 marks.
Part 2 is marked out of 5.
Part 3 is marked out of 15.

Part 1	Transformations	5 questions	Students rewrite five sentences.
Part 2	Short communicative message	35–45 words	Students write short messages, giving three pieces of information.
Part 3	Continuous writing – an informal letter or story	100 words	Students choose to write either an informal letter or a story.

Paper 2 Listening 30 mins

The Listening paper has four parts with 25 questions. There is one mark for each question.

Part 1	Multiple-choice questions based on pictures	7 questions	Students listen to seven short recordings and identify the relevant picture from a choice of four.
Part 2	Multiple-choice questions	6 questions	Students listen to a monologue or an interview with one main speaker.
Part 3	Note-taking	6 questions	Students listen to a monologue and fill in missing information.
Part 4	True/false	6 questions	Students listen to an informal conversation and decide whether statements are true or false.

Paper 3 Speaking 10–12 mins

There are four parts with 30 marks weighted to 25. The Speaking test involves two examiners and two candidates. One examiner asks the questions (the interlocutor) and the other is the assessor. The assessor does not take part in the conversation. Students are assessed throughout the Speaking test on their language skills, not on their knowledge of the world.

Part 1		2–3 mins	Questions and answers on personal information between candidates and interlocutor.
Part 2 Shared task		2–3 mins	Students work on a shared task based on visual prompts.
Part 3 Individual long turn		3 mins	Each candidate speaks alone about a photograph.
Part 4 Discussion		3 mins	The candidates discuss a topic related to the photographs in Part 3.

Note: In the PET exam, the consistent use of American pronunciation, spelling and vocabulary is acceptable.

The FCE exam

The FCE exam tests the use of language skills in Reading, Writing, Listening and Speaking in real-life situations. The exam falls within level 3 of the ALTE framework (Common European Framework B2).

Aims of FCE

Success at FCE may be used as proof that the student can work or study in English. It is widely recognised in commerce and industry, and for entry to some universities.

Assessment and marking

In the exam, the four skills components are tested in five papers with a total of 200 marks. Each paper is weighted to 40 marks. There is no minimum pass mark for individual papers and the overall FCE grade is based on the total score gained in all five papers. There are three passing grades, A, B and C, and three failing grades, D, E and U. A Grade C pass corresponds to about 60% of the total mark.

Paper 1 Reading 1 hour 15 mins

The Reading paper has four parts. There are 35 questions. Questions in Parts 1, 2 and 3 carry two marks and questions in Part 4 carry one mark.

Part 1	Multiple matching	6 or 7 questions	Students match a prompt from a list to a prompt in another list, or to elements in a text.
Part 2	Multiple choice	7 or 8 questions	Students read a text and answer four-option multiple-choice questions.
Part 3	Gapped text	6 or 7 questions	Students reconstruct a text, replacing sentences or paragraphs that have been removed.
Part 4	Multiple matching	13 or 15 questions	As Part 1

Paper 2 Writing 1 hour 30 mins

The Writing paper has two parts, and candidates have to complete two tasks. Part 1 is compulsory. In Part 2 students choose one task from four. Each question carries equal marks.

Part 1	Transactional letter	Compulsory task, 120–180 words	Students read input material which may include ads, letters, diaries, etc. and write a letter.
Part 2	Students choose from: an article a non-transactional letter a report a discursive composition a descriptive/ narrative short story. In Q5 students can choose to write about a set text, using one of the formats above.	Students choose one task from four, 120–180 words. Q5 has two options.	

Paper 3 Use of English 1 hour 15 minutes

There are five parts with 65 questions. Questions 31–40 carry two marks.

Part 1	Multiple-choice cloze	15 questions	Students choose from four options for each gap.
Part 2	Open cloze	15 questions	Students fill in gaps in a text.
Part 3	'Key' word sentence transformations	10 questions	Students complete a sentence using a given word.
Part 4	Error correction	15 questions	Students identify lines in a text which contain extra or grammatically incorrect words.
Part 5	Word formation	10 questions	Students change the form of a given word to complete a sentence.

Paper 4 Listening 40 mins

The Listening paper has four parts with 30 questions. There is one mark for each question.

Part 1	Multiple-choice questions (3 options)	8 questions	Students listen to short dialogues or monologues and answer multiple-choice questions.
Part 2	Note-taking	10 questions	Students listen to a dialogue or monologue and fill in missing information.
Part 3	Multiple matching	5 questions	Students listen to a series of unrelated short extracts and choose options from a list of six.
Part 4	Choice of task from T/false, yes/no, which speaker said what, etc.	7 questions	Students listen to a monologue or dialogue.

Paper 5 Speaking 14 mins

The Speaking test involves two examiners and two candidates and there are four parts. One examiner asks the questions (the interlocutor) and the other is the assessor. The assessor does not take part in the conversation. As with PET, students are assessed throughout the Speaking test on their language skills, not on their knowledge of the world.

Part 1 Interview	3 mins	The interlocutor interviews the candidates.
Part 2 Individual long turn	4 mins	Each candidate speaks alone for about a minute, then their partner reacts to what they have said.
Part 3 Collaborative task	3 mins	Candidates work together to discuss a task.
Part 4 Three-way discussion	4 mins	Discussion including the interlocutor.

Note: In the FCE exam, the use of American pronunciation, spelling and vocabulary is acceptable.

The CELS exams

The aim of the CELS exams is to assess a candidate's language competence through a variety of authentic tasks using authentic texts. Students can take the exams at different levels in different skills, and gain a certificate for what they can do rather than being penalised for what they can't do. CELS is offered at three levels, Preliminary (Common European Framework B1, ALTE Level 2) and equivalent to PET, Vantage (Common European Framework B2, ALTE Level 3) and equivalent to FCE and Higher (Common European Framework C1, ALTE Level 4) and equivalent to CAE.

Each test consists of one paper at each level.

Reading

The task focus is the same at all levels. The aim of the test is to assess the candidate's ability to read a variety of authentic texts, using skills found in reading in daily contexts. The text types include advertisements, forms, letters, leaflets, newspapers, magazines, diaries and timetables. The skills tested include:
- locating and understanding specific information
- understanding the overall message of a text
- recognising emotion and attitude of the writer
- reacting to information in a text.

At Vantage and Higher levels, candidates may also have to:
- decide what a text is based on – fact or opinion
- understand implication
- identify accurate summary of information
- trace the development of an argument.

At all levels there is a balance of multiple-choice and open questions.

Preliminary 1 hour 20 minutes
Vantage 1 hour 40 minutes
Higher 2 hours

Parts	Task focus
1	skimming/scanning
2	use of discourse markers, referencing
3	detailed comprehension

Writing

This tests the candidate's ability to write in various real-life contexts such as employment, education and training. The tasks reflect real-life situations and test a wide range of writing skills and styles. There is always a specified target reader to establish a purpose for writing. Separate papers are set at the three levels, and the task is as authentic as possible.

Preliminary 1 hour 10 minutes – two tasks
Vantage 1 hour 40 minutes – three tasks
Higher 2 hours 10 minutes – four tasks
Task types include:
Preliminary – form, letter, fax, message, note, postcard, set of instructions
Vantage and Higher – as Preliminary + summary, CV, memo, report, article, biography, proposal, advertisement.

Listening

This test assesses a candidate's language competence though a variety of tasks that reflect real-life situations. There is a specified context to give a purpose for listening.
Preliminary – 30 minutes + 7 minutes' transfer time to an answer paper
Vantage – 33 minutes + 7 minutes' transfer time
Higher – 37 minutes + 7 minutes' transfer time

Parts	Task types	Text type
1 (30 items)	Productive tasks, e.g. sentence/note completion, short answers, error correction	Short, factual informational monologues
2 (35 items)	Productive tasks, e.g. sentence completion, correcting factual information	Discursive
3 (40 items)	Objective tasks, e.g. multiple-choice questions, true/false questions, ordering information	Discursive

Text types may include: weather reports, news reports, sports reports, phone-ins, quizzes, interviews, public announcements, lectures/talks.

Speaking

The test takes place with two candidates and two examiners (interlocutor and assessor), and is divided into two parts. In the first part, candidates speak directly to the interlocutor, and in the second part they discuss something together and then with the interlocutor. Each paired test lasts 20 minutes.

Part 1 Candidates choose a topic to talk about alone and have $1\frac{1}{2}$ minutes to prepare. They then talk individually with the Interlocutor for seven minutes on the topic they have chosen.

Part 2 Candidates choose a topic to talk about together and have $1\frac{1}{2}$ minutes to prepare. They then discuss the topic together for four minutes and then continue the discussion with the interlocutor for four minutes on the topic they have chosen.

UNIT 1 A question of family

Reading 1 p. 4

Aims:
- **to introduce the theme of the unit**
- **to help students to predict the content of a reading passage**
- **to help students identify specific information**

Exam information PET CELS

In the Reading paper of the PET and CELS exams, students have to read statements and decide if they are true or false. In the CELS they have to decide if the information is true, false or not given.

Teaching tip

Using the technique of predicting the content of a text before actually reading it makes all reading texts easier to handle. Students can be encouraged to do this regularly, by using the title or layout of a text, or by reading the first paragraph and predicting what the rest of the text might be about.

---

1 Students could discuss this exercise in pairs. The connections are family ones. Picture A shows Sophie Dahl, a supermodel, who is the granddaughter of the novelist Roald Dahl, shown in picture D. He is now dead but he wrote well-known children's stories including *Charlie and the Chocolate Factory* and *The BFG*. Picture B shows the supermodel Kate Moss and Picture C is her brother Nick Moss.

2 Remind students that Sophie Dahl is now a famous well-paid model. She is well-known for not being exceptionally thin as many other models are. Explain that the text is made up of questions and answers, and ask them to think of questions they would like to ask her. Suggestions:
How did she start modelling?
Does she enjoy it?
How did she get on with her grandfather?

What was her childhood like?
Predicting what the questions might be makes it easier for students to understand the general content of a text when they first read it.

3 Ask students to look at the questions in the text. When they have finished reading them, ask them to tell you how many of the questions were the same as theirs. Were the other questions less interesting than theirs?

4 This true/false exercise focuses on specific detail in the text. Ask students to work in pairs. Then check answers with the whole class.

5 This speaking exercise personalises the content for students.

ANSWERS

Ex. 4
1 false   2 true   3 true   4 false   5 false
6 false   7 true   8 true

Vocabulary 1: working out meaning from context p. 5

Aims:
- **to start students thinking about the value of guessing the meaning of a word from its context**
- **to give them practice in using this skill**

1 This is important learner training. The discussion starts students thinking about how they approach reading. Make sure that they talk about each option in each question and don't just choose an answer quickly. Give them enough time to discuss the questions and think about their choices in pairs.

Check question 4 as a class discussion so that every student has a chance to understand the point of the exercise.

There are obviously no 'right' answers to questions 1 and 2 but students may be interested in what the others say. Discuss the potential problems with the options in question 3:

A: They might not understand the meaning of the text.

B: They will not get a sense of the tone or 'flow' of the text.

C: They may not know which are the 'important' words.

D: They may need to check in a dictionary whether they are right.

It is important that they understand that options C and D are both more useful to their language learning than either A or B. Option D would be the best choice.

2   Ask students to do this exercise in pairs. When they have finished, ask them which words they found most difficult and discuss why. This will help them to develop the confidence not to use a dictionary each time they don't understand a word.

Point out that words like *terribly* can mean different things in different contexts, so even if they use a dictionary they will need to choose the best meaning from several for the particular text they are reading.

3   This follow-up exercise could be set for homework.

▶ Photocopiable Activities 1A and 1B pp. 168 and 169.

ANSWERS

Ex. 2
spotted – seen
huge – very big
dreadful – very bad
terribly – a lot
guy – man

See also: *Going for Gold Language Maximiser* Unit 1.

Grammar 1: questions (1) p. 6

Aims:
- **to focus students' attention on question forms**
- **to give practice in asking and answering questions in PET exam format**

Exam information PET FCE

In Part 1 of the PET and FCE Speaking papers, students will have to ask and answer questions about personal information such as hobbies, family and occupation. In the PET exam, they will also have to spell a word, which may be their name, the place where they live or any other word they may have to spell in real life.

Teaching tip

It is a good idea for students intending to take the PET exam to practise these questions and areas of discussion regularly during the course so that they become very familiar and confident with them.

---

1   Students should work in pairs to complete the questions. Check their answers before going on to the listening. Remind them that they can check the Grammar reference on p. 136 if they need to.

2   Give students enough time to practise in Exercise 2.3, and check their pronunciation of the alphabet again at the end.

➡ Tapescript p. 101

3 , **4** , **5**   These exercises all provide preparation for the PET Speaking paper. Students should do them in pairs, and change partners for Exercise 5 to give maximum practice.

ANSWERS

Ex. 1
1 What   2 How   3 Where   4 What
5 How many   6 How often   7 When
8 How long   9 Why   10 How much
11 What   12 Who   13 Whose

Ex. 2
1 Aitchison   2 Roxburgh   3 Olearski

Ex. 3
home town: Where are you living at the
    moment?

---

school: How much does it cost to travel to your school from your home by public transport?

job: What do you do?

free time: How often do you go to the cinema? When did you last see a band live? Who is one of your favourite actors at the moment?

holidays: Which country would you most like to go on holiday to?

learning English: How long have you been learning English? Why are you learning English?

family: How many brothers and sisters have you got? (In your family) Whose views do you most respect and listen to?

See also: *Going for Gold Language Maximiser* Unit 1.

Listening p. 6

Aims:

• **to train students to identify specific information while listening**

Exam information PET

In Part 1 of the PET Listening paper, students have to listen to seven short conversations or monologues and identify which picture of four relates to what they hear. The recording is played twice.

---

1   This discussion about the pictures prepares students for the type of information they will hear in the Listening paper and for question 1. Do it with the whole class. For Exercise 1.2, play the recording twice. When you check the answers, point out that students did not need to understand every word as the information was given in one or two key words – in this case, the numbers. Tell them that there will always be such key words in this type of listening.

➡ Tapescript p. 101

2   Look at each question in Exercise 2. Ask students what type of key word they will listen for, e.g.

1 time
2 present, dad (there may be several presents mentioned, or presents for another person)
3 activity, tonight (names of different activities – there may be another day mentioned)

4 words for describing people
5 different forms of transport and ways of getting to school

3   Play the recording twice. Check the answers and then ask students to tell you what key words they were listening for.

➡ Tapescript p. 101

ANSWERS

Ex. 1
She has one brother and one sister.
Picture C matches her description.
Students did not need to understand every word, only the key words.

Ex. 2
1 the time
2 names of possible presents
3 names of evening activities
4 words for describing people
5 ways of getting to school

Ex. 3
1 A   2 C   3 C   4 A   5 C

Vocabulary 2: family and friends p. 7

Aims:

• **to provide topic vocabulary**
• **to give students ideas about the topic through discussion**

1   Go through the family tree with the whole class so that they all understand how it works. Then ask them to work in groups of three or four to explain the differences between their own families and Paula's.

2 , **3**   Students could stay in the same groups to do Exercises 2 and 3 so that they can check their answers together. Tell them to practise saying the words aloud.

4   Students should think by themselves for a moment about the people they want to talk about. Then they should work with a partner and talk to them about the people they have chosen.

5   This discussion could be done in the same groups as Exercise 1 or as a general class discussion.

You could also use the first question as the basis for a formal debate. Divide the class into halves. Tell group A that they have to think of the advantages, and group B that they should think of the disadvantages of the given statement. Then write the statement on the board:

There are more advantages than disadvantages in being an only child.

Give students five minutes to think of ideas. Then choose a representative from each group to make a short statement about the ideas they have thought of. Then ask all students to join the discussion.

At the end, ask the class to vote on whether they agree or disagree with the statement.

ANSWERS

Ex. 2

1 cousin   2 grandfather   3 niece
4 stepmother   5 sister-in-law   6 aunt
7 widow

Ex. 3

grandfather – grandmother
aunt – uncle
cousin – cousin
sister-in-law – brother-in-law
father-in-law – mother-in-law
niece – nephew
widow – widower
stepmother – stepfather

Speaking p. 8

Aims:
• **to extend ideas introduced in the unit**

Exam information PET

This section provides practice for Part 4 of the PET Speaking paper, in which students have to talk about different aspects of a given topic, which is related to a photograph they have already described.

---

1   Focus attention on the photograph and encourage students to think of as many reasons as possible why they like (or don't like) this sort of occasion. This will help them with the listening, and with ideas for the topic.

2   Tell students to listen only for who likes this type of occasion, and not to listen for detail this time. Play the recording once.

➡ Tapescript p. 101

3   Ask students to listen for details and to fill in the missing words in the expressions. Play the recording again. Discuss which expressions are the strongest.

Play the recording again for students to listen and repeat.

➡ Tapescript p. 101

4   Ask students to work in pairs and to use their own ideas from Exercise 1 to discuss the topic. They should ask each other about what they like or don't like as well as giving their own opinions.

ANSWERS

Ex. 2
Katia

Ex. 3
1 love (very strong)
2 quite like (not very strong)
3 really like (strong)

Writing 1: short answers p. 9

Aims:
• **to focus on the real-life task of filling in a form**
• **to help students to see what information is required**
• **to check for spelling and punctuation mistakes**

1   Ask students to read through the form and decide what type of information is required for each space. Tell them not to fill in any answers yet.

2   Ask students to work with a partner to discuss the two extracts. Alternatively, do this with the whole class so that all the students can see the differences clearly. Remind them that the Writing reference on p. 151 will help them with spelling.

3 , **4** , **5**   For Exercises 3 and 4, ask students to work alone and to think of their own answers before they work with a partner. Exercise 5 could be set for homework, so that students have the chance to revise the work done in class later.

ANSWERS

Ex. 2

1 Extract A is not good.
2 Extract A has problems with: punctuation (capital letters for *Italian* and *August*); spelling (*Italian, August, student, secondary*); unnecessary complete sentences (I born on ...); unnecessary information (I am in my last year ...).

Grammar 2: indirect questions p. 9

Aims:

- **to introduce the form of indirect questions**
- **to provide speaking practice of indirect questions**

1   Do this with the whole class so that students understand the difference between direct and indirect questions (indirect questions are usually polite).

2, **3**   Ask students to work in pairs. Explain that there may be more than one possible answer. Go over all the possibilities when you check the answers.

4   Explain that students should use indirect questions when they are speaking to strangers as in the given situations. Ask them what they might say for the first situation to give them ideas. Write suggestions on the board. Roleplay the first situation with a student in front of the class. Then ask them to work in pairs to do the same with the other situations. If you have time, ask a pair to act out their roleplay in front of the class.

ANSWERS

Ex. 1

1 The questions in picture B are more polite as they are indirect questions.
2 Differences:
   The order of subject – verb – object in an indirect question is the same as in a normal statement.
   Auxiliary *do* is omitted in indirect questions. You have to add *if* or *whether* in an indirect question that needs a *yes/no* answer.

Ex. 2

  1 What's your full name? Could you tell me what your full name is?

2 What's your title? Could you tell me what your title is?
3 What's your home address (including post code)? I'd also like to know what your home address (including post code) is.
4 What's your telephone number? Could you tell me what your telephone number is?
5 What's your nationality? Could you tell me what your nationality is? / Could you tell me where you are from?
6 What's your date of birth? I'd also like to know what your date of birth is. / I'd also like to know when you were born.
7 What's your present occupation? / What do you do? Could you tell me what your present occupation is? / Could you tell me what you do (at the moment)?
8 How many brothers and sisters do you have? Could you tell me how many brothers and sisters you have?
9 Do you still live with your parents? I'd also like to know if you still live with your parents.
10 Which member of your family are you closest to? Could you tell me which member of your family you are closest to?
11 Are you closer to your family or your friends? Could you tell me if you are closer to your family or your friends?
12 How often do all the members of your family come together? On what occasions? I'd also like to know how often all the members of your family come together and on what occasions.

See also: *Going for Gold Language Maximiser* Unit 1.

Reading 2 p. 10

Aims:

- **to start students thinking about the elements of a good story**
- **to provide ideas for the Writing section**

Exam information PET FCE CELS

This section is a good introduction to the matching exercises in the Reading Papers of the PET, FCE and CELS exams.

1 Remind students that there may be more than one meaning for some words in the dictionary. They should choose the right one when they read the text.

2 Before you ask students to read the text, ask them what they think makes a good beginning to a children's book. Write their ideas on the board. Some suggestions might be:
• interesting situation
• something unusual or frightening
• something supernatural.
Ask them to read the text and decide if any of their ideas fit this story. Do they have any other ideas why this is (not) a good beginning to a children's book?

3 This exercise focuses on the main point of each paragraph. Ask students to work in pairs. They should look for the main point of each picture and the key words for these in the text.

4 This exercise focuses on detail in the text. Students should work in pairs and should underline the evidence in the text for their answers. They should give this evidence when the answers are checked.

ANSWERS

Ex. 1
1 doze off – fall asleep
2 hide – be somewhere that no one can see or find you
3 whisper – say something quietly
4 witch – a woman who has magic powers
5 lean – move or bend your body
6 freeze – suddenly stop and stay very still

Ex. 3
A paragraph 3   C paragraph 1
B paragraph 6   D paragraph 4

Ex. 4
2 There was no whispering as everyone else was asleep. (Someone once whispered to Sophie about the witching hour, but that was in the past.)
3 Sophie didn't open the curtains – she went underneath them to look out.
4 it wasn't quite dark in the village, there was 'silvery moonlight' and she could see the village street where 'everything was pale'.
5 Sophie didn't scream: 'no sound came out'.

Writing 2: a story (1) p. 11

Exam information PET FCE

In the Writing paper of the PET and FCE exams, students may have to write a short story. In the PET exam, they will be given the first line, and they may be given the first line in FCE.

Teaching tip

When students try to write a short story they may have problems with thinking of ideas and using interesting vocabulary. It is a good idea to read short extracts with them regularly. Ask them if they like the extract and why, what vocabulary is interesting and how the story might continue. This will help them with the problem areas above.

1 Before you do this exercise, ask students to think about what might happen next in the story they read in the last section. Then ask them to decide which options they think are the most interesting and why.

2 Explain that they are going to write the next part of the story. Ask them to work in pairs and discuss the questions. This will help them with ideas and they should make notes. Then either ask them to write the story from their notes in class, or set the story for homework and ask them to bring it to the next lesson. Ask them to read and check each other's work.

Tell them to look at the Writing reference on pp. 150 and 152 for more help.

ANSWERS

Ex. 1
Option 3 is the best. It includes:
• linking words: *then, However*
• interesting vocabulary: *suddenly, looked straight at her, to her amazement*
• Sophie's thoughts
• longer interesting sentences with correct punctuation: capital letters, commas, full stops, speech marks

---

Your students are now ready to do Unit 1 test on p. 111.

UNIT 2 Time out

Listening p. 12

Aims:
- to help students to predict the content of a listening text
- to practise answering multiple-choice questions

Exam information PET FCE CELS

In the Listening papers of the PET and FCE exams, students have to listen to a recording of a conversation or monologue and answer multiple-choice questions. In the CELS exam, they have to listen to short extracts and answer multiple-choice questions.

1, **2** The discussion in Exercises 1 and 2 will help students with predicting and dealing with the content of the listening. They should work in pairs or small groups. They should work through all the questions, discussing their ideas.

3 Before you play the recording, ask students to read carefully through all the questions. Have they already talked about any of these areas in Exercise 1? Remind them that when they listen to the recording, the answers will always come in the same order as the questions. Play the recording twice and ask students to compare their answers with each other before you check them with the whole class. Discuss any answers they got wrong, explaining why the other options are not possible. Play the recording again if necessary.

➡ Tapescript p. 101

ANSWERS
Ex. 3
1 C   2 A   3 C   4 B   5 C   6 A

See also: *Going for Gold Language Maximiser* Unit 2.

Grammar 1: present simple p. 13

Aims:
- to introduce the form and use of the present simple tense
- to introduce adverbs of frequency

1 Explain that this exercise focuses on the rules for using the present simple. It could be done with the whole class, so that all students understand the rules. Explain that there are some verbs that are not used in the continuous form. Draw students' attention to the Watch Out box and ask them to do the exercise there. Tell them that they can refer to the Grammar reference on p. 137 for further help.

2 Ask students to work in pairs to complete the text with words from the box. They can look back at the rules in Exercise 1 if they need help.

3 Explain that adverbs of frequency are usually used with the simple tense. Ask students to do Exercise 3 together.

4 Students should write their sentences alone and then compare with a partner. They could discuss any ideas that are similar or very different.

5 Ask students to think about the form of the questions they should ask in order to complete the table. Tell them to ask as many other students as possible. Then go round the class asking each student to tell you one thing that they have found out.

ANSWERS
Ex. 1
1 C   2 D   3 A   4 B
Watch Out: state verbs
1b) and 2b) are not correct because *understand* and *love* are state verbs not usually used in the continuous.

Ex. 2
1 spends   2 goes   3 take   4 wakes
5 don't drink   6 eat   7 practise
8 don't practise   9 like   10 listen
11 travel   12 don't dream

Ex. 3
2 They are **always** late.
6 I **never** have toast for breakfast.

▶ Photocopiable Activity 2A p. 170.

See also: *Going for Gold Language Maximiser* Unit 2.

Vocabulary 1: free time activities p. 14

Aims:
- **to provide topic vocabulary**
- **to introduce the idea of collocations**

Exam information PET
This section provides vocabulary that will be useful for Part 1 of the PET Speaking test.

1   Students could do the matching activity in pairs. Alternatively, you could write the verbs across the board to make five columns and ask students to work in pairs and come and write the activity under the appropriate verb. They could then tell the class which activities they enjoy doing and why.

2   If the words are written on the board, ask students to say how many syllables each has and to mark the stress on them. If students are working in their books, then ask them to mark the stress in pairs. Read the words around the class to check the answers.

3   This exercise reinforces the vocabulary, and puts it into a personal context for the students. This should make the collocations easier to remember.

4   This exercise extends students' knowledge of collocations. They could use a good monolingual dictionary such as the *Longman WordWise Dictionary* to help them with this.

5   The discussion allows students to practise collocations with the adverbs of frequency taught in the grammar section. After they have worked in pairs, choose one or two pairs to give feedback to the class.

ANSWERS

Ex. 1
going to: the cinema, museums
playing: football, table tennis, chess, the
    guitar, basketball, the piano
collecting: stamps
going: jogging, camping
taking: photographs

Ex. 2
Stressed syllables are underlined.
One syllable: stamps, chess
Two syllables: jogging, football, guitar,
    camping
Three syllables: cinema, photographs,
    museums, basketball, piano
Four syllables: table tennis

Ex. 3
1 play   2 took   3 playing   4 collecting
5 playing   6 go   7 went   8 play

See also: *Going for Gold Language Maximiser* Unit 2.

Speaking p. 15

Aims:
- **to provide topic vocabulary for interests and hobbies**
- **to provide a model for talking about hobbies**

Exam information PET FCE
In the PET and FCE Speaking paper, students may have to talk about their interests and hobbies.

1, **2**, **3**   These exercises provide ideas and vocabulary for the topic. Ask students to do Exercises 1 and 2 in pairs. Then play the recording for them to check their answers.

➡ Tapescript p. 102

4   Tell students that when they talk on their own about something, it is more interesting for the listener if the talk is structured. Tell them to look back at the text in order to do Exercise 4 and then play the recording again so that they can listen and check their ideas.

5   Tell students they should use the structure identified in Exercise 4 as a model, and think of some ideas about their own favourite free time activity. They should make notes. They should then put their notes away and talk to a partner who should listen and ask further questions about their favourite activity.

ANSWERS

Ex. 1

She is talking about tennis.

Ex. 2

1 doing   2 times   3 started   4 member
5 play   6 outdoors   7 exercise   8 game

Ex. 4

1 how long she has been doing it
2 when and how often she does it
3 how she first became interested in it
4 where she does it
5 why she likes it

▶ Photocopiable Activity 2B p. 171.

Reading   p. 16

Aim:

- **to provide an approach to multiple-matching tasks**

Exam information PET CELS FCE

In the PET Reading paper, students have to match descriptions of people with summaries of books, videos, holidays, activities and so on. They have to choose the most appropriate summary for each person described. In the CELS exams, students have to match information to a particular text or piece of information. In the FCE exam, they have to match statements or questions to part of a text or texts and say where the information or statement is mentioned. The work in this section follows the PET format.

Teaching tip

Suggest the following standard procedure for this PET task to students

1 Read the descriptions of the people and mark key words (there should be two areas to mark in each description).

2 Read the descriptions of the things and mark key words.
3 Read the descriptions of the people again and match them to the best thing.
Warn students to be careful of distracters – here, there may be more than one film possible for one of the key words they have underlined, but only one film will fit both the key words.

---

1   This exercise starts students thinking about films and should activate some of the vocabulary they may meet in Exercise 2.

2   Do the first one with the whole class so that they get the idea. Then ask students to work in pairs to complete the task. Check the answers and make sure that students can justify their answers from the text. Discuss any wrong answers and show why they are not possible.

3   If students are interested, extend the discussion into films in general. What type of films do they like? Why? What don't they like? Why? etc.

ANSWERS

Ex. 2

2 E (policeman)   3 A (sorcery, magical powers)   4 D (adventure, sea)
5 B (horror, tension, suspense)

Vocabulary 2: recording vocabulary
p. 17

Aim:

- **to help students choose an appropriate method of recording vocabulary**

Teaching tip

It is important that students think about the best ways of recording vocabulary for themselves. If they develop a system that suits them, they will find it easier to remember and learn words later.

---

1   Ask students to do the discussion in small groups.

2   Ask students to work in the same groups and to look at the six different ways of recording vocabulary. They should tell each other about the advantages and disadvantages of any way they have tried. Then discuss ideas with the whole class. Remind students that they should record vocabulary in the way that suits them best, but that writing a list of single words with no context or connection will not help them to remember new vocabulary.

3   Ask students to work alone to choose words to record and to decide in what way they will record them. Then ask them to explain their choices to a partner.

See also: *Going for Gold Language Maximiser* Unit 2.

Grammar 2: present continuous or present simple? p. 18

Aims:

- **to focus on the uses of the present simple and present continuous**
- **to provide practice in identifying mistakes in verb form**

1 , **2**   Do these exercises with the whole class.

➡ Tapescript p. 102

3 , **4**   Ask students to work in pairs, and then check the answers with the class.

5   Ask students to work in pairs but have a feedback session with the whole class. Refer them to the Grammar reference section on p. 137 if they need help.

6   Ask students to work in pairs. For homework, they could write a short paragraph summarising what they have found out about their partner.

ANSWERS

Ex. 1

are you doing	am reading
you thinking	are you doing
am not doing	

Ex. 2

There were five examples of the present continuous. The first three have use 1 (temporary situation). The last two have use 2 (for future arrangements).

Ex. 3

1 'm having   **2** Are ... going   **3** isn't raining
4 's watching   **5** are ... getting   **6** 'm not working   **7** 're speaking   **8** is ... looking

Ex. 5

Sally:	I take the train to school.
Ruth:	Today I'm wearing green and blue.
Jenny:	I don't usually do anything. (word order)
Tom:	I always have cereal for breakfast.
Tom:	My friends think I'm crazy.

See also: *Going for Gold Language Maximiser* Unit 2.

Writing: informal letter (1) p. 19

Aim:

- **to introduce the form, layout and organisation of an informal letter**

Exam information PET FCE CELS

In the Writing paper of the PET, FCE and CELS exams, students may have to write an informal letter.

Teaching tip

Identifying topic sentences in reading texts is good practice for developing awareness of text organisation. Ask students to look for topic sentences whenever they are reading any new texts. This will help them with their reading skills, particularly dealing with questions on specific information as they will understand where to find the answers in the text. It will also develop their productive writing skills and help them to organise their own writing more clearly.

1, **2** Do these exercises with the whole class as they are crucial to understanding the rest of the section. Refer students to the Writing reference on p. 149 for work on paragraphs.

3 Ask students to work in pairs to identify the topic sentences, but check the answers with the whole class.

4 This could be set for homework. It is a good idea to write a model outline on the board, and remind students of the clear separate sections of the task given in Exercise 2.

ANSWERS

Ex. 1

1 The letter begins *Dear David* and ends *Love, Elena*.
2 Each paragraph begins under the end of the opening line.
3 Paragraph 1 is about the party. Paragraph 2 is about the travel arrangements. Paragraph 3 is saying how much the writer is looking forward to seeing David.

Ex. 2

There should be three paragraphs. Paragraph 1 should begin with *My name is Marcia* and end with *getting to know you*. Paragraph 2 should begin with *Let me tell you a little* and end with *starting my homework*. Paragraph 3 should begin with *I like doing lots of different things* and end with *takes up a lot of time*.

Paragraph 2 topic sentence: *Let me tell you a little about my everyday life.*

Paragraph 3 topic sentence: *I like doing lots of different things in my free time.*

See also: *Going for Gold Language Maximiser* Unit 2.

Your students are now ready to do Unit 2 test on p. 113.

UNIT 3 The senses

Reading 1 p. 20

Aims:
- **to practise reading for specific information**
- **to extend students' vocabulary about personality and colour**

Exam information PET CELS

In the Reading paper of the PET and CELS exams, students have to read statements and decide if they are true or false. In the CELS they have to decide if the information is true, false or not given.

1 This discussion introduces the ideas in the reading text. Encourage students to discuss all the questions in Exercise 1.1 before reading the first paragraph and discussing the highlighted questions. Explain that it is always easier to understand a reading text if you already have some ideas about the topic.

2 Remind students that they do not need to understand every word in the text, and that they can often work out the meaning of unknown words from their context. (In the PET exam, they will not be allowed to use a dictionary, although monolingual dictionaries are allowed in CELS exams.)

3 Ask students to work through the statements in pairs so that they can discuss the different possibilities and justify their answers to each other. This will mean that they have to read the text carefully and use evidence from it to support their answers.

4 When students have found the missing words, you could encourage them to discuss whether they think they are positive or negative. This will help them to use the words appropriately.

5 When the students have discussed these questions in pairs, check the conclusions of the whole class. You could make a list of the most popular/ unpopular colours in the class.

ANSWERS

Ex. 2
You should wear yellow to help you win (a football match, etc.).
You should wear blue to help you succeed (in an interview, etc.).

Ex. 3
1 true   2 true   3 false (it is blue)   4 true
5 false (you may be seen as aggressive)
6 false (only yellow is)   7 true   8 true

Ex. 4
1 Confident   2 efficient   3 hard-working
4 strong   5 assertive   6 aggressive

Grammar 1: gerunds p. 21

Aim:
- **to provide rules and practice for the use of gerunds**

1 This matching activity focuses on the rules for using gerunds. Do the Watch Out box with the whole class to avoid possible common problems.

2, **3**, **4** Ask students to work in pairs, but check the answers with the whole class.

5 Ask students to complete their own sentences, and then compare their ideas with a partner. Ask some pairs to give feedback to the whole class. Suggest they use the form:
... is really (interested in) ... but I'm (interested in) ...
... and I are both really (interested in) ...
Students could write a short paragraph comparing and contrasting their answers.

See also: *Going for Gold Language Maximiser* Unit 3.

ANSWERS

Ex. 1

1   1A   2B. They are both gerunds (or -ing forms).

2   Sentence 1: We use gerunds when an activity is the subject of a sentence.
Sentence 2: We use gerunds after prepositions.

Watch Out: gerund or infinitive?

1   It's fun to go shopping. We use the infinitive when the second clause is the subject, following expressions like *it's fun, it's difficult, it's interesting*, etc.

2   I'm looking forward to going to the party. We use the gerund, because *to* is a preposition in the verb expression *look forward to*.

3   I'd like to go to the party. We use the infinitive after *I'd like* (though we use the gerund after *I like*).

Ex. 2

1   I told my best friend the news before <u>telling</u> everyone else.

2   (Being) afraid of flying means I usually go on holiday in this country.

3   (Living) with other people is often quite difficult.

4   He's using it for <u>keeping</u> old newspapers in. (*using* is a present participle)

5   I'm looking forward to <u>hearing</u> from you. (*looking* is a present participle)

Ex. 3

1   Speaking another language well is difficult.

2   Eating a lot of fat and sugar isn't healthy.

3   Writing clearly in an exam is important.

4   Going shopping is one of my favourite things.

5   Getting a video is cheaper than going to the cinema.

6   Talking about things that worry you is a good idea.

7   Driving a car when you're 15 is illegal.

8   Do you think buying CDs is a waste of money?

Ex. 4

1 waiting   2 playing   3 use   4 getting
5 cooking   6 seeing   7 give   8 arriving

Vocabulary: word formation p. 22

Aim:

• **to introduce students to some common suffixes**

Exam information FCE

In the Use of English paper of the FCE exam, students have to complete gaps in a text with a given word in the correct form.

Teaching tip

Students often think that it is enough to know one form of a word, and they may make mistakes such as *I am learning the England language*. Make sure they realise the importance of using words in their correct form, as mistakes can lead to misunderstanding. Suggest that when they make a note of a new word, they write down its other forms as well. In class, ask them what the noun form is, or the adjective, of new words. You could also give regular short dictations where you read the noun form of ten words and they have to write down the adjective form. This is useful exam preparation, recycles vocabulary and is a good way of improving the accuracy of their speaking and writing. Remind students that there is general help with spelling in the Writing reference on p. 151.

1   Discuss the words with the class so that they can see the different suffixes for the different forms of the words.

2 , **3**   Ask students to work in pairs. Then check the answers with the whole class. As a follow-up you could ask them to find three words in their dictionary to test the others in the class by asking *What's the noun?* or *What's the adjective?*

▶ Photocopiable Activity 3A p. 172.

See also: *Going for Gold Language Maximiser* Unit 3.

ANSWERS

Ex. 1
1 improve = verb   2 improvement = noun
3 weak = adjective   4 weakness = noun

Ex. 2
Verb to noun:
excite – excitement
enjoy – enjoyment
inform – information
impress – impression
reduce – reduction

Adjective to noun:
lazy – laziness
secure – security
flexible – flexibility

Ex. 3
1 improvements   2 reduction
3 information   4 flexibility   5 excitement

Speaking p. 23

Aims:
- **to help students organise their ideas when describing a picture**
- **to provide language to compare ideas**

Exam information PET FCE

In Part 3 of the Speaking paper of the PET exam, students have to describe a single picture. In Part 2 of the Speaking paper of the FCE exam, they have to compare and contrast two pictures, and talk about an aspect of the pictures such as how the people are feeling.

Teaching tip

Students often feel that they lack vocabulary when they are asked to talk about a picture, but they may only lack the confidence to organise their thoughts coherently. Take pictures into the class regularly, and use them for a five-minute activity with the whole class. Ask students to suggest things to say about the picture, write these ideas on the board, and then organise them into a logical description. Then ask students to practise the talk in pairs.

1, **2**   These exercises are very useful for giving students the confidence to talk about a picture. Work through them with the whole class. Ask students to do Exercise 2.2 in pairs, and then they can read their sentences to the class.

3   Students should work in pairs. Remind them to follow the model in Exercise 1.

Ex. 1
1
Possible answers
B This photo shows the inside of a typical supermarket.
A I think it was taken in a hot country because it looks sunny and some of the people are wearing T-shirts and short-sleeved shirts. It could be in Brazil but I'm not sure.
2
Picture A: 3
Picture B: 1, 2, 4
Ex. 2
1 –   2 like   3 as if

▶ Photocopiable Activity 3B p. 174.

Listening 1 p. 24

Aim:
- **to practise listening for specific information**

Exam information PET

In Part 1 of the PET Listening paper, students have to listen to seven short conversations or monologues and identify which picture of four relates to what they hear. The recording is played twice.

1   This discussion should start students thinking about the topic of the listening and using the vocabulary they will hear in it. They should work in pairs, but then share some ideas with the class.

2   This first task identifies the main tone of each extract and the attitude of the speakers. Play the recording once and ask students for their answers.

➡ Tapescript p. 102

3   This activity asks students to identify specific information, as in the PET task. Play the recording twice.

ANSWERS
Ex. 2
1 negative   2 positive   3 negative
4 neutral   5 neutral
Ex. 3
1 C   2 B   3 A   4 C   5 B

Reading 2: labels p. 24

Aims:
- **to focus on the exact meaning of real-life signs and labels**
- **to provide practice in dealing with multiple-choice questions**

Exam information PET

In the Reading paper of the PET exam, students have to read five signs, notices or messages and decide what each one means, choosing from three options.

Teaching tip

The signs, notices and messages in the PET exam are from real life. Students should be encouraged to take note of signs outside the classroom and think about their meaning – even if these are not in English. This practice will help them to decide which options are not possible when they do the task in the exam, and may help them to choose the right one. If students find any examples of notices in English, in magazines or when they travel, they could bring them into class, so that they get used to the type of information given in signs and notices in real life.

1   This activity starts students thinking about the real-life situations in which they might read signs and labels. They should do this discussion in small groups to get as many ideas as possible, but then they should share their ideas with the whole class.

2   Ask students to do this exercise in pairs. Suggest the following procedure:
1 Look at the label.
2 Try to imagine where the label is taken from, and what the correct meaning would be in real life.
3 Read each option, and choose the most sensible answer.
Note: Warn students that the words on the label may appear in some or all of the options, and they should not be distracted by this.

3   The follow-up discussion extends the topic and should be done in pairs.

ANSWERS
Ex. 1
1 You might see a similar label on deodorants, hair sprays, cleaning sprays, etc.
2 1 a and d 2 b
Ex. 2
2 A   3 C   4 B   5 A   6 C

Grammar 2: gerunds and infinitives
p. 25

Aims:
- **to build on work done in Grammar 1 by introducing verbs that can be followed by either a gerund or an infinitive**
- **to provide practice in a format similar to the PET exam**

Exam information PET FCE

In the Writing paper of the PET exam, students have to rewrite five sentences so that they mean the same as the original. They are given the beginning of the new sentence. Different structures are tested, and the five sentences usually make a complete text. In the FCE exam they have to rewrite discrete sentences, but they are given the beginning and the end of the sentences and a keyword that they have to use.

Teaching tip

Paraphrasing is a useful skill for all students to acquire, even if they are not taking any exam. It is a good idea to do quizzes or tests made up of sentences from students' work which can be written in another way, just to help them to realise that there is usually more than one way to say the same thing. In speaking activities in class, a spontaneous question *Can you put that another way?* is a useful means of developing this skill.

1 Remind students that they have already looked at uses of the gerund. Explain that now they are going to look at words that can be followed by either the gerund or the infinitive. Ask them to work out the rules in pairs, and check the answers with the class.

2 Students should do this in pairs, discussing the different possibilities and justifying their answers.

3 Go through the example with the whole class so that they understand the point of the exercise, and then do the first one with them as well. Then ask them to complete the exercise in pairs.

ANSWERS

Ex. 1
A gerund   B infinitive

Ex. 2
1 having   2 doing   3 doing   4 to help
5 using   6 to make   7 to go   8 to find
9 to finish   10 doing

Ex. 3
1 I offered to help her with the shopping.
2 I'm hoping to buy some shoes today.
3 I agreed to go with him.
4 I'm considering asking Jessica to help me.
5 We finally managed to finish the project.
6 I suggested going to the cinema.
7 I want to avoid seeing Manuel.
8 The holiday involves walking a lot.
9 We arranged to meet at 6 o'clock.
10 I've finished doing all the cooking.

See also: *Going for Gold Language Maximiser* Unit 3.

Listening 2: song p. 26

Aims:
- **to stimulate students' imagination**
- **to recycle words related to the senses**

1 Give students time to think about their story, and to share their ideas with others. They could discuss their ideas in pairs first, instead of thinking alone. Ask them to give reasons for their ideas, using the pictures as evidence – this will help them practise describing a picture and saying how people are feeling.

2 Play the recording and ask the students to check their ideas and to confirm the order of the pictures in the song.

➡ Tapescript p. 102

3 Tell them to read the words of the song and to fill in the spaces with words from the box. Then play the recording again so that they can check their answers. .

4 Before you play the recording again, ask students to discuss the questions to see what they think the answers will be. Then play it so that they can check.

Encourage students to sing along with the song if they can, as this will help their pronunciation.

ANSWERS

Ex. 2
Order: B, D, A, C

Ex. 3
1 felt   2 seen   3 feels   4 say   5 feeling
6 voice   7 touch

Ex. 4
1 No, she doesn't.   2 No, it's happened a lot before.   3 Because she thinks he'll leave her again.   4 Because she will believe him and then get hurt if it's not true for ever.
5 hearing him (his voice)

Writing: informal letter (2) p. 27

Aims:

- to help students to organise their ideas in paragraphs
- to focus on spelling

Exam information PET FCE CELS

In the Writing paper of the PET, FCE and CELS exams, students may have to write an informal letter.

Teaching tip

Tell students to read the instructions for any writing task carefully. If they are taking an exam, they will lose marks if they don't include all parts of the task. It is worth checking that they understand what is required whenever you set a writing task. Remind them to check with the Writing reference on pp. 149 and 151 for help with paragraphs and spelling.

1   This exercise focuses on what is actually required in the task. Ask students to do both parts of Exercise 1 in pairs, but then check the answers with the whole class. Remind students how important it is to complete the whole task.

2   This exercise provides a model outline for this type of writing.

3   This exercise focuses on topic vocabulary and on spelling rules. Remind students that there are spelling rules in the Writing reference p. 151.

4, **5**   These are preparation exercises for the writing task in Exercise 6. They should be done in class. Students can work in pairs so that they help each other and check their notes for spelling or vocabulary mistakes.

6   The task can be completed in class or set for homework. Remind them that there is help with layout in the Writing reference p. 154.

ANSWERS

Ex. 1

1 You should write 100–120 words.

2

1 She's seen the film *Chocolat*.

2 She doesn't tell her the ending because she thinks Marianne should go and see the film and she doesn't want to spoil it for her.

Ex. 2

a) 2   b) 3   c) 1

Ex. 3

1 1 main star   2 to play (someone)   3 plot 4 acting

2 1 writing (not writeing)   2 angrier (not angryer)   3 planning (not planing)

Your students are now ready to do Progress test 1 on p. 115.

Units 1–3 Progress check p. 28

ANSWERS

Ex. 1

1 k 2 l 3 a 4 h 5 g 6 e 7 j 8 i
9 b 10 d 11 f 12 c

Ex. 2

1 I usually have cereal and toast for breakfast.
2 correct
3 She is visiting her sister in Australia next week.
4 I don't know what time the match starts.
5 correct
6 correct
7 They are travelling around Italy at the moment.
8 I am staying with some friends for a few days until I find my own place.

Ex. 3

1a) Could you tell me how much that jacket is, please?
 b) I'd also like to know if you have this jacket in other colours.
2a) Could you tell me what time the film starts, please?
 b) I'd also like to know how long the film lasts.
3a) Could you tell me if you have any English–English dictionaries, please?
 b) I'd also like to know how much this grammar book is.
4a) Could you tell me how to get to the nearest post office, please?
 b) I'd also like to know how far it is from here.

Ex. 4

1 She bought two pairs of jeans, six T-shirts, some shoes and a black jacket.
2 correct
3 We drove to Paris, found a hotel and then had a fantastic meal in a local restaurant.
4 I've left my keys in John's car.
5 If I see Harriet, I'll tell her you want to talk to her.

Ex. 5

1 grandmother 2 nieces 3 cousins
4 stepfather 5 photographs 6 chess
7 jogging 8 guitar 9 smell 10 touch
11 noise 12 taste

Ex. 6

1 information 2 thoughtfulness
3 happiness 4 enjoyment 5 efficient
6 security 7 emotional 8 protection

Ex. 7

1 visiting 2 to move 3 watching
4 to tidy 5 to live 6 applying 7 going
8 to teach

UNIT

4 Practice makes perfect?

Reading p. 30

Aims:

- **to help students predict the content of what they read**
- **to provide practice in dealing with multiple-choice questions**

Exam information PET FCE CELS

In the Reading paper of the PET and FCE exams, students have to read a passage and choose the correct answer from four options. In the CELS exam, they may have to choose the correct answer from three options. These questions can be about detail, attitude of writer, reference or the meaning of a word. They could also be connected with the writer's intention or the overall purpose of the text.

Teaching tip

Suggested procedure for dealing with multiple-choice questions:

1 Read the title of the passage to see what it's about.
2 Read the questions or stems to see if you can predict any detail.
3 Read the text, referring to the questions. Mark the text where you think the answers are. Look for key words.
4 Read the text again, this time stopping at the relevant marked parts and checking all the options carefully. Remember that some options may be half true, or may be true but may not answer the question. Only one will answer the question completely.
5 Read the text again, referring to the questions, to check answers.

1, **2** These exercises help students to predict the content of the text. Encourage them to talk about their ideas, particularly in Exercise 2.2. Students often ignore titles but this exercise will show them how useful a title can be in helping them understand what a text is about.

3 Encourage students to tell you what they had thought before they read the text and what they found out as they read it.

4 Ask students to do the exercise in pairs so that they can talk about the different options and discuss which one is the right answer. Remind them that:

- The questions themselves are in the same order as the information appears in the text.
- The options are in the same order as they appear in the text.
- Some words may appear in both the text and an option but may not be the right answer.
- Although some options may be half answers to the question, only one option will be absolutely correct.

Check the answers with the whole class, and discuss why the other options were wrong.

5 Do these discussion points either as a whole-class discussion or in small groups, so that students hear as many opinions as possible.

ANSWERS

Ex. 2

1 The photos suggest that Sian is a cellist and that she also mixes records as a nightclub DJ.
2 The title suggests that the text is about someone who is pretending to be something that they are not.

Ex. 4

2 B   3 A   4 B   5 C   6 A

Ex. 5

1 It means that the more you practise, the better you get; to be very good at something, you have to practise a lot.

Grammar 1: past simple and past continuous p. 31

Aims:

- **to provide students with the rules for using the past simple and the past continuous**
- **to give controlled and free practice in using these tenses**

1 This exercise gives students the chance to work out the rules for themselves. Ask them to work in pairs, then check the answers with the whole class.

2 When students have completed the sentences for themselves, ask them to move around and compare their ideas with other students in the class. If there are any problems with form, then they can check the rules again. Remind them that they can also look at the Grammar reference p. 138.

3 , **4** These exercises provide very controlled practice of the form of the tenses. Students should work in pairs.

5 This provides freer practice. Tell students to read the questions silently and think about their answers, both for themselves (as they will have to answer their partner's questions), and for their partner. They should then compare their ideas with their partner by saying what they think their partner will say, and asking and answering questions.

ANSWERS

Ex. 1

1 1 c   2 a   3 b

2

Sentence 2 is incorrect because we only use *while* with long actions in the past continuous, not finished actions in the past simple.

Ex. 2

Possible answers

1 ... was watching the TV.
2 ... were driving to the shops.
3 ... was having a shower.
4 ... was having a bath.
5 ... was running for the bus.
6 ... was sending me an email.

Ex. 3

1 was living, went
2 started
3 was tidying, were playing
4 wasn't looking, walked
5 didn't study, didn't pass
6 cut, was cooking

Ex. 4

2 was going   3 waited   4 was trying
5 were talking   6 started   7 got
8 was cycling   9 ran   10 fell   11 broke

See also: *Going for Gold Language Maximiser* Unit 4.

Listening p. 32

Aim:

- **to help students identify specific information in a listening text**

Exam information PET CELS

In the Listening paper of the PET and CELS exams, students have to read a series of statements and listen to a text to decide if the statements are true or false.

Teaching tip

When you check the answers to a listening exercise, you should try to play the recording again so that students can actually hear the correct answer, and identify why they made a mistake. Maybe they heard the wrong word or didn't understand the pronunciation. If it is not possible to play the recording again, or if students want to do further detailed work, then let them look at the tapescript.

A suggested procedure:

1 Read the statements carefully.
2 Listen to the recording.
3 If they can't hear the answer to a statement the first time, they should leave it and go on to the next one. They may hear it better the second time.

---

1 This exercise helps students to start thinking about the topic.

2   The question in this exercise asks students to identify the main point of the listening text. If they are familiar with the general topic before they start listening for specific information, they will find the task easier.

➡ Tapescript p. 102

3   Remind students of the procedure before you play the recording and that they will hear the information in the same order as it is written in the task.

Play the recording twice, then check the answers with the whole class.

4   Ask students to do these games in small groups.

ANSWERS

Ex. 2

Only Daniel is sure.

Ex. 3

2 true   **3** false   **4** true   **5** false   **6** true

7 false

Ex. 4

1 Start in the bottom left-hand corner and follow the arrows:

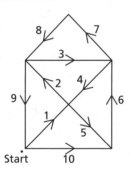

2 The next number is 46. The gap between each number is the last number + multiples of 3: 1 + (3 × 1) = 4; 4 + (3 × 2) = 10; 10 + (3 × 3) = 19; 19 + (3 × 4) = 31; 31 + (3 × 5) = 46

3 cat, on, one, tone, eat, ate, tied, action, tin, dine, dice, cane, cute, ten, dent, into, ace, not, note, etc.

Vocabulary 1: education p. 33

Aims:

- **to introduce key topic vocabulary**
- **to give students information about the education system in Britain so that they can compare it with their own country**
- **to develop dictionary skills**

Exam information CELS

In the CELS exam, students have to talk on their own about a topic which they can choose from a list given to them by the examiner. They have preparation time for this. The work in this section will help students to prepare a short talk on the topic of education.

Teaching tip

The work in this section gives students useful information about using a dictionary. Remind students about this information frequently during the course, and encourage them to use monolingual dictionaries such as the *Longman WordWise Dictionary*.

---

1   Ask students to do this exercise in pairs, but check their answers with the whole class. This is important training for them. Discuss question 6 in detail, to show them how useful a dictionary can be.

2   Encourage students to discuss the key words and share their ideas before they use their dictionaries. They could think about the answers to the questions for their own country before moving on to Exercise 3.

3   After students have matched the questions to the answers, ask them if they were surprised by any of the answers. Were any answers very different from in their own country? How? Which do they think is better? Why?

4   Students should work in pairs to prepare a short talk. If there is time, they could give their talk to the rest of the class; otherwise they can practise in small groups.

> **ANSWERS**
>
> **Ex. 1**
> **1** noun **2** three **3** on the first syllable (time) **4** yes **5** the train timetable
> **6** yes, because it is very clear
>
> **Ex. 3**
> **1** B **2** J **3** G **4** C **5** E **6** A **7** D **8** H
> **9** I **10** F

See also: *Going for Gold Language Maximiser* Unit 4.

Speaking p. 34

Aims:
- **to help students describe and compare things in a photograph**
- **to provide useful language for speculating**
- **to help students organise a short talk**

> **Exam information** PET
>
> In the PET exam, students have to describe a picture. They have to talk about what they can see, and then think about why the people might be there or how they might be feeling. The work in this section prepares students for this task. PET students will find it useful to learn the stages for describing a photograph presented in Exercise 2 to use in the exam.

1   Suggest that students underline or highlight the phrases in italics so that they can use this language of speculation in other situations.

2   Tell students that it is easier to listen to someone giving information if it is organised clearly. (The organisation of the information can be very similar to the approach used in writing.) Tell them to use the stages identified in Exercise 2.1 for the practice in Exercise 2.2.

3   The discussion extends the topic into interesting related areas. The questions could be discussed with the whole class. Alternatively, put students into pairs or small groups and ask them to think of ideas for the questions. Then ask them to report back to the class. For question 2, put the subjects suggested on the board to see whether the students all agree on the important ones.

▶ Photocopiable Activity 4 p. 175.

> **ANSWERS**
>
> **Ex. 1**
> **1**
> Probably true: 1, 2, 3, 5
> Probably false: 4 (It's probably a very boring lesson.) 6 (They seem to be listening to the teacher and taking notes.)
> **2**
> **1** to **2** as **3** might **4** if **5** is ('s)
> **6** looks/seems
>
> **Ex. 2**
> **1** 1 C 2 A 3 B

Use of English: vocabulary (cloze) p. 35

Aim:
- **to provide techniques to help students to complete a gapped text**

> **Exam information** PET FCE
>
> In the PET and FCE exams, students have to complete a multiple-choice cloze. In each case the focus is on vocabulary, although there may be some grammar areas tested, such as connectors or prepositions.

> **Teaching tip**
>
> When students do this kind of exercise, they should always read the whole text through first without trying to fill in any spaces so that they understand what the text is about. Encourage students to think of these cloze passages as reading texts and approach them in the usual way.

1   These questions start students thinking about the topic of the cloze passage.

2   This task focuses students on the main idea of the passage. It is very important, and students should think carefully about their answer. They will find it much easier to fill in the spaces if they have a clear general understanding of the text itself.

3   Ask students to work in pairs and read through the text filling in the spaces. Tell them to think about what the word might be before they look at the options – they may be able to guess the word and then if they find it as a choice, this will confirm their answer. When they have completed the task, tell them to read it through again to check that it makes sense. Check the answers with the whole class and discuss any wrong answers.

4   This discussion exercise extends the topic of the text. Do it as a class discussion or in pairs.

ANSWERS

Ex. 2

c

Ex. 3

2 D   3 B   4 B   5 A   6 D   7 D   8 B   9 C
10 B   11 A

Grammar 2: past perfect simple p. 35

Aim:

- **to present and practise the rules for using the past perfect tense**

1   Do this task with the whole class.

2 , **3**   Ask students to do these exercises in pairs. Then check the answers with the whole class.

4   The matching activity should be done in pairs, so that students can discuss their answers. The discussion enables them to use the structures in a natural way.

ANSWERS

Ex. 1

A first   B second

Ex. 2

1 1 I'd finished, 2 went

2 1 had landed, 2 phoned

3 1 he'd spoken, 2 left

4 1 had finished, 2 went

5 1 she'd gone out, 2 tried

6 1 had gone, 2 arrived

Ex. 3

1 had brought, came

2 had met, saw

3 felt, hadn't flown

4 had seen, started

5 arrived, had closed

6 saw, hadn't eaten

Ex. 4

1 c   2 e   3 a   4 b   5 d

See also: *Going for Gold Language Maximiser* Unit 4.

Vocabulary 2: adverbs of manner p. 36

Aims:

- **to present the rules for using adverbs of manner**
- **to provide controlled practice in using them**

1   Do this task with the class and complete the rules together.

2   Ask students to work in pairs to complete the sentences.

3   Put students in small groups so that they can talk about the situations together.

ANSWERS

Ex. 1

1

speaks = verb, confidently = adverb, confident = adjective, person = noun

2

A adverbs   B adjectives

Ex. 2

1 careful   **2** happily   **3** nervously
4 serious   **5** loudly   **6** quietly

See also: *Going for Gold Language Maximiser* Unit 4.

Writing: story (2) p. 37

Aims:

- **to help students think of ideas for their writing**
- **to help students use linking words**

Exam information FCE

In the FCE exam, students may be asked to write a story from a title. The work in this section will help them to plan and organise this type of story.

1   Remind students that they should always try to predict what they are going to read about as this will make it easier to understand the text.

2   Ask students to work in pairs, but then to share their ideas with the class. Discuss the wrong answers so that students understand how the sequence of ideas links together.

3   This task links back to the grammar section, to remind students of how to identify the order of events.

4   Go through the example with the class, to show them how linking the ideas makes the sentences easier to understand and more interesting. Ask them to complete the exercise in pairs.

5, **6**   Students could plan their story in class and complete it for homework. Remind them to learn the preparation stages and use them whenever they write a story.

ANSWERS

Ex. 2
Paragraph 2: G, E, F
Paragraph 3: I, J, H

Ex. 3

1

It sets the scene:
time – One afternoon
place – were walking along the river
introduces people – Marek and Jon
It gives interesting information and a reason to continue reading – they saw a rowing boat

2

The first sentence introduces the people, but doesn't set the scene or provide interest. The second one sets the scene, but doesn't introduce the people.

Ex. 4

1

At first, soon, After a while, Finally

2

1 At first
2 After a while
3 Finally
4 One afternoon
5 soon

See also: *Going for Gold Language Maximiser* Unit 4.

Your students are now ready to do Unit 4 test on p. 118.

UNIT 5 Behind the mask

Listening 1 p. 38

Aims:
- to help students identify and make notes on specific information in a listening text
- to show how a talk is organised, and how the introduction can help students to predict and understand what follows

Exam information PET FCE CELS

In the Listening papers of the PET, FCE and CELS exams, students have to complete notes based on a listening text, usually a monologue. They may only have to write one or two words.

Teaching tip

Remind students that predicting what they will hear will always make listening easier. They can do this by reading the notes through before they listen.

1 , **2** The initial discussion introduces the topic of the talk the students will listen to. Listening first to the introduction will help them to predict what they might hear from the way the talk is organised and what is said.

Tell students to read through the different uses for masks in Exercise 2.3 before you play the recording through. When they have put them in order, they should check their answers with a partner.

➡ Tapescript p. 103

3 Tell students to read through all the notes carefully. They should think whether the missing words are nouns, verbs or adjectives (they are often nouns). What kind of information is missing? Is it a number? A country? A date?

Tell them that they will hear the information in the same order as it appears in the task. Then play the

recording twice. Ask them to compare what they have written with a partner before you check the answers with the whole class.

4 This discussion extends the topic of the talk.

ANSWERS

Ex. 1

1

The masks come from North America, Egypt and Italy.

Ex. 2

3

curing illness: 2
dressing up for parties: 4
helping farmers grow food: 3
representing characters in drama: 5
remembering people from the past: 1

Ex. 3

1 1350 **2** medicine **3** America **4** dancers
5 Carnival **6** Italy

Grammar 1: reported statements p. 39

Aims:
- to give students the rules for making reported statements
- to show the difference between *say* and *tell*
- to provide controlled practice in using reported statements

Exam information PET

Exercise 3 is similar to the format of the task in the PET exam. Transforming sentences is a quick way of giving students practice in using a structure and allowing them to practise paraphrasing at the same time. This technique can be used with other structures or for quick tests.

1   The different sections of this exercise show students the differences between reported and direct speech. Ask them to work in pairs, but check the answers with the whole class.

2   This exercise focuses on the difference between *say* and *tell*, a common mistake made by students at this level. Refer them to the Grammar reference on p. 139, and ask them to work in pairs.

3   Go through the example and do the first one with the class, and then ask students to work in pairs.

4   This is a slightly freer activity which allows students to personalise the target structure. Ask them to work in small groups. Alternatively, ask them to write down their five things individually and then read them to the rest of the class. They could also write the sentences for homework, bring them to the next lesson and work in small groups at the start of the lesson. This would provide a quick revision of the grammar.

ANSWERS

Ex. 1

1 1 have   2 had   3 will   4 can

2

	Direct speech	Reported speech
Verb tenses	present simple	past simple
	past simple	past perfect
	will	*would*
	can	*could*
Time phrases	*last year*	*the year before*
	next month	*the following month*

Ex. 2

1 When we use *tell*, we use an object. When we use *say*, we do not use an object.

2 1 said   2 told   3 told   4 said   5 said   6 told

Ex. 3

(**Note:** the example uses *me*, but any object pronoun would be acceptable here.)

1 He said he wanted to go on holiday the following month.

2 She told me she had studied Italian for three years.

3 She told me she could speak very good French.

4 They said they would have a party that month.

5 She told me she hadn't done her English homework the week before.

6 He said he didn't like Chinese food very much.

7 They said they wouldn't bring the car back until the next/following day.

8 She said she couldn't go to the class that afternoon.

See also: *Going for Gold Language Maximiser* Unit 5.

Vocabulary 1: phrasal verbs with *get* p. 40

Aims:

- **to show students the meaning and use of phrasal verbs using *get***
- **to allow students to personalise the verbs and so remember them more easily**

Exam information PET FCE

Phrasal verbs are often tested in the PET and FCE exams. They may be tested as part of a reading text or in a cloze passage.

Teaching tip

Students often find phrasal verbs difficult to remember and benefit from a lot of recycling and practice. It is easier for them to learn and remember the whole verb as a single item, so encourage them to note verbs down in this way, e.g. *get through = make contact*. As any phrasal verb may have more than one meaning, it is useful if students can also note down an example sentence to show the particular meaning of the verb clearly from its context.

---

1   This matching exercise focuses on the meaning of the phrasal verbs and provides students with definitions. They should do the exercise in pairs and then write out the verbs and definitions in their vocabulary note books.

2   This exercise allows students to use the verbs in different contexts.

3   This task allows students to personalise the contexts. Suggest that they work in pairs, and if the sentence is false for them they use the same phrasal verb in a sentence of their own that is true for them. Give an example, e.g. *It takes me a long time to get over a cold.*

ANSWERS

Ex. 1
2 2 a   3 b   4 d   5 e   6 c

Ex. 2
1 Last time I had a cold, I got over it very quickly.
2 I don't want to be rich. I just want to be able to get by.
3 When I have a problem, I usually got round it by asking my best friend for help.
4 When I get through to someone's answer phone, I never leave a message.
5 When I was a child, I did really naughty things and usually got away with them.

▶ Photocopiable Activity 5A p. 176.

See also: *Going for Gold Language Maximiser* Unit 5.

Reading p. 40

Aims:
- **to review narrative tenses**
- **to practise story telling**

1, **2**   Ask students to work in pairs. Tell them not to look at the reading text yet. Don't give them the correct order of the pictures. When they have discussed the possible order of the pictures, they should tell their story to each other, describing each picture alternately. Alternatively, they could write their story down, using just one or two sentences for each picture.

3   Ask them to read the story, and compare it with the ones they told in Exercise 2. As a follow-up, you could ask them to underline the tenses in the story.

4   This exercise revises the work already done on tenses.

5   This discussion puts the story into a wider context for the students. You could do it as a whole-class discussion or in small groups.

ANSWERS

Ex. 1
Correct order of pictures: D, C, A, E, B

Ex. 4
1   1 b   2 a   3 c

Ex. 5
The aim of the story is to teach that being ugly does not mean someone is a horrible person, and that it is wrong to judge someone by his or her appearance.

Writing: story (3) p. 41

Aim:
- **to show students how to improve their story by using interesting vocabulary and varying sentence structures**

Exam information PET FCE

In the Writing paper of the PET and FCE exams students may have to write a short story. In the PET exam they will be given the first line, and they may be given the first line in the FCE exam.

1, **2**, **3**   Each exercise focuses on a different aspect of writing. They should all be done in pairs with feedback with the whole class. Refer students to the Writing reference on p. 147 for work on sentences to help them with these exercises.

Exercise 1 shows students how longer sentences with linked ideas and specific vocabulary are more interesting to read than simple sentences.

Exercise 2 allows students to link ideas in sentences. Before they do the task, point out that:
and links similar ideas
although and *but* link contrasting ideas
so and *because* give reasons.

Exercise 3 focuses on interesting vocabulary. When students have done the task, you could discuss other words that might be more interesting. Write the words below on the board and ask students to suggest alternative words. Which one do they think is most interesting?
pretty (beautiful)
afraid (terrified/frightened)
small (tiny)

Suggest that students make a note of these words and try to use them when they write stories.

4   Ask students to plan their story in pairs. Refer them to the Writing reference on p. 152.

5, **6**   Students should write their stories alone. When they have finished, they could exchange them with their partner to check the things listed in Exercise 6. Alternatively, set the story for homework and ask students to exchange and check each other's work at the start of the next lesson.

ANSWERS

Ex. 1

1 Sentence b is more interesting because it has two clauses joined by a linker (not just two ordinary Subject/Verb/Object-type sentences).

2 Sentence b is more interesting because *big* is a common and general word. *Enormous* is more precise and not used so much. *Very ugly* also adds precise and interesting information.

Ex. 2

1 He picked a rose and a terrible Beast appeared.

2 The Beast wanted to marry Beauty so her father took her to the Beast's castle.

3 At first she was frightened but there were lots of interesting things to do. / At first she was frightened although there were lots of interesting things to do.

4 Although the Beast was kind, he was very ugly. / The Beast was kind although he was very ugly. / The Beast was very kind but he was very ugly.

Ex. 3

The words in the box are more interesting because their meaning is more specific and they are not so commonly used as the words in brackets.

1 enormous   2 furious   3 entertaining
4 generous

See also: *Going for Gold Language Maximiser* Unit 5.

Listening 2   p. 42

Aims:
• to listen for specific information
• to practise giving opinions and agreeing and disagreeing about ideas

---

Exam information PET FCE CELS

In the Listening papers of the PET and FCE exams, students have to listen to a recording of a conversation or monologue and answer multiple-choice questions. In the CELS exam, they have to listen to short extracts and answer multiple-choice questions.

Teaching tip

Remind students to read through statements or multiple-choice questions carefully before they listen to the recording. This will help them to predict what they are going to hear and make the listening task easier.

---

1   This discussion starts students thinking about the topic. It could be done in pairs or with the whole class. The photos show Ben Affleck, Brad Pitt, Anna Kournikova and Julia Roberts.

2   This first listening exercise focuses on the main ideas. Ask students to read through the items before you play the recording. Ask them what they think they are going to hear. When they have done the task, ask them to compare their answers in pairs before you check the answers with the whole class.

➡ Tapescript p. 103

3   Ask students to read through the questions and all the options before you play the recording again. Remind them that they will hear the information in the same order as it appears in the task, and that there will be key words to listen for.

Ask them to discuss what they think the key words are. Then play the recording. Ask them to compare their answers with each other before you check the answers with the whole class. Play the recording again if necessary, so that students can check again.

4   Ask students to work in pairs or small groups and then take feedback from the whole class. If they can suggest any similar sayings (or any sayings which give opposite ideas), write these on the board. They can then say which ones they agree with.

ANSWERS

Ex. 2
They talk about 1, 2, 3, 5, 6 (not 4 or 7)

Ex. 3
1 A   2 B   3 A   4 C   5 B   6 C

Ex. 4
1 1e   2d   3c   4b   5a

Grammar 2: reported questions p. 43

Aims:
- **to give students the rules for reported questions**
- **to provide controlled practice in using reported questions**

1   This exercise demonstrates the difference between direct and reported questions. Do it with the whole class.

2   Ask students to look back at the examples and discuss the questions. Write the rules on the board if necessary. Refer students to the Grammar reference on p. 139.

3   Ask students to work in pairs to find the mistakes and correct them.

4   Do the example and the first question with the whole class. Then ask them to work in pairs to complete the exercise.

ANSWERS

Ex. 1
2 What things do beautiful people have in common?
3 Is this a personal opinion?
4 Do you agree with that opinion?

Ex. 2
Reported questions:
a) *Wh-* questions: question word + subject + verb
b) *Yes/No* questions: if (or *whether*) + subject + verb

Ex. 3
1 Jack asked his teacher when the class finished. (not *did*)
2 Three people asked me how old I was. (word order: not *was I*)
3 The taxi driver asked me where I wanted to go. (verb tense: past simple)
4 She asked me if I knew Michael's phone number. (not *did*)
5 Kate asked her mother if she had seen Maria. (verb tense: past perfect)
6 They asked me whether I could speak French. (word order: not *could I*)

Ex. 4
1 She asked me if I liked swimming.
2 My friend asked me who I had met at Jim's party the week before.
3 He asked me if I could drive.
4 She asked me if I would tell Gerry.
5 They asked me what I usually did on Friday evenings.
6 He asked me if I could phone him that evening.
7 My friend asked me if I had seen my teacher the day before.
8 She asked me where I would go on holiday the following year.

See also: *Going for Gold Language Maximiser* Unit 5.

Vocabulary 2: physical appearance p. 44

Aims:
- **to provide key topic vocabulary**
- **to extend students' knowledge of alternative (interesting) vocabulary**
- **to introduce the idea of appropriate language and connotation**

Exam information PET FCE

This vocabulary will be useful for PET and FCE students to use in the Speaking paper when they are describing a picture.

---

1   This task starts students thinking about the appropriacy of some words. This could be done with the whole class so that all the students understand the concept of register and appropriacy.

2 , **3** , **4**   These exercises can be done in pairs. Check the pronunciation of the words with the whole class. Point out that these words are useful when describing a picture.

5   Do one question and answer task first with the whole class as an example. Then ask students to work in pairs.

ANSWERS

Ex. 1

2

1 men: good-looking; women: beautiful; both: attractive

2 slim

Ex. 2

beauty	height	weight/ build	hair (face and head)
attractive	medium height	skinny	beard
beautiful	short	slim	blonde
good-looking	tall	thin	curly
plain		well-built	moustache
		overweight	straight
			wavy

Ex. 3

Possible answers

Picture A: moustache, slim

Picture B: well-built, overweight

Picture C: well-built, beautiful, blonde, wavy

Ex. 4

2 f   **3** b   **4** a   **5** h   **6** e   **7** d   **8** g

---

See also: *Going for Gold Language Maximiser* Unit 5.

Speaking   p. 45

Aim:

- **to provide useful language for agreeing, disagreeing and giving opinions**

Exam information   PET FCE CELS

In the Speaking paper of the PET, FCE and CELS exams, students have to discuss a task or solve a problem. The work in this section provides functional language to help students complete these tasks.

Teaching tip

The short phrases that are used to agree, disagree and give opinions are very useful. Students should make a note of them, learn them and try to use them whenever they have a discussion.

▶ Photocopiable Activity 5B p. 177.

1   This exercise gives students the language they need. Ask them to work in pairs but don't check their answers before playing the recording.

➡ Tapescript p. 103

2   This task shows students the way the phrases are actually used in a conversation.

3   This discussion allows students to practise using the phrases. Tell them to read through the statements alone and decide what they think about each one. Then put them into small groups for their discussion. Remind them to use the phrases they have learned in Exercises 1 and 2.

ANSWERS

Ex. 1

2 Oh, I don't really agree.

3 in my opinion

4 I agree up to a point, but

5 That's right.

6 I don't agree at all!

Ex. 2

1 I think, in my opinion

2 That's right (= stronger agreement), I agree up to a point, but ...

3 I don't really agree, I don't agree at all (= stronger disagreement)

See also: *Going for Gold Language Maximiser* Unit 5.

Your students are now ready to do Unit 5 test on p. 120.

UNIT
6 Whatever next?

Listening 1 p. 46

Aims:
- to introduce the theme of the unit
- to provide practice in listening for specific information

1 This discussion enables students to predict the content of what they will listen to. It could be done as a whole-class discussion.

2 Tell students that they are going to hear the answers to the questions they have discussed. Play the recording and check their answers.

➡ Tapescript p. 103

3 Remind students that before they listen to a recording they should read through the questions or statements in the task. This will help them to identify the information they need. Give them time to discuss whether they can guess if the statements are true or false, then play the recording and check their answers.

4 This discussion extends the topic of the listening. It can be done with the whole class, or in small groups. When discussing question 3, students should be encouraged to link their ideas in complex sentences as in the example.

ANSWERS

Ex. 2
1 His real name is Mitch Maddox and he spent a year living by just using the Internet to get what he needed.
2 The Internet first started in 1969.

Ex. 3
1 false (30)   2 false (mid seventies)   3 true
4 false   5 true   6 false

See also: *Going for Gold Language Maximiser* Unit 6.

Vocabulary 1: computers p. 46

Aim:
- to introduce topic vocabulary

1, **2** The matching exercise can be done in pairs. Check the answers with the whole class before asking students to do Exercise 2.

3, **4** These exercises will give students ideas and vocabulary for talking about the advantages and disadvantages of computers. When they have completed the notes, ask them to read the sentences again and decide whether they are true for them individually. Then ask them to work in small groups and compare their ideas.

ANSWERS

Ex. 1
1 D   2 F   3 B   4 G   5 E   6 H   7 C   8 A

Ex. 2
1 print   2 copy, paste   3 save   4 opened
5 existing   6 cut

Ex. 3
A: check my email; visit a website; word-processing; make a back-up copy; send/receive emails; surf the Net; buy online
B: get a virus; crash (your computer); lose a document

Reading p. 47

Aim:

• to practise looking for specific information

Exam information PET FCE CELS

In the Reading paper of the PET and FCE exams, students have to read a passage and choose the correct answer from four options. In the CELS exam, they may have to choose the correct answer from three options. These questions can be about detail, attitude of writer, reference or the meaning of a word. They could also be connected with the writer's intention or the overall purpose of the text.

Teaching tip

Suggesting that students try to predict the content of any reading or listening text will make the task easier for them. They should be encouraged to do this as a habit before starting any task. They can do it by reading the title of a reading text or the multiple-choice questions and options of a listening task.

1   This discussion starts students thinking about the topic of the reading text.

2   Point out to students that scanning is extremely useful as it helps them to deal with difficult texts. It is obviously important that they scan for something specific and the questions in Exercise 1 provide this stimulus.

3   Point out that when doing multiple-choice questions, students should always read the questions (though not necessarily all the options) before they look at the text. This will help them to scan the text and find the relevant parts of it to find the answers. When they read the text through first, they could mark relevant sections so that when they read again in detail they know where to look. Ask them to do the multiple-choice questions in pairs, following the suggested procedure, and then check the answers with the whole class.

4   Ask students to choose their answers, compare and discuss in pairs, and then discuss them with the class.

ANSWERS

Ex. 2

1 Stanley Kubrick originally wrote the film.
2 It is set in the distant future.
3 It's not a good film for young children because some bits of it are frightening and disturbing.

Ex. 3

1 D   2 A   3 C   4 B   5 B

Grammar 1: *will* and *going to* p. 49

Aim:

• to show the difference in use between *will* and *going to* for planning and predicting future events

1   This task contextualises the uses of *will* and *going to* for making plans or spontaneous decisions about the future. Do it with the whole class to make sure that all students understand the difference.

2, **3**   Ask students to work in pairs to complete these tasks, which check their understanding of the rules.

4   This exercise focuses on *will* and *going to* for different types of prediction. Do it with the whole class.

5   This task puts the uses of *will* and *going to* for prediction into a context. Ask students to work in pairs. For further practice, you could ask them to make up their own mini situation which they read to a small group and ask the others if they think it should be *will* or *going to* and why.

6   Ask students to discuss the predictions in small groups. Explain that they may need to use either *will* or *going to*, depending on whether they think there is evidence or whether they just believe it.

ANSWERS

Ex. 1

1
Situation 1: at the moment of speaking
Situation 2: before the moment of speaking
2
A: *will (not)* + infinitive
B: *am/are/is (not) going to* + infinitive

Ex. 2
1 's going to   2 'll   3 'll   4 is going to
5 'll   6 'm going to

Ex. 3
1 's going to   2 'll   3 's going to
4 isn't going to   5 won't   6 'll

Ex. 4
1
Situation 1: some evidence she can see now
Situation 2: something she knows or believes
2
A: *am/are/is (not) going to* + infinitive
B: *will (not)* + infinitive

Ex. 5
2 will (something you know or believe)
3 is going to (based on some evidence)
4 will (something you know or believe)
5 is going to (based on some evidence)
6 will (something you know or believe)
7 will (something you know or believe)
8 will (something you know or believe)
9 are going to (based on some evidence)
10 will (something you know or believe)

See also: *Going for Gold Language Maximiser* Unit 6.

Speaking p. 50

Aims:
- **to give students the chance to talk about their own future plans**
- **to give students other ways of talking about the future**

PET

1   Tell students that they are going to listen to a boy telling his friend about his future plans. Ask them to read the questions. Tell them to tick (✓) the ones he talks about. Play the recording.

➡ Tapescript p. 104

2   Tell students to look at the gaps in the sentences and see if they can complete any of them using words from the box. Then play the recording again so that they can check their answers.

3   This exercise focuses on accuracy and recycles the phrases taught in Exercise 2. Ask students to work in pairs and then play the recording so that they can check their answers. Play the recording again, stopping to do choral pronunciation of the sentences.

➡ Tapescript p. 104

4   Encourage students to interact with each other, and to ask questions, so that they don't just give each other information. Remind them of phrases they can use to sound interested,
e.g. *Really? That's interesting! Me too!*
and to ask questions, e.g.
How about you? And you? What do you think?
Do choral pronunciation of these phrases, putting emphasis on the intonation. Then ask students to work in pairs to do the exercise.

ANSWERS

Ex. 1
He talks about questions 2 and 3 (this weekend and the summer holidays).

Ex. 2
1 like   2 probably   3 sure   4 idea
5 depends   6 thinking

Ex. 3
1 I'd like to go to university.
2 I'm thinking about having a party.
3 It depends on my exam results.
4 I'm probably going to go travelling.
5 One idea is to buy a new computer.
6 I'm not sure but I think I'll get a job.

Vocabulary 2: collocations (adjective + preposition) p. 51

Aims:
- **to raise students' awareness of the importance of collocations**
- **to teach some collocations**

Exam information PET FCE

These types of collocation are often tested in the PET and FCE exams, in the cloze passage.

Teaching tip

Students often don't realise how important it is to make a note of words with their collocations, and not alone. If they do this, it will make the words easier to remember and use, and easier to remember in an exam situation. Encourage them to note new words in phrases.

1   Tell students what collocations are and why they are important. Do this exercise with the whole class, so that you can deal with any questions about collocations.

2   Ask students to do this matching exercise in pairs. Ask them to underline the collocations so that they can refer to them in the future.

3   This exercise allows students to use the collocations in a personal context, which should make it easier for them to remember them. Ask them to complete the questions, and then ask a partner. They can then exchange roles. For further practice, they could write a short paragraph about their partner.

▶ Photocopiable Activities 6A and 6B p. 178 and 179.

ANSWERS

Ex. 1
1 C   2 A   3 D

Ex. 2
1 j   2 h   3 e   4 g   5 i   6 d   7 f   8 c
9 a   10 b

Ex. 3
1 on   2 at   3 to   4 to   5 in   6 about
7 from   8 of

See also: *Going for Gold Language Maximiser* Unit 6.

Listening 2 p. 51

Aim:
• to listen for specific information

Exam information   PET   FCE   CELS

In the Listening papers of the PET and FCE exams, students have to listen to a recording of a conversation or monologue and answer multiple-choice questions. In the CELS exam, they have to listen to short extracts and answer multiple-choice questions.

1   This discussion introduces the topic of the listening. Ask students to work in pairs.

2   Tell students to read through the list of things talked about before you play the recording. Check answers with the class.

➡ Tapescript p. 104

3   Remind students that they should read through the questions and the options before they listen, and that they will hear the answers in the same order as they are in the task. Play the recording twice and check answers. Discuss any wrong answers and play the relevant part of the recording again if necessary so that students can hear why they made a mistake.

4   These discussion points extend the topic of the listening. Ask students to work in pairs or small groups. Alternatively, run a formal debate on the topic of questions 3 or 4. Write one of them in the form of a statement on the board, e.g.
Computer games have a negative effect on children's health.
Parents should have total control over the computer games children play.
Ask students to think of ideas for and against and then have a formal debate. At the end, students can vote on whether they agree or disagree with the statement.

ANSWERS

Ex. 2
The speaker talks about: 1, 2, 4, 5 and 6 (3 and 7 are not mentioned).

Ex. 3
1 B   2 C   3 C   4 B   5 A   6 B

Grammar 2: present simple and present continuous for future p. 52

Aim:

- **to present and practise the uses of the present simple and present continuous for future time**

1 Ask students to read the dialogue through, ignoring the gaps and to say what is happening on Saturday morning. Then play them the recording and ask them to write the correct verb in the spaces. Check answers with the class.

➡ Tapescript p. 104

2 Ask students to use their answers to Exercise 1 to work out the rules. Check that the whole class understands. Refer them to the Grammar reference p. 140 if they need more help.

3 Students could complete Exercise 3 in pairs. Check answers with the class.

4 This exercise allows freer practise of the target structures. As a follow-up to the discussion in pairs, students could write a short paragraph about their partner's future plans.

ANSWERS

Ex. 1
1 The final of the computer games competition.
2 1 finishes   2 are going   3 'm meeting   4 starts

Ex. 2
1
Verbs 1 and 4: present simple
Verbs 2 and 3: present continuous
2 A: present continuous   B: present simple

Ex. 3
1 timetable – starts
2 arrangement – 'm going
3 timetable – arrives
4 arrangement – 'm playing
5 timetable – does this programme finish
6 arrangement – are having
7 arrangement – are you meeting
8 arrangement – 'm not studying
9 arrangement – 'm staying
10 timetable – closes

See also: *Going for Gold Language Maximiser* Unit 6.

Writing: messages and notes p. 53

Aims:

- **to show the differences in style between a note and a letter**
- **to teach the meaning of common abbreviations**

Exam information PET CELS

In the PET and CELS exams students may have to write a short note. In the Reading paper of the PET exam they have to understand the meaning of a note or sign.

Teaching tip

Students need to be aware of the style differences between different types of writing. Try to show them as many different types of text as possible, so that they can recognise these differences.

1 Emphasise that writing a note is a real-life task.

2 This task focuses on the style differences between a note and a letter. Ask students to do it in pairs, and then discuss the answers with the whole class.

3 Do this with the whole class. Ask them to look at the sentences and see if they can guess from the context what the abbreviation means. Tell them that these abbreviations are very common and would be used in informal notes.

4 Ask students to work together to change the style of the notes. Suggest that they start by underlining any phrases or expressions that are too formal before trying to change anything.

ANSWERS

Ex. 1
Suggestions:
When we go out and want to tell something to someone who lives with us.
When we can't speak, e.g. in a library.
When we want to warn people of something, e.g. photocopier out of order.
When we want to remind someone (or ourselves) to do something.

Ex. 2
Message B is more appropriate because it is short and uses informal language and abbreviations. Auxiliary verbs and articles are not used much.

Ex. 3
1 Sat. = Saturday; p.m. = afternoon/evening
2 a.s.a.p. = as soon as possible
3 tel. no. = telephone number
4 N.B. = important – take note! (from the Latin: *Nota bene*)
5 e.g. = for example; etc. = and so on (more examples of the same thing)

Ex. 4
Suggested answers:
Tony,
Dave phoned 9 p.m. Are you free on Sat.?
If yes, he'll get an extra ticket for football match. Call him.
Paul

Sally,
V. sorry – have to meet my sister this a.m. Can you do shopping for party? We need all the things we talked about – I'll pay for half.
There is some money in my bedroom on desk.
See you later. Hope to be home 2–3 p.m.
Eva

See also: *Going for Gold Language Maximiser* Unit 6.

Your students are now ready to do Progress test 2 on p. 122.

Units 4–6 Progress check p. 54

ANSWERS

Ex. 1
1
1 I fell asleep while I was watching the television.
2 While I was travelling in Europe, I met some interesting people.
3 I saw two buses go past while I was running to the bus stop.
4 He fell off his bike while he was cycling to a friend's house.
2
1 Olivia offered to pay for the meal, but David had already paid.
2 When I arrived, I had missed the beginning of the film.
3 By the time he was four, he had learned to read perfectly.
4 After closing the door, I realised I had left my key in the house.

Ex. 2
1 happy   2 carefully   3 easy   4 well
5 beautiful   6 happily   7 careful   8 good
9 beautifully   10 easily

Ex. 3
1 tall   2 skinny   3 blonde   4 wavy
5 attractive   6 medium height   7 well-built
8 moustache   9 beard   10 curly
11 good-looking

Ex. 4
1 been   2 didn't   3 wanted   4 would
5 had   6 could   7 if/whether   8 hadn't
9 could   10 wouldn't

Ex. 5
1 C   2 A   3 B   4 B   5 B   6 B   7 C   8 A
9 C   10 B   11 A

Ex. 6
1 'm going to   2 is going to   3 are going to
4 is going to   5 'll   6 'll   7 is going to
8 'll   9 'll   10 are going to

Ex. 7
1 'm going   2 correct   3 correct
4 is working   5 depart   6 finishes
7 correct   8 Are you seeing   9 correct
10 'm staying

UNIT
7 Body works

Vocabulary 1: sports p. 56

Aims:
- **to provide topic vocabulary**
- **to provide vocabulary to help students with the listening**

1 This could be done with the whole class. Write the topic areas on the board and ask students to come up and write a word in the correct column. Ask students to mark the stress on the words and do choral pronunciation practice with the whole class.

2 Ask students to work in pairs to complete the sentences.

3 This exercise will help students to use the context to identify the topic of a sentence or the meaning of words. Ask them to underline the words that helped them to identify the sport, e.g. *ball, racket*.

4 Do the Watch Out box with the whole class, as these words are often confused.

5 This discussion will enable students to use the words they have learned. Ask them to work in small groups, and report back to the rest of the class.

See also: *Going for Gold Language Maximiser* Unit 7.

ANSWERS

Ex. 1
Sport: basketball, motor racing, tennis, athletics
Equipment: football, crash helmet, net, racket
People: captain, umpire, spectators
Place: court, pitch, track

Ex. 2
1 racket 2 pitch 3 net 4 crash helmet
5 spectators 6 umpire 7 captain 8 track
9 court 10 athletics

Ex. 3
1 tennis (ball, net, racket, court)
2 motor racing (track, drivers, flag, race off)
3 football (season, manager, players, score goals)
4 basketball (tall, ball, basket)

Watch Out: *win* or *beat*?
1 win 2 beat

Speaking p. 57

Aims:
- **to give students vocabulary for describing pictures**
- **to help students to keep a conversation going by asking for opinions and giving their own**

Exam information PET

In Part 3 of the PET exam, each student has to describe a picture. In Part 4, they then discuss a related topic (given to them by the examiner) with their partner. It is particularly important that in the discussion they ask each other's opinions and don't just say what they think themselves. The work in this section will help students with both of these parts of the Speaking paper. The final task in this section (Exercise 5) is a typical PET task for the discussion following the pictures.

---

1 This exercise gives students key vocabulary for talking about the pictures.

2 Ask students to read the table before playing the recording. Then ask them to listen and fill in the missing information.

➡ Tapescript p. 104

3 This focuses students on ways of asking for opinions or information. Ask them to predict what the missing words might be before playing the recording. Practise saying the questions to help their pronunciation and intonation.

4 Ask students to work in pairs to discuss the topics. Remind them to ask for their partner's views as well as giving their own.

5 This provides free practice and should be done in pairs.

ANSWERS

Ex. 1
Picture A: a gym, an exercise machine
Picture B: to go jogging, traffic, the weather, street
Both: to get exercise, trainers

Ex. 2

	Carla		Gerhard	
Gym	Likes	✓	Likes	✓
	Dislikes	☐	Dislikes	☐
	Why?		Why?	
	Near my home		Go with friends	
	Can watch MTV		Can have coffee after	
Jogging	Likes	☐	Likes	✓
	Dislikes	✗	Dislikes	☐
	Why?		Why?	
	Boring		Peaceful	
	Weather can be bad		Relaxing	

Ex. 3
1 about you   2 don't you   3 what, you like

Reading 1 p. 58

Aims:
• to practise reading for specific information

Exam information PET CELS

In the Reading paper of the PET and CELS exams, students have to read statements and decide if they are true or false. In CELS they have to decide if the information is true, false or not given.

---

1 Discussion of the pictures should raise students' interest in the topic of the reading text.

2 Ask students to read the text and match the people to the opinions.

3 Ask them to read through the statements. They should then read the text again and decide if each statement is true or false. Ask students to check their answers with a partner before checking with the class.

4 This is a general discussion. Encourage students to ask for each other's ideas as well as giving their own opinions.

ANSWERS

Ex. 2
a) a good thing: Tara
b) a bad thing: Thomas
c) can be good or bad: Rachel, David

Ex. 3
1 true   2 false   3 false   4 true   5 true
6 true   7 false   8 true

Grammar 1: *must, mustn't, have to, don't have to* p. 59

Aim:
• **to present and practise the use of modal verbs of obligation and prohibition**

1 Explain the meaning of the words in rules A, B, C and D. Then ask students to suggest which rule matches each example sentence 1–4.

2 Ask students to work in pairs. Remind them to read the whole text through before they try to complete the spaces.

3 Ask students to work in pairs to rewrite the sentences. Check answers with the whole class.

4 When students have written down their two things they have to do, don't need to do and mustn't do, ask them to compare their ideas with other students. Are they the same or different? Is there anything that everyone in the class has to do, or mustn't do?

See also: *Going for Gold Language Maximiser* Unit 7.

ANSWERS

Ex. 1
1 D   2 C   3 B   4 A

Ex. 2
2 have to swim
3 have to go
4 don't have to do
5 don't have to change
6 mustn't eat

Ex. 3
1 You don't have to go up the stairs. There's a lift.
2 Hannah mustn't eat fish. She's allergic to it.
3 He doesn't have to go to work today because it's a public holiday.
4 You mustn't be late. They close the door at 9 o'clock.
5 You don't have to pay to go into this museum. It's free.

Listening p. 60

Aims:
• **to listen for specific information**

Exam information PET FCE CELS

In the Listening papers of the PET, FCE and CELS exams, students have to complete notes based on a listening text, usually a monologue. They may only have to write one or two words.

1 This discussion introduces the topic of the listening. Do it with the whole class.

2 Ask students to read through the list of subjects before you play the recording. After they have done the task, ask them to compare their answers with a partner before you check with the whole class.

➡ Tapescript p. 104

3 Tell students that they are going to fill in some missing information. Ask them to read through the notes and see if they can guess any of the missing words. Encourage them to think about what kind of information it might be, and what form of the word they might need to use.

4 See if students can remember this information – if not, then play the recording again.

5 Ask students to do the puzzle in pairs.

6 Students could do this in small groups.

▶ Photocopiable Activities 7A and 7B pp.180 and 181.

ANSWERS

Ex. 2
He talks about 1, 3, 5, 6, 7 and 9.

Ex. 3
2 himself   3 stars   4 hearts   5 happy
6 coffee   7 bicycle   8 teachers
9 shoulders   10 very expensive

Ex. 4
back, face, shoulders, arms

Ex. 5
Across: 1 toe   **5** thumb   **6** skin   **7** ankle
Down: 1 shoulder   **2** eyebrows   **3** neck
5 tongue   **8** nose   **9** lips

Grammar 2: requests with *can*, *could* and *would* p. 61

Aim:
• **to present and practise using modal verbs for making polite requests**

1 , **2** Ask students to do the matching exercise in pairs. Then play the recording so they can check their answers. Practise pronunciation of the phrases, and encourage students to think about intonation so that they sound polite.

➡ Tapescript p. 105

3 This exercise allows students to practise polite requests in different situations. You could ask them to roleplay their dialogues to the class.

ANSWERS

Ex. 1
2 d   3 c   4 e   5 a   6 b   7 f

See also: *Going for Gold Language Maximiser* Unit 7.

Reading 2 p. 62

Aim:

- **to provide practice in scanning for specific information**

Exam information PET CELS FCE
In the PET Reading paper, students have to match descriptions of people with summaries of books, videos, holidays, activities and so on. Students have to choose the most appropriate summary for each person described. In the CELS exams, students have to match information to a particular text or piece of information. In the FCE exam, they have to match statements or questions to part of a text or texts and say where the information or statement is mentioned. The work in this section follows the PET format.

Teaching tip

Remind students that there are key words in both the descriptions of the people and the descriptions of the books. They may find a match for one of the key words in several options, but only one option will match all the key words.

1   Read through the instructions carefully with the class. Then ask them to do the reading task in pairs.

2   This discussion allows students to react to the texts in a personal way. If they aren't interested in reading any of the books described, ask them what type of books (or magazines) they do like reading.

ANSWERS
Ex. 1
1 C   **2** H   **3** B   **4** E   **5** D

Vocabulary 2: phrasal verbs (health and fitness) p. 63

Aims:

- **to introduce phrasal verbs connected with the topic of health and fitness**
- **to provide practice in using phrasal verbs in natural contexts**

1 , **2**   Ask students to do the matching exercise in pairs. Check their answers before asking them to do Exercise 2.

3   This discussion allows students to use the phrasal verbs to give personal information. Ask them to work in small groups, and encourage them to share information in the same way as in the Speaking sections.

ANSWERS
Ex. 1
2 c   **3** a   **4** e   **5** g   **6** f   **7** d
Ex. 2
1 come   **2** pass   **3** worn   **4** getting   **5** get
6 come   **7** carry

▶ Photocopiable Activity 7C p. 182.

See also: *Going for Gold Language Maximiser* Unit 7.

Writing: informal letter (3) p. 63

Aims:
- **to focus on punctuation**
- **to help students edit their work**

Exam information PET FCE CELS
In the Writing paper of the PET, FCE and CELS exams, students may have to write an informal letter.

1   Ask students to correct the punctuation in pairs. They can refer to the Writing reference on p. 148 if necessary. To check their answers, you could ask a pair to come and write their corrected sentence on the board so that all the students can see it and check their own answers.

2 , **3**   Students have to read the letter to identify what its main point is before going on to correct any punctuation mistakes.

4   Read through the plan with the students. Then tell them that they are going to write their own letter, following the plan. Ask them how many things they have to do in the task. Then ask them to write the letter. Remind them to check their punctuation when they have finished.

ANSWERS

Ex. 1
1 She went to Germany with Martin on Friday.
2 He wrote some emails, arranged a meeting, spoke to his manager and then left the office.
3 Jeremy will eat potatoes, carrots, peas and tomatoes but he won't eat mushrooms.
4 I'll put these clothes on Rachel's bed.

Ex. 2
He mentions the swimming pool, the basketball, tennis and badminton courts, the gym and the café.

Ex. 3
Dear Kerry,
Thank you for your letter. It sounds like you had a great holiday!
I'm just writing to invite you to come with me to a great new leisure centre which has just opened near my house. It's got a huge swimming pool and courts for basketball, tennis and badminton. They've also got a very modern gym and a really nice café where you can get drinks and snacks.
Let me know if you're interested. It would be great to see you and hear all your news!
Love,
Tim

See also: *Going for Gold Language Maximiser* Unit 7.

Your students are now ready to do Unit 7 test on p. 125.

Reading p. 64

Aims:

- **to help students identify the topic of a paragraph**
- **to help students to identify specific information**
- **to help students understand reference**

Exam information FCE CELS

In the Reading paper of the FCE exam, students have to match headings to paragraphs. The headings give the main idea of the paragraph. In the CELS exam, students may have to identify a paragraph by a sentence which gives the main topic. This section provides some practice for this. There is also help with multiple-choice questions, in particular identifying the relevant part of the text for each multiple-choice question.

Teaching tip

It is useful to ask students to identify topic sentences in paragraphs in any reading text. This will help them with the exam task types above, but will also enable them generally to understand the way texts are organised.

1 These discussion points introduce ideas and vocabulary to help students with the reading task.

2 Read the questions with the class and then ask students to read the text quickly to find the answers.

3 This task focuses students on the organisation of the text and on topic sentences. Refer students to the Writing reference on p. 149 for help with paragraphing. Exercise 3.2 shows students how the questions are spread through the text. Ask students to read only the question, and then mark the relevant paragraph. This will make it much easier for them to do the task in Exercise 3.3.

ANSWERS

Ex. 1

1 Tom Hanks in *Cast Away*

2 looking for food, being alone, missing his family and friends, being frightened of dangerous animals, etc.

Ex. 2

1 They are living on a Scottish island. They are staying there for a year as part of a television programme/project.

2 Tom Hanks was playing a real castaway (someone who escapes from a shipwreck and reaches a desert island). The people in the TV programme were taken to an island for a specific reason and length of time (so they are not real castaways).

Ex. 3

1

Paragraph 1: In the year 2000, a television company did an experiment called Castaway 2000.

Paragraph 2: One of the 'castaways' was Roger Stephenson.

Paragraph 3: Two other castaways were a couple, Dez and Liz.

2

Question 1: Paragraph 1
Question 2: Paragraph 1
Question 3: Paragraph 2
Question 4: Paragraph 2
Question 5: Paragraph 2
Question 6: Paragraph 3

3

1 B   2 D   3 C   4 D   5 B   6 A

Optional activity

To provide further free practice, ask students to choose four people in their class (not including themselves) who they think should live on the Castaway island with each other. Tell them to think about why the people they choose would make a good group together. Then ask them to work with a partner and tell each other about the group they've chosen and why. Explain that they have to give detailed reasons why they think the people in their group would be good together. Then they have to discuss whether they agree with each other's ideas or not, and why.

Grammar 1: present perfect (for indefinite past) p. 65

Aim:

- **to present and practise the use of the present perfect for expressing actions that took place at an indefinite time in the past**

1 , **2** Do the matching activity with the whole class so that all students understand the rules. Then ask them to do Exercise 2 in pairs.

3 When students have filled in the missing verbs in the dialogue, they could read it aloud. Remind them about intonation patterns, and ask them to try to make the dialogue sound as interesting as possible. Do choral pronunciation of some of the useful ways of showing interest as students can use these in the Speaking paper of the PET, FCE and CELS exams.

4 Ask students to unjumble the questions by themselves. Then they can work with a partner and take turns to ask and answer the questions.

ANSWERS

Ex. 1
I've lived = B (present perfect)
I lived = A (past simple)

Ex. 2
1 Have you ever lived in an unusual home?
3 Has she done the shopping yet?
4 I've already bought some more bread – look, it's there!
5 He's just decided to move house.
6 Have you ever grown your own vegetables?
8 She's already finished making the dinner.

Ex. 3
2 've never been   3 Have you been
4 have just booked   5 told
6 Have you done   7 haven't done
8 have already written   9 bought

Ex. 4
1 What's the most exciting thing you've ever done?

---

2 What have you never done that you'd like to do?
3 Did you make any New Year Resolutions?
4 Have you broken any of your New Year Resolutions yet?

See also: *Going for Gold Language Maximiser* Unit 8.

Vocabulary 1: town and country p. 66

Aims:

- **to provide key topic vocabulary**
- **to provide practice in using the vocabulary to discuss the advantages and disadvantages of living in the country**

1 , **2** Ask students to work in pairs to do these exercises and then check answers with the whole class.

3 Tell students to read the questions in 1, then play the recording and elicit answers. Then ask them to fill in the missing words in 2, and play the recording again to check their answers.

➡ Tapescript p. 105

4 Encourage students to use complete sentences for this, e.g. *The country isn't too crowded but there aren't many facilities.*
Remind them of linking words they can use to contrast ideas: *but, on the other hand, whereas, though*. Refer students to the Writing reference on p. 147 for help in linking sentences together.

5 This discussion gives students ideas for the topic. Ask them to work in small groups.

ANSWERS

Ex. 2
1 peaceful   2 crowded   3 built up
4 polluted   5 facilities   6 public transport
7 open space   8 traffic   9 nightlife

Ex. 3
1
1 from the country to a city
2 generally happy
2 2 peaceful   3 open space   4 built up
   5 traffic   6 polluted   7 facilities
   8 public transport   9 nightlife

Speaking p. 67

Aim:

• to show students how to compare and contrast pictures

Exam information   FCE

In the FCE exam, students have to compare and contrast photographs.

1, **2**   Ask students to work in pairs. Check answers with the class.

3   This writing task focuses students on linking ideas and giving reasons.

4   This provides a framework for doing the task. Go through it with students to remind them of how to organise their talk. Then ask them to do the task in pairs. Tell them to listen to each other and comment on the way their partner organised their talk, and how well the ideas in the sentences were linked.

ANSWERS

Ex. 1

1 on the right – on the left; at the bottom – at the top
2 the right way up – upside down or the wrong way up
3 in the background – in the foreground
4 under – over or above
5 in front of – behind

Ex. 2
Picture C: cottage
Picture D: block of flats

▶ Photocopiable Activity 8A p. 183.

Writing: transactional letter (1) p. 68

Aims:

• to show how a transactional letter is organised
• to provide some linking words for use in transactional letters
• to show students what is required of them in a task like this

---

Exam information   FCE   CELS

In the Writing paper of the FCE exam, there is a compulsory question. Students are given some information and they have to write a letter in response to this. In their letter they may have to give information, request information, make a complaint, correct some incorrect information or respond to suggestions. There is also a transactional letter in the CELS exam.

Teaching tip

When students do a writing task, it is very useful if they compare their answers. Checking another student's work develops good editing skills and reinforces the things they have to be careful of in their own writing.

---

1   This exercise focuses on the requirements of the writing task. Do it with the whole class.

2   Ask students to work in pairs. Tell them that important parts of the letter are missing. Tell them to look back at the task itself, and at the ideas mentioned in Exercise 1.

3   This exercise focuses on useful linking words for contrasting ideas. After students have identified the linking words in the letter, write them on the board. For further practice, students could choose one of the linking words and write a sentence linking ideas. They could then compare their sentence with a partner to see if it is correct or not.

4   This task also focuses on linking words, but this time with typical student mistakes. Ask students to work in pairs.

5 Rewriting the sentences allows students to use linking words in controlled sentences. Ask them to work in pairs.

6 Before students write their letter, remind them to:
- check all parts of the task – they have to give information, and make suggestions with reasons
- include all the necessary information
- include correct layout features
- plan their ideas and organise them into paragraphs
- link ideas with appropriate linking words.

Then either set the task for homework or ask students to write their letter in class.

7 If students do the task for homework, then do this exercise at the start of the next lesson. It is important that students read and check each other's work as it will help them to develop good editing skills.

▶ Photocopiable Activity 8B p. 184.

ANSWERS

Ex. 1
1 a friend 2 yes 3 yes 4 100–120 words

Ex. 2
1 You should start a letter with *Dear* ...
2 You should say why you're writing in the first paragraph.
3 You should include your opinion in a final paragraph.
4 You should finish an informal letter with *Love* ... or *Best wishes* ...

Ex. 3
1 contrasting views
2 but: ... the people are very friendly but I think the Scottish accent is difficult to understand
3
Although there are lots of interesting places to visit, the public transport is very expensive.
In Brighton, *on the other hand*, the buses are quite cheap and the beaches are free!
There aren't as many tourist places in Brighton. There is, *however*, a good funfair and lots of nice cafés.

Ex. 4
1 Both are correct.
2 Sentence b is incorrect because we don't use commas around *but*.

---

3 Sentence b is incorrect because the clause with *however* should be a separate sentence.
4 Sentence b is incorrect because the clause with *on the other hand* should be a separate sentence.

Ex. 5
1 Although I leave the house on time, I'm often late for school. / I'm often late for school although I leave the house on time.
2 We went to Paris but we didn't see the Eiffel Tower.
3 I like learning English. However, I sometimes find it difficult. / I like learning English. I sometimes find it difficult, however.
4 There aren't any cinemas. On the other hand, there are lots of sports facilities.

See also: *Going for Gold Language Maximiser* Unit 8.

Listening p. 69

Aims:
- **to help students decide whether something is a fact or an opinion**
- **to practise note-taking**

Exam information PET FCE CELS

In the Listening papers of the PET, FCE and CELS exams, students have to complete notes based on a listening text, usually a monologue. They may only have to write one or two words.

---

1 This discussion prepares students for the topic of the listening text. It also revises some useful topic vocabulary. Students should discuss the questions in small groups. Suggest that they make a note of the reasons why they do or don't have routines.

2 Tell students that they are going to hear two people discussing their own routines. Ask them to listen and decide whether the two speakers have the same or different opinions.

➡ Tapescript p. 105

3   Explain that it is important to be able to tell when someone is giving factual information or stating their opinion. Ask students to look at the statements. Go through the example with them, and then ask them to work in pairs. Check their answers, then practise saying the expressions that give opinions.

4   Ask students to read through the sentences in 1 and decide what kind of word is missing. What kind of information should they listen for? Can they guess what any answers might be? This will help them to identify the missing information when they listen. Then play the recording for students to complete the sentences. Ask them to compare their answers in pairs before checking with the whole class. Ask them to check each other's spelling and word formation.

5   Ask students to work in pairs or small groups. When they have discussed the statements, get feedback from the whole class. Which statement do most of the class agree with?

ANSWERS

Ex. 2
They have different opinions.

Ex. 3
1 opinion   2 opinion   3 fact   4 fact
5 opinion   6 fact

Ex. 4
1
1 number (of years)   2 place   3 noun
4 meal / food   5 type of food   6 type of food
7 age   8 adjective
2
1 nine   2 different places   3 routine
4 breakfast   5 sandwich   6 eggs, bacon and tomatoes   7 25   8 depressing (awful / boring)

Grammar 2: present perfect (unfinished past) p. 70

Aims:
- **to present uses of the present perfect for the unfinished past**
- **to present uses of the present perfect with *for* and *since***
- **to provide controlled practice**

1   Do this with the whole class and explain the time lines. Explain that this visual idea for showing time can help them to remember what the different uses of the present perfect actually refer to.

2   Ask students to do this exercise in pairs, and check the answers with the whole class.

3, **4**   Ask students to complete these exercises in pairs, and then check answers with the whole class.

5   This activity allows students to use *for* and *since* in natural contexts so that they will find it easier to remember the differences between them.

ANSWERS

Ex. 1
1 B   2 A

Ex. 2
1
1 and 2: 1 is correct because we use the present perfect (with *for* and *since*) to talk about events which started in the past and continued to the present. We use the present simple to talk about habits/repeated events (but without saying how long this has continued).
3 and 4: 3 is correct because we use *for* with a period of time (e.g. *two months, five minutes*). We use *since* with a point of time (e.g. *January, when I was a child*).
5 and 6: 5 is correct because we use the phrase *How long ...?* to ask about the duration of an action from the past to present. *How long time ...?* is incorrect.

2
A for
B since

Ex. 3
1 for   **2** since   **3** since   **4** since   **5** for
6 since

Ex. 4
1 I've known her since I was nine.
2 She's worked there for two years.
3 How long have you had it?
4 They lived in Rome for ten years.
5 He hasn't played football since he broke his leg.
6 How long have you been in this class?

See also: *Going for Gold Language Maximiser* Unit 8.

Vocabulary 2: adjectives ending -*ed* and -*ing* p. 71

Aims:
- **to show the difference between adjectives that end in -*ed* and -*ing***
- **to provide controlled and free practice in using these adjectives**

1   Do this exercise with the whole class so that they understand the difference between the adjective endings. Do some work on pronunciation. Explain:
interested: 3 syllables /ˈɪntrəstɪd/ -*ed* is pronounced separately
amazed: 2 syllables, /əˈmeɪzd/ -*ed* is not pronounced separately
bored: 1 syllable, /bɔːd/ -*ed* is not pronounced separately
depressed: 2 syllables, /dɪˈprest/ -*ed* is not pronounced separately

2   Ask students to work in pairs and choose the correct form of the word.

3   This exercise provides freer practice. Remind students to ask each other about their experiences and not just explain their own. Remind them of some of the phrases they can use, such as *What do you think? How about you?*

ANSWERS

Ex. 1
1 adjectives ending -*ing*
2 adjectives ending -*ed*

Ex. 2
1 a confusing   **b** confused
2 a surprising   **b** surprised
3 a boring   **b** bored
4 a frightened   **b** frightening
5 a annoyed   **b** annoying
6 a exciting   **b** excited

See also: *Going for Gold Language Maximiser* Unit 8.

Your students are now ready to do Unit 8 test on p. 127.

More than words

Use of English: vocabulary (cloze)
p. 72

Aims:
- **to provide information about the topic of communication**
- **to prepare students for the work in the Grammar section**
- **to provide practice in completing multiple-choice cloze passages**

Exam information PET FCE

In the PET and FCE exams, students have to complete a multiple-choice cloze. In each case the focus is on vocabulary, although there may be some grammar areas tested, such as connectors or prepositions.

1 This discussion introduces the topic of the reading text. Do it with the whole class.

2 Remind students to read the title of the passage as this will help them to decide what it is about. Then ask them to read the text quickly without filling in any spaces, to find out where whistling is used for communicating. Remind them that they should always follow this procedure with a gapped text.

3 Students read the text again to see if they can fill in any spaces without looking at the options. When they have done this, tell them to work through the text again, choosing the best option for each space. Suggest that they write the actual word in the space, not just the letter so they can use it later for revision. Ask them to compare with a partner before checking the answers with the whole class.

ANSWERS

Ex. 1
Possible answers: by signalling with boards or flags; sign language; body language; facial expressions; smoke signals; Morse code; noises, e.g. *Sssshh!* etc.

Ex. 2
Oaxaca, Mexico; north eastern Turkey; La Gomera (one of the Canary Islands)

Ex. 3
2 D   3 A   4 B   5 D   6 D   7 C   8 C
9 B   10 D   11 A

Grammar 1: defining relative clauses
p. 73

Aim:
- **to present and practise defining relative clauses**

1 Explain that defining relative clauses tell us exactly which person or thing is being described. Ask students to read the example sentences and then answer the questions in Exercise 1.2. Discuss their answers.

2 Ask students to work in pairs to join the sentences.

3 Do the Watch Out box with the whole class. Then ask students to do Exercise 3 in pairs.

4 This exercise allows students to use defining relative clauses to give personal information. Ask them to complete the sentences for themselves, and then to compare their answers with a partner. They can ask each other questions to find out further information about their answers. Remind them to respond in an interested way to what their partner says.

ANSWERS

Ex. 1

1 *the man* is replaced by *who*

2 *it* is replaced by *which*

3 *there* is replaced by *where*

4 no commas are used

Ex. 2

1 The book is about a young man who travels around the world.

2 Have you got the pen which I lent you yesterday?

3 That's the café where we went for a drink last night.

4 He was the man whose corn leaves I bought.

5 I don't like the new boy who is tall and has long black hair.

6 She works for a company which makes microchips for computers.

7 Here is a photo of the party where I met my boyfriend.

8 They are the people whose flight was cancelled.

Watch Out: *that* (1)

Both alternatives are possible in each sentence because they are both defining clauses.

Ex. 3

1 Where is the newspaper which was in the living room?

2 These are the keys (that) I was looking for.

3 The girl who lives next door has a motorbike.

4 The village where I was born has a beautiful old church.

5 What was the name of the CD (which) you bought yesterday?

6 Losing my job is the best thing that has ever happened to me.

7 The guy (who) I met on holiday sent me an email last night.

8 Do you know a shop where I can get an English newspaper?

See also: *Going for Gold Language Maximiser* Unit 9.

Vocabulary 1: sounds p. 74

Aim:

• to introduce vocabulary that can help students to make their story telling more interesting

1 , **2**   This can be a fun activity. Play the recording and see if students can match the sounds. Then ask them to work in pairs to decide who or what makes the noise. Ask them to justify their answers – they may disagree!

3   Ask students to work in pairs to complete the sentences.

Optional activity

Explain that this kind of vocabulary makes stories more interesting. Ask students to work in small groups to think of a story using the vocabulary in Exercise 1. They should each say a sentence that continues the story and try to get in as many words as possible.

4   Explain that if students are aware of sounds around them, then they are more likely to think of them when they are writing a story. Ask the class to listen and to write down as many sounds as possible that they can actually hear in the classroom. Then give each group the name of a different place (such as a supermarket, a train station, a forest, a city centre) and ask them to think of the sounds that they could hear in that place. Get feedback from the groups and collect words for each place.

ANSWERS

Ex. 1

1 whisper   2 crash   3 ring   4 yawn

5 bang   6 scream   7 whistle   8 sneeze

Ex. 2

whisper a   crash a, b, c   ring c   yawn a, b

bang c   scream a, b   whistle a, b, c

sneeze a, b

Ex. 3

1 screaming   2 yawning   3 whispering

4 ringing   5 crash   6 whistles   7 bang

See also: *Going for Gold Language Maximiser* Unit 9.

Listening 1: song p. 75

Aims:
- **to develop understanding and use of a lexical set**
- **to listen for pleasure**

1   This pre-listening activity helps students to predict the content and topic of the song.

2   Explain that all the words are connected with communication, but they are used in different ways and have different meanings. Encourage students to discuss the differences.

3, **4**   Students could sing along as they listen for the second time. This is excellent pronunciation practice, and fun. Elicit answers to the questions around the class.

➡ Tapescript p. 105

ANSWERS

Ex. 1
Sometimes people communicate better when they don't use words, e.g. by using facial expressions, body language and so on.

Ex. 2
1 speak   2 saying   3 explain   4 hear
5 know   6 saying   7 says   8 talking
9 define   10 said

Reading p. 75

Aims:
- **to help students to understand the writer's attitude**
- **to scan for specific information in different texts**

Exam information FCE CELS

In the FCE exam, students are given four or five different texts, or one text divided into sections. They have to read statements and decide which text or part of the text it relates to. In the CELS exam they have to relate statements to paragraphs of a text.

Teaching tip

Students should read the text(s) quickly to get an idea of what they are about. Then they should read the statements, and then try to match them up. The statements do not appear in any order, so students should take each statement in turn and try to find it in any of the text(s).

---

1   This question focuses on the writers' attitudes. Make sure that students understand the difference between *very* and *quite* in this context. Ask them to tell you which is stronger (*very*).

2   Ask students to work in pairs. Check their answers with the whole class.

3   This discussion question allows students to talk about the topic of the reading texts.

ANSWERS

Ex. 1
1 Lia and Rajmund are very positive.
2 Pierre and Sylvia are quite positive.

Ex. 2
2 Lia   3 Pierre   4 Rajmund   5 Sylvia
6 Pierre   7 Lia   8 Sylvia   9 Pierre

See also: *Going for Gold Language Maximiser* Unit 9.

Speaking: negotiating p. 76

Aims:
• **to give students language for negotiating**
• **to provide free speaking practice**

Exam information   FCE   PET   CELS
The final task in the section gives specific practice for Part 3 of the FCE Speaking paper, but it is also useful practice for PET and CELS.

1 Write suggestions on the board so that students can compare their ideas with the recording.

2 Tell students that they are going to listen to a group of young people discussing the same problem. Play the recording and ask them to listen for:
• any ideas that are the same as theirs
• what the young people decided to buy.

➡ Tapescript p. 106

3 Tell students that when they are negotiating they have to:
• make suggestions, e.g. *How about ...*
• give opinions, e.g. *I think ...*
• agree, e.g. *That's a good idea ...*
• disagree, e.g. *I'm sorry, I don't agree ...*
• make decisions, e.g. *So we're going to ...*
Elicit some ideas for these language functions and write them on the board. Then ask students to complete the questions using words from the box. Finally, add the expressions from the box to the list on the board.

4 This activity gives students controlled practice in using the target language. Ask them to work in pairs. For further practice, ask them to think of three more suggestions. Then in groups of four, they have a conversation using their own suggestions.

5 , **6** These tasks allow students to use the language in a problem-solving task.

▶ Photocopiable Activities 9A and 9B pp. 185 and 186.

ANSWERS
Ex. 2   some travel books about Italy
Ex. 3
1 how about   2 interesting suggestion
3 what about   4 bad idea
5 Why don't we   6 really good idea

Listening 2 p. 77

Aim:
• **to provide practice in listening for specific information**

Exam information   PET   FCE   CELS
In the Listening papers of the PET and FCE exams, students have to listen to a recording of a conversation or monologue and answer multiple-choice questions. In the CELS exam, they have to listen to short extracts and answer multiple-choice questions.

1 These questions introduce the topic of the listening and enable students to predict what might be discussed. Go through them with the whole class.

2 Listening for the answer to this global listening question will help students to understand the general meaning of what they hear.

➡ Tapescript p. 106

3 Remind students to read through the questions and all the options before they listen, and that they will hear the answers in the same order as in the task. Then play the recording. As a follow-up discussion, you could ask them whether they think it is useful to be able to speak other languages, and why. Write their suggestions on the board. Then ask them to choose one or two ideas and work in pairs to discuss the advantages of each.

ANSWERS
Ex. 2
Isabella: very well/bilingual
Christina: pretty well but not completely   fluent
Natalia: not very well
Ex. 3
1 B   2 C   3 A   4 B   5 C   6 A

Grammar 2: non-defining relative clauses p. 77

Aims:
- **to present the rules for using non-defining relative clauses**
- **to give controlled and free practice**

1   Tell students they are going to look at clauses which are introduced by the same words but do not define the subject of the sentence. Go through the examples and show how the information is not necessary to understand who or what is the subject of the sentence.

2   Do the example with the whole class. Show them how the main clause (*Anna is studying economics*) makes sense without the extra information.

3   Do the Watch Out box with the whole class. Then ask students to do the task in pairs.

ANSWERS

Ex. 1

1 who   2 where   3 which   4 where
5 which   6 whose

Ex. 2

1 Dublin, where I was born, has always attracted a lot of tourists.
2 Terry, who was already half an hour late, finally arrived at 8 p.m.
3 My next door neighbour, whose dog I've always been afraid of, is leaving.
4 We stayed in this fantastic hotel in Istanbul, which a friend had recommended to us.
5 Professor Burton, who I've always respected, is going to be my tutor next term.
6 I'm going to visit friends in Mexico City, where I used to live.
7 My friend Simon, whose job means he is away a lot, has said I can stay in his flat.
8 A new car park, which will have space for 5,000 cars, will be built here by the end of the year.

Watch Out: *that* (2)

In sentence 1, only *who* is possible because we don't use *that* in non-defining clauses.
In sentence 2, only *which* is possible because we don't use *that* in non-defining clauses.

Vocabulary 2: phrasal verbs (communication) p. 78

Aim:
- **to introduce phrasal verbs around the topic of communication**

Teaching tip

Students find it easier to remember phrasal verbs if they are linked in theme. Suggest that they group them in this way in their notebooks. Remind them of the work done on recording vocabulary in Unit 2 p.17.

---

1   This task links verbs to their meanings. Students should work in pairs and then check their answers with the rest of the class.

2   This task helps students to get a 'sense' of the phrasal verb by asking them to find the missing word that goes with the verbs. They should work in pairs.

3   This exercise allows students to put the verbs into a personal context, so that they are easier to remember. They could work in pairs or small groups and then explain their answers to each other.

ANSWERS

Ex. 1

1 to make contact with   2 to speak louder
3 to check in a reference book   4 to invent
5 to stop talking   6 to reprimand

Ex. 2

1 I wish my dad wouldn't always tell **me** off for being untidy!
2 When you get through **to** David, can you tell him about the party?
3 He was so surprised at what they were saying that he just shut **up** and said nothing.
4 She was a good storyteller and could make **up** wonderful stories about animals.
5 I looked **up** this word in my dictionary but it's not there. / I looked this word **up** in my dictionary but it's not there.
6 She's good at getting a difficult idea **across** very quickly. / She's good at getting **across** a difficult idea very quickly.

Writing: discursive composition p. 79

Aims:
- **to help students plan and organise their writing**
- **to provide useful linking expressions for adding further information to a point**

Exam information FCE

In Part 2 of the FCE Writing paper, students may have to write a discursive composition.

Teaching tip

There are three main problems that students have when writing a discursive composition:
- thinking of ideas
- planning and organising the ideas
- linking the ideas in sentences.

The work in this section will help with all of these problem areas.

---

1 , **2**   These discussions are very important for helping students think of ideas for the topic. Ask them to work in small groups, but then discuss the ideas with the whole class so that students hear as many ideas as possible.

3   This task focuses on the organisation of a discursive composition. Suggest that students make a note of the three stages so that they can refer to them when writing other discursive compositions:
Introduction (giving the topic of the composition)
The main points (in this case, the advantages)
Conclusion, with the summary of the writer's opinion.
Refer them to the Writing reference on p.156 for more work on this.

4   This task focuses on phrases that are used to add information to a point already made. Point out that they have already used phrases to add contrasting information, e.g. *however*, *but*, *though*. Remind them of these by writing a sentence on the board:
I like tea <u>but</u> I don't like coffee.
Contrast this with:
I like tea <u>and</u> I like coffee.
Ask students to do the task in pairs.

5   Ask students to work in pairs. For further practice, they could write their own sentences and ask their partners to add some information to them.

6   This writing task could be set for homework. If it is done in class, ask students to show each other their compositions so that they can check them.

ANSWERS

Ex. 3
1 c **2** a **3** b

Ex. 4
Films are **also** usually only two hours long.
In addition, it is difficult to carry a film around with you ...

Ex. 5
Possible answers
1 This book is easy to read. It's also got a great ending.
2 We went to lots of great places in Florence. In addition, the weather was fantastic.
3 The job was boring. As well as that, the pay was terrible.
4 His sister is very clever. In addition, she's captain of the basketball team.
5 My bedroom is quite big. It's also got a great view of the city.

See also: *Going for Gold Language Maximiser* Unit 9.

Your students are now ready to do Progress test 3 on p. 129.

Units 7–9 Progress check p. 80

ANSWERS

Ex. 1

1 I'm so tired, I just can't stop *yawning*.
2 I love going to watch the motor *racing* on Saturdays.
3 I couldn't hear what she was saying because she was *whispering*.
4 My *racket* broke when I was playing tennis with Peter yesterday.
5 Atishoo! Could I have tissue, please? I've been *sneezing* all day.
6 There's a new *track* in the park where you can practise running.
7 He's a good leader so they've made him *captain* of the football team.
8 When you play doubles in tennis, there are four players on the *court*.
9 It's really important that you wear a *helmet* when you're on a motorbike.
10 There were 50,000 *spectators* watching last week's football match.
11 Please don't *bang* the door. Can't you close it more quietly?
12 If there is a problem with a point in a tennis match, the *umpire* has the final decision.

Ex. 2

1 B   2 A   3 B   4 C   5 A   6 B   7 A   8 C
9 A   10 A

Ex. 3

1 have worked   2 has never been   3 moved
4 have just tidied   5 Have you ever seen
6 did you learn   7 have already seen
8 have had   9 Have you told   10 went

Ex. 4

1 annoyed   2 crowded   3 nightlife
4 tiring   5 built-up   6 amazed
7 open spaces   8 frightened   9 polluted
10 traffic   11 boring   12 embarrassing

Ex. 5

1 ... all students have to register ...
2 You mustn't touch that ...
3 correct
4 You don't have to ask me.
5 Do we have to bring ...
6 correct
7 I must try to do ...
8 We don't have to wear ...
9 correct
10 You mustn't tell Fiona.

Ex. 6

1 up   2 came down   3 up   4 passed
5 getting   6 came out   7 off   8 shut

Ex. 7

1 who   2 when   3 whose   4 which
5 where   6 when   7 which   8 whose
9 who   10 where

Reading 1 p. 82

Aims:
- to practise scanning for key words
- to use information from a text in a discussion

1, **2** Students could do these reading tasks alone, and then compare their answers.

3, **4** The follow-up discussion could be done in pairs or small groups.

ANSWERS

Ex. 1
1 a termite 2 a killer whale 3 a flea
4 a cheetah 5 an American polyphemus moth 6 a marmoset

Ex. 2
2 This is how big our heads would be if we had bodies and brains like marmosets.
3 This is how much a baby would eat if it ate like the larva of an American polyphemus moth.
4 If we could jump like a flea, we could jump over St. Paul's Cathedral.

Vocabulary 1: numbers p. 83

Aim:
- to help students recognise and pronounce numbers

Teaching tip

Students often find it difficult to recognise and pronounce numbers. The exercises in this section allow students to listen to numbers and recognise them, pronounce them and then use them in a personal context.

1 This task can be done in pairs. Do choral pronunciation of the numbers after students have listened to the recording, to reinforce both recognition and pronunciation.

➡ Tapescript p. 106

2, **3** These exercises should be done in pairs.

ANSWERS

Ex. 1
1
54 mph – speed
86.9 km/h – speed
2.75 seconds – time
183 and 274 m – distance
100-metre – distance
9.85 seconds – time
1994 – year
80 – number
150 – number
1/4 mile – distance
0.4 km – distance
56 hours – time
86,000 – number
7 lb – weight
3.175 kg – weight
273 tons – weight
1,087,146 – number
20 ft – height
6.096 m – height
1958 – year
34.5 mph – speed
55.5 km/h – speed
55.5% – percentage

See also: *Going for Gold Language Maximiser* Unit 10.

Grammar 1: conditionals (1) p. 83

Aims:

- **to introduce the form of zero, first and second conditional structures**
- **to present and practise the uses of these conditionals**

1   This exercise allows students to work out the rules for the conditionals from sentences that use the structures naturally. Ask students to work in pairs, but discuss the differences in use between the structures with the whole class. Emphasise that the sentences all refer to present or future time, and that the difference lies in how likely the event is to happen. Refer them to the Grammar reference on p. 143 for more information about conditionals.

Each of the next three exercises focuses on a different conditional structure. Ask students to work together to complete them.

2   Encourage students to react to what their partner has said. Remind them of useful phrases, e.g. *Really? That's interesting*, and tell them to ask for more details.

3   Ask pairs to get together with other pairs to check their answers.

4   Encourage students to react to what their partner has said, to ask for more details and to say what they think about the ideas. You may need to remind them of phrases for giving opinions, e.g. *I don't agree at all, In my opinion*, etc.

5   This exercise allows students to work with a variety of conditional sentences. It also gives them practice in looking for errors and editing.

6   This allows students to make their own decisions on the correct structure to use. Ask them to work in pairs, but get feedback with the whole class. Make sure that students explain why they chose the conditional structure they used in their sentences.

▶ Photocopiable Activity 10A p. 187.

See also: *Going for Gold Language Maximiser* Unit 10.

ANSWERS

Ex. 1

1 1 c, d   2 b, e   3 a, f

2 a) 2nd conditional   b) 1st conditional
c) zero conditional   d)   zero conditional
e) 1st conditional   f) 2nd conditional

Ex. 3

If you do the washing-up, I'll dry.

If you go for a walk, you can take my umbrella.

If you have time, you should go on the London Eye.

If you leave now, you'll just catch the last train.

If you're hungry, we'll stop and get a sandwich.

If you want to come, you'll be very welcome.

Ex. 5

2 We *would* go travelling if we had the money.

3 *If* you mix the colours blue and red, you get purple.

4 What will you do *if* it rains?

5 If I had more time, I *would* help you fix your bike.

6 If I finish my work, I *will* meet you at the cinema.

7 If I lived near the sea, I *would* go swimming every day.

8 If you don't *do* your homework, our teacher gets annoyed.

Ex. 6

1 1st conditional: If you can come to the meal tonight, will you ring me?

2 zero conditional: If you press that button, you get extra sugar.

3 2nd conditional: Would you mind if I opened the window?

4 2nd conditional: I would cycle to school if it wasn't quite so far.

5 1st conditional: If you go shopping this afternoon, will you buy me a white T-shirt?

6 2nd conditional: If I knew his telephone number, I would phone him.

7 1st conditional: I'll give you a lift to the party, if I get back from college in time.

8 zero conditional: If I eat oysters, I feel sick.

Use of English: grammar (open cloze) p. 84

Aim:
- **to help students complete a cloze passage by providing graded practice (students are given words to choose from to fill in the spaces)**

Exam information FCE

In Part 2 of the Use of English paper in the FCE exam, students have to complete a cloze passage. They will not be given any multiple-choice options. The focus of the task is more grammatical than the multiple-choice cloze, which is more focused on vocabulary.

Teaching tip

Make sure that students always read a cloze passage through before they attempt to fill in any spaces. If they understand what kind of text it is and what it is about, they will find it easier to choose the missing word.

1 This discussion starts students thinking about the topic of the text. Do it with the whole class.

2 Remind students how important it is to read the title of a text. Ask them to read the title and tell you what they think the text will say about pets. Then tell them to read the whole text without attempting to fill in any missing words. Elicit the groups of people who have benefited from their relationship with animals and write them on the board so that students can see the point of the question. Explain that this gives them the topic and that the rest of the passage provides supporting detail for this topic.

3 Tell students that if they take the FCE exam, they will have to fill in a cloze passage without any multiple-choice options. Explain that to help them this time, the missing words are provided, but suggest that they try to fill in the spaces before looking at the words in the box. Write a checklist for them to refer to:
Is the missing word
- a noun, verb, adverb or adjective?
- in positive or negative form?
- a preposition or a pronoun?
- part of a structure e.g. *if* (conditional), *most* (comparative/superlative)?

When they have completed the cloze, ask them to compare with a partner and justify their choices.

4 This task reminds students that it is a real text with something to say. You could ask them to make notes on the main ideas before discussing them in small groups.

ANSWERS
Ex. 2
people with heart disease; disabled children; hospital patients
Ex. 3
2 most   3 the   4 is   5 of   6 their
7 in   8 with   9 as   10 and

Speaking: coming to a decision p. 85

Aims:
- **to focus on the language functions of suggesting, agreeing, disagreeing and reaching a decision, and their pronunciation**

Exam information PET FCE CELS

In the Speaking papers of the PET, FCE and CELS exams, students have to complete a task involving decision making.

Teaching tip

Decision making is important for the speaking papers of the PET, FCE and CELS exams. However, this language is also necessary for everyday life, and students should be encouraged to use it regularly and not just for exam practice.

1 This discussion introduces the topic. Do it with the whole class.

2 Ask students to read the possibilities before you play the recording. This establishes the topic of each conversation.

➡ Tapescript p. 106

3   This task focuses students on the specific language used in the conversations. When they have filled in the missing phrases, ask them to compare their answers before you check them.

4   Reading aloud focuses the students on pronunciation. Ask them to read the conversation they have chosen before you play the recording again. Ask them to listen to compare their pronunciation of individual sounds and intonation. When they have the conversation again without reading the transcript, ask them if they feel that they sound more natural.

5   This discussion provides free practice for students. Remind them to think about intonation.

ANSWERS

Ex. 1

The photo is of the Rainforest Café. You can eat and drink there.

Ex. 2

Conversation 1: going to the Rainforest Café; going to see a film
Conversation 2: going to another friend's house: going for a pizza

Ex. 3

Conversation 1: good idea; agree; so let's
Conversation 2: right; so; idea

▶ Photocopiable Activity 10B p. 188.

See also: *Going for Gold Language Maximiser* Unit 10.

Listening p. 85

Aim:

• **to help students with ideas and vocabulary for story telling**

1, **2**   These exercises provide vocabulary and generate ideas for telling a story. Students' answers to Exercise 2 will vary. Ask them to say why they think each word is connected to a particular picture.

3   The listening task identifies key vocabulary and information in the pictures that is useful for telling each story.

➡ Tapescript p. 107

4   These questions focus students on the details of the stories. After completing the questions, students could tell each other the stories again in their own words.

ANSWERS

Ex. 3

Story 1: B   Story 2: D   Story 3: C   Story 4: A

Ex. 4

Story 1: 1 up to the top of her legs   2 a child pretending to have seen a shark
Story 2: 1 the garden and a pond   2 She became too interested in the fish in the pond.
Story 3: 1 on a camping weekend   2 She nearly trod on a large spider in her shoe.
Story 4: 1 in a country field   2 The bull lost interest in them.

Vocabulary 2: story-telling devices p. 86

Aim:

• **to help students make their stories more interesting**

1   This task focuses on the way vocabulary can make stories interesting by helping the reader to become involved in the narrative. Ask students to work in pairs. You could play the recording again to check the pronunciation and intonation of the phrases identified by the students.

2   Ask students to work in pairs to complete the sentences.

3   Ask students to work in pairs and tell each other their stories. They should tell each other whether the phrases from Exercise 1 made the story more interesting to listen to.

ANSWERS

Ex. 1

a) Can you believe it?; You cannot believe ...
b) Anyway ...
c) In the end; Eventually
d) just as ...; suddenly
e) Honestly; Really
f) Well; you know; you see
g) So; then

Ex. 2
1 suddenly   2 can you believe it?
3 Anyway   4 in the end   5 Honestly
6 you know

▶ Photocopiable Activity 10C p. 189.

See also: *Going for Gold Language Maximiser* Unit 10.

Reading 2   p. 86

Aims:
- **to show students how a text is organised**
- **to help students complete a text which has missing sentences or paragraphs**

Exam information FCE

In the Reading paper of the FCE exam, students have to replace paragraphs or sentences into a text. The missing paragraphs or sentences are jumbled.

Teaching tip

Work done on text organisation will help students with this task. Other important areas to focus on are linking words and referents (*this*, *that*, etc.). It is important that students understand that when they work on organising their writing it will also help them improve their reading skills. A procedure to follow for this task is:

1 Read the title and predict what the text is about.
2 Read the whole base text without worrying about the missing parts. This text should make sense without the missing information, which provides extra detail.
3 Decide what kind of information is missing, and what it might be about.
4 Read the sentences or paragraphs that have to be replaced and see if there are any topic matches.
5 Look at the grammar, time references, etc.
6 Go through the base text carefully and choose the best paragraph or sentence to insert.
7 Finally, read the whole text through to check that it makes sense.

1   This discussion will start students thinking about the topic of the reading text.

2 , **3**   Tell students to read through the whole text and decide what it is about.

4   The first part of this exercise will help students to identify what kind of information is missing. Ask them to work in pairs and identify what kind of information they can find in the sentences A–F, and, therefore, which one is the best for the gap.
Note: in the FCE exam there will be one sentence which they will not need to use.

5   This discussion is very important as it focuses students on the techniques they have used to complete the task. Discuss it with the whole class once students have compared their answers.

6   This exercise reminds students of the importance of context for guessing the meaning of words or identifying missing information.

7   The discussion allows students to discuss the topic giving their own personal opinions. Question 3 could be done as a class discussion or debate.

ANSWERS

Ex. 1
The chimpanzee's name is Cheetah and he is famous for appearing in Hollywood movies.

Ex. 3
Yes, he does.

Ex. 4
2 E   3 F   4 B   5 D   6 A

Grammar 2: conditionals (2) p. 88

Aim:
- **to present and practise the form and uses of the third conditional structure**

1   This exercise presents the form of the third conditional through context.

2   This task tests students' understanding of the structure by asking them to identify mistakes in sentences. They should work in pairs and explain their answers to each other.

3   This controlled practice allows students to produce conditional sentences. Play the recording so that they can check their own answers.

➡ Tapescript p. 107

4   This allows students to use the third conditional in free practice. After they have written about their decisions, ask them to talk about them to a partner. Encourage them to ask for more details. Then they could share their ideas with the whole class.

ANSWERS

Ex. 1

1 a) past   2 c) past perfect

Ex. 2

2 I would have *been* very happy ...

3 If he *had* worked harder, ...

4 I would *have* phoned her ...

5 She wouldn't have left him if he *hadn't* spent so much time at the office.

6 *Would* they have known what to ...

7 I couldn't have gone to university if my parents *hadn't* given me ...

8 If he'd got in the team, he would *have* had to go ...

Ex. 3

2 I would have helped them if they had asked.

3 If I hadn't gone to the party, I wouldn't have seen Antonia.

4 I would have sent you a postcard if I had had time.

5 If the weather hadn't been so bad we would have gone out.

6 I would have missed tennis practice if you hadn't woken me up.

See also: *Going for Gold Language Maximiser* Unit 10.

Writing: a report p. 88

Aims:

- **to show students how to organise information in a report**
- **to show students how linkers of consequence are used in a report**

Exam information FCE CELS

In the Writing paper of the FCE and Vantage and Higher CELS exams, students may have to write a report.

Teaching tip

Writing reports is easier if students follow a fixed format. Suggest they use headings for the different sections (which they can take from the instructions for the task) and use these to show the main topic of the paragraphs. This is good practice for revising topic sentences and will help students with their reading as well as their writing.

---

1   Refer students to the Writing reference on p.157. This tells them the principles of report writing.

2, **3**   The discussion starts students thinking about the topic of the report. In pairs students explain and justify their ideas to each other.

4   When students have identified the linker, you could ask them to write a sentence for each one, which they could compare with a partner.

5   Ask students to work in pairs. Exercise 5.1 should provide ideas for their report, and then they can plan their ideas under the headings they choose. They can write the report in class or for homework.

ANSWERS

Ex. 1

use headings; use formal language; don't give personal opinions until the conclusion

Ex. 3

Notes do not have a title. There are no headings for the paragraphs. The second paragraph is different from the one in the final report.

Ex. 4   consequently

See also: *Going for Gold Language Maximiser* Unit 10.

Your students are now ready to do Unit 10 test on p. 132.

UNIT
11 Danger!

Reading p. 90

Aims:
- to help students to identify the purpose of a text, and the writer's attitude
- to scan for specific information

Exam information PET FCE CELS

In the Reading paper of the PET and FCE exams, students have to read a passage and choose the correct answer from four options. In the CELS exam, they may have to choose the correct answer from three options. These questions can be about detail, attitude of writer, reference or the meaning of a word. They could also be connected with the writer's intention or the overall purpose of the text.

1   This discussion introduces the topic of the reading passage. Discuss the questions with the whole class.

2   The words in this activity come from the reading text. Student A's words are verbs and Student B's are nouns. Remind them of the information they can find in a dictionary.

3   This global question focuses students on the writer's attitude in the text. It is important that students sometimes read for a purpose other than identifying information.

4   The multiple-choice questions in exams sometimes ask about the writer's purpose or attitude. Remind students about the technique of reading the questions first, then identifying the part of the text where the answers are. Then ask them to answer the questions in pairs.

5   This task focuses on word formation. Ask students to work in pairs.

ANSWERS

Ex. 3
She liked the book a lot.

Ex. 4
1 B   2 C   3 D   4 B   5 A   6 D

Ex. 5
2 living   3 dangerous   4 threats   5 fear
6 weigh

Grammar 1: making comparisons p. 91

Aims:
- to focus on language used for making comparisons
- to provide controlled and free practice in using the language of comparisons

1 , **2** , **3**   These activities focus on the form of the words. Ask students to work in pairs.

4   This exercise allows students to recognise mistakes in the use of the target language. Ask them to work in pairs and to check their answers with other students before you go through them with the whole class.

5 , **6**   These activities allow students to produce the target language in free practice. Ask them to work in pairs.

ANSWERS

Ex. 1
1 most   2 more   3 as

Ex. 2
1 (the) oldest   2 bigger (than)
3 (the) quietest   4 happier (than)
5 more boring (than)   6 (the) most exciting
7 more intelligent (than)   8 (the) best
9 worse (than)

Ex. 3

1 one   2 by adding -er and -est   3 two
4 by removing y and adding -ier and -iest
5 exciting has three; intelligent has four
6 by adding more and the most   7 irregular

Ex. 4

2 This is one of the oldest universities in the world.
3 The film was definitely more exciting than I thought it would be.
4 You look terrible and your cough sounds worse than it was yesterday.
5 Tina speaks better French than her sister.
6 My schooldays were certainly not the 'happiest days of my life'!
7 This new armchair is a lot more comfortable than our old one.
8 The book certainly isn't as good as the film.
9 Isn't Paul thinner than he was before the holidays?
10 There's nothing more boring than doing homework on a sunny evening.

See also: *Going for Gold Language Maximiser* Unit 11.

Vocabulary 1: describing jobs and qualities needed for jobs p. 92

Aim:

• **to give students key topic vocabulary**

1, **2** Encourage students to help each other understand the meaning of the words before resorting to the dictionary. Remind them that a good way to show the meaning of a word is to use it in a sentence as this gives it a context. Remind them too of the different ways of recording vocabulary in their notebooks.

3 This matching exercise encourages students to expand their vocabulary. They could work in the same groups and write down the words that they suggest.

4 This task allows students to use the vocabulary they have just been working with. Students should work in pairs, but Exercise 4.2 could be set for homework. Students could write a short paragraph about the chosen job and the kind of person who

would do it well. They could then read out their paragraphs to the class without naming the job. The other students have to guess.

ANSWERS

Ex. 1

Group 1: well-paid, exciting, dangerous, stressful
Group 2: brave, patient, good with people, imaginative, good with numbers, curious, fit

Ex. 3

Possible answers

Firefighter: exciting, dangerous, stressful; brave, fit
Actor: stressful; imaginative
Teacher: stressful; patient, good with people
Nurse: stressful; patient, good with people
Police officer: exciting, dangerous, stressful; brave, patient, good with people, fit
Accountant: well-paid; patient, good with numbers
Journalist: exciting, dangerous; good with people, curious
Photographer: patient, imaginative

See also: *Going for Gold Language Maximiser* Unit 11.

Use of English: vocabulary (cloze) p. 93

Aim:

• **to provide practice in dealing with a multiple-choice cloze passage**

Exam information PET FCE

In the PET and FCE exams, students have to complete a multiple-choice cloze. In each case the focus is on vocabulary, although there may be some grammar areas tested, such as connectors or prepositions.

Teaching tip

Remind students to follow the procedure already practised (read title and text for meaning and topic, try to guess missing words, check options, complete task).

1   Ask students to read the text, ignoring the gaps, and then elicit suggestions around the class for what the headline means.

2, **3**   Ask students to work in pairs and justify their answers to each other.

> **ANSWERS**
> **Ex. 1**
> The headline refers to a father and son who were caught by storms in the mountains and had to dig a snow hole where they stayed for three nights until rescue came.
> **Ex. 3**
> 2 D   3 A   4 C   5 D   6 A   7 B   8 C
> 9 A   10 C   11 B

Listening p. 94

Aim:
- **to practise listening for specific information**

> **Exam information** PET CELS
>
> In the Listening paper of the PET and CELS exams, students have to read a series of statements and listen to a text to decide if the statements are true or false.

> **Teaching tip**
> Remind students of the procedure already practised (read the statements, try to predict content, listen to the recording).

1   Do this discussion with the whole class as it introduces the topic of the listening. Put students' suggestions on the board so that they can write down any new words which may be useful for the listening task and also useful when describing a picture.

2   The questions give students a general understanding of what they will hear. Play the recording, and check their answers.

➡ Tapescript p. 107

3   Give students time to read through the statements. Then play the recording again and ask them to decide if the statements are true or false.

4   This discussion allows students to react personally to the information in the task. It could be done in groups or with the whole class.

> **ANSWERS**
> **Ex. 2**
> b) two newspaper articles
> **Ex. 3**
> 1 true   2 false   3 true   4 false   5 true
> 6 false (two: mirror and whistle)
> 7 false (carbohydrates)

Grammar 2: giving advice p. 94

Aim:
- **to introduce language for giving advice**

> **Teaching tip**
> This language is especially useful for the Speaking papers of the PET, FCE and CELS exams. Remind students of the language (and how important it is to respond to advice or opinions) and encourage them to use this language whenever they do a task that involves suggesting or giving advice.

1   Go through the examples. Then ask students to do this exercise in pairs. Remind them that there is more information in the Grammar reference on p. 144.

2   You could write some problems on the board, ask each student to choose one and then ask as many other students as possible for their advice. You could then get feedback on the problems and find out what the best advice was. Suggested problems:
I never seem to have enough time to do my homework.
I want to get fit.
I want to improve my listening in English.
I find it difficult to use a computer.
I want to play more sport.

3   Students should do this discussion in small groups.

▶ Photocopiable Activities 11A and 11B pp. 190 and 191.

See also: *Going for Gold Language Maximiser* Unit 11.

ANSWERS

Ex. 1

1 Sentences 1, 2 and 4 advise you to do something. Sentence 3 advises you not to do something.

2

1 You should/ought to take an umbrella. / Why don't you take an umbrella?

2 You should/ought to buy it. / Why don't you buy it?

3 You should/ought to come to the cinema with me. / Why don't you come to the cinema with me?

4 You should/ought to take some aspirin and lie down. / Why don't you take some aspirin and lie down?

5 You should/ought to do some revision. / Why don't you do some revision?

Vocabulary 2: survival p. 95

Aims:
- **to provide key topic vocabulary**
- **to provide practice in word formation**

1 This matching activity focuses on the meaning of key words. Ask students to work in pairs. To check understanding, you could ask them to use the words in sentences.

2 This gap-filling exercise focuses on form. Ask students to work in pairs and then check their ideas with other students.

3 This focuses on pronunciation. Students should practise in pairs before you play the recording. If necessary, do choral pronunciation with the class and play the recording again.

➡ Tapescript p. 107

ANSWERS

Ex. 1

1 g)   **2** j)   **3** d)   **4** i)   **5** b)   **6** f)   **7** a)
8 e)   **9** h)   **10** c)

Ex. 2

1 bandage   2 first aid   3 earthquake
4 blood   5 frostbite   6 signal   7 attacked
8 injury   9 poisoned   10 escaped

Speaking p. 96

Aim:
- **to allow students to use the language of giving advice in a natural context**

1 , **2** , **3** Students should work through these exercises in pairs or small groups.

ANSWERS

Ex. 2

a) 1   **b)** 3   **c)** 2   **d)** 3   **e)** 1   **f)** 2

Writing: informal letter (4) p. 96

Aim:
- **to focus on style and layout of paragraphs in an informal letter**

Exam information FCE CELS

In the Writing paper of the FCE and CELS exams, students may lose marks if their work does not answer the question, is not in a consistent and appropriate style, or is too long (and therefore possibly irrelevant). The work in this section deals with these aspects of exam technique.

Teaching tip

Writing clearly and in an appropriate style is not just an exam skill. Students should always be encouraged to check their work for any mistakes in these areas.

1 The first question asks students to think about what the task is actually asking them to do. This will help them to avoid the mistake of writing about things that are irrelevant to the task.

2 Each picture is an important part of the narrative. By asking students to order them, you are focusing them on how the narrative is organised, and helping them to see why it is clear and dramatic.

3 Question 1 focuses on the layout. Question 2 focuses on style. Ask students to underline the inappropriate parts. Discuss the possible improvements with the whole class. Question 3 focuses on editing down work that is too long. Students should look for repetition or irrelevant ideas.

4   The writing task could be set for homework or done in class in pairs. Students should then exchange their answers and check each other's work for style and accuracy.

ANSWERS

Ex. 1
Yes.

Ex. 2
Correct order = C, D, B, A

Ex. 3
1 Yes.
2 I must apologise for not having responded sooner to your previous letter. – I'm really sorry for not replying sooner to your last letter.
   Please write in the near future and inform me about what is happening in your life.
   Yours faithfully, – Please write soon and tell me all your news. Best wishes,
3 About 20–25 words need to be cut.
   Suggestions for editing:
   Cut *We have a favourite place not far from our house* – irrelevant to task.
   Cut out repetition of *shouting*.
   Combine sentences, e.g. *I looked out to sea and there was a young man swimming alone who was waving and shouting.*
   Use more reference words, e.g. *it* for *the branch*.

See also: *Going for Gold Language Maximiser* Unit 11.

Your students are now ready to do Unit 11 test on p. 134.

UNIT

12 Do you remember?

Reading p. 98

Aims:

- **to remind students of the technique for doing this type of reading task**
- **to focus on organisation of a text**

Exam information FCE

In the Reading paper of the FCE exam, students have to replace paragraphs or sentences into a text. The missing paragraphs or sentences are jumbled.

> **Teaching tip**
> Remind students of the techniques they looked at in Unit 10 Reading 2 and that this type of exercise will help them to understand organisation within a text.

1 These pre-reading questions introduce the topic of the reading text. Do them as a general discussion with the whole class so that all students share their ideas.

2 Ask students to read the text quickly to find the answer to the general question. Remind them that the text should make sense without the missing sentences, so it will be easy to understand the main idea.

3 This exercise shows students how to work out which sentences will fit the space. Do it with the whole class and discuss all the options so that students understand exactly how to find the best answer.

4, **5** Ask students to do these exercises in pairs. It is important that they discuss their answers to reinforce the technique they are using.

6 This discussion question allows students to respond personally to the text.

> **ANSWERS**
>
> **Ex. 2**
> He has problems remembering everyday events, e.g. people's holidays, recent telephone conversations, appointments, meal times, etc.
>
> **Ex. 3**
> **1** 1 true   2 true   3 false
> **2** 1 C
>
> **Ex. 4**
> **2** F   **3** A   **4** E   **5** B   **6** D

Grammar 1: *can, could, be able to* p. 99

Aim:

- **to focus on the uses of *can, could* and *be able to* for expressing ability**

1 Ask students to do this exercise in pairs. Then check answers with the whole class. Go through the Watch Out box with the whole class so that students can see the difference between the structures.

2, **3** Ask students to work in pairs and then compare their answers with other students. Encourage them to discuss and justify their ideas.

4, **5** These production activities could also be done in small groups. Encourage students to respond to what others say as naturally as possible. Remind them of phrases they can use.

6 These short dialogues could be done spontaneously. The students could be given a piece of paper with a note on, e.g. *open window, borrow pen, leave room*. Each has to make a request and nominate another student to answer.

ANSWERS

Ex. 1

1 true   **2** false   **3** true

Watch Out: *able to* or *could*?

1 was able to   **2** could

could means something is generally true

able to means something is possible on one particular occasion

Ex. 2

2 Can, come   **3** couldn't go   **4** can see

5 could swim   **6** can't hear   **7** could, do

8 couldn't answer

Ex. 3

2 I was able to escape through the bedroom window.

3 I was able to use a friend's computer.

4 She wasn't able to get tickets for the Madonna pop concert.

5 I wasn't able to get to sleep last night.

6 They were able to throw her a lifebelt.

See also: *Going for Gold Language Maximiser* Unit 12.

Vocabulary 1: memory p. 100

Aims:

- **to introduce some key topic vocabulary**
- **to show the differences between words often confused**

1   Ask students to match the words and definitions in pairs. Then go through the Watch Out box with the whole class.

2   Ask students to work in pairs to complete the sentences and to compare their answers with other students.

3   The discussion questions could be done in small groups. The groups could report back to the class, who could then vote for the most forgetful person, or the most difficult thing to remember.

▶ Photocopiable Activity 12A p. 192.

See also: *Going for Gold Language Maximiser* Unit 12.

ANSWERS

Ex. 1

1 remember   **2** memorise   **3** remind

4 memory   **5** forget   **6** forgetful

7 unforgettable   **8** reminder

Watch Out: *forget*

Sentence 2 is not possible. *Forget* cannot be used in the same way as *leave*.

Ex. 2

1 reminder   **2** unforgettable   **3** memorise

4 forgetful   **5** forget   **6** memory

7 remember   **8** remind

Use of English: grammar (error correction) p. 101

Aim:

- **to show how to identify unnecessary words in a text**

Exam information FCE

In the Use of English paper of the FCE exam, students have to read a text and identify lines that have an extra or unnecessary word in them.

Teaching tip

Any practice that students have in editing work and identifying errors will help them with their own writing. Remind them that they should read the whole text through before they try to identify any unnecessary words, so that they understand what it is about. Then they should read the text sentence by sentence rather than line by line, as this will mean that they will be working with meaning rather than just looking for individual words.

1   Remind students that, as with any reading task, they should read the title first, and then read the whole text to get an idea of what it is about *before* they attempt to complete the task. Ask them to read the text, and then ask the whole class about whether there was any information in it that was new to them.

2 Ask students to work in pairs to complete the task. Make sure that they follow the suggested procedure in the Coursebook and that they read the whole text through again at the end to check that it makes sense.

ANSWERS

Ex. 2

1 to   **2** that   **3** us   **4** been   **5** whose
6 more   **7** with   **8** are   **9** a   **10** up
11 this   **12** in   **13** if   **14** the (before *life*)
15 of   **16** to

See also: *Going for Gold Language Maximiser* Unit 12.

Listening p. 102

Exam information FCE

In the Listening paper of the FCE exam, students have to listen to different people talking about a related topic. They then have to match some given information to the appropriate speaker.

---

1 The pre-listening discussion starts students thinking about the general topic that all the speakers will mention. Do this discussion with the whole class.

2 Ask students to read through the subjects listed before you play the recording for them to do the task. Ask them to compare their answers with each other before they look at the transcript. Reading the transcript reinforces the technique of listening for key words and makes the task easier.

➡ Tapescript p. 107

3 Tell students that they are going to listen to three more people talking about their childhood memories. Tell them to listen for key words, and identify which subject in Exercise 2 each speaker is talking about.

➡ Tapescript p. 107

4 The pictures reinforce the notion of key words and ideas. Ask students to work in small groups. They could also discuss any other words that could have been key ideas.

ANSWERS

Ex. 2
1 B

Ex. 3
Speaker 2 E
Speaker 3 D
Speaker 4 C

Ex. 4
Picture B (Speaker 1) shows a family in a full
   car arriving at a 'Bed and Breakfast' hotel.
   They are being greeted by the owner.
Picture C (Speaker 1) shows a young girl
   running into the sea.
Picture D (Speaker 2) shows a young boy
   eating the leftovers in a cake mixing bowl.
Picture E (Speaker 3) shows two parents
   starting to decorate a Christmas tree.
Picture F (Speaker 3) shows a Christmas tree
   with presents underneath.
Picture G (Speaker 4) shows a teenage boy
   holding his baby brother.
Picture H (Speaker 4) shows a young boy
   laughing as his feet are being tickled.

Grammar 2: *used to* p. 102

Aim:
• **to present and practise *used to* for past habits and states**

1 When you have discussed this activity with the class, refer them to the Grammar reference on p. 144.

2 Ask students to work in pairs to correct the mistakes. They must justify their answers by referring to the rules in the Grammar reference.

3 , **4** These question and answer activities put the structure into a personal context for the students and make it easier for them to remember. They should work in pairs to do them.

ANSWERS

Ex. 1

a) a past habit or state

Ex. 2

A: So, what did you use to be like when you were at school?

B: Oh terrible. I *used to* be really cheeky to the teachers and I never used to do my homework on time.

A: Did they *use to* get cross with you?

B: Yes, and once the headmaster asked for my parents to go to the school to see him. It was so embarrassing. I also used to hate getting my annual report from school. My parents *used to be* very upset when I didn't do well in my school exams.

A: Were they surprised when you told them what job you wanted to do?

B: Yes. They couldn't believe I wanted to be a teacher!

See also: *Going for Gold Language Maximiser* Unit 12.

Vocabulary 2: prefixes p. 103

Aims:

• to help students form negative adjectives by using negative prefixes

• to help students with word formation

1   Discuss the example sentences with the class and see if they can think of any other words that use the same prefixes.

2   Ask students to work in pairs to match the words in the box with the prefixes in Exercise 1. Check answers with the whole class.

3   Ask students to work in pairs to complete the sentences. As a follow-up activity, they could choose two words and write similar sentences for their partner to guess the missing word. This would help them to understand whether they have provided enough context for the word or not, and would help them to see how to use context more effectively.

ANSWERS

Ex. 1

The effect is to make each main word negative.

Ex. 2

unhappy, dislike, impossible, illegible, unfriendly, unlock, impolite, invisible, unemployed, dishonest, irresponsible

Ex. 3

1 illegible   2 invisible   3 agree
4 impossible   5 unlock   6 polite
7 irresponsible   8 dislike

Speaking p. 104

Aim:

• to help students to compare and contrast pictures

Exam information PET FCE

In Part 3 of the Speaking paper of the PET exam, students have to describe a single picture. In Part 2 of the Speaking paper of the FCE exam, they have to compare and contrast two pictures, and talk about an aspect of the pictures such as how the people are feeling.

Students should work through all the activities in this section in pairs as this is what they will have to do if they are taking an exam. Exercise 5.2 can be done in groups.

➡ Tapescript p. 108

ANSWERS

Ex. 4

Because it's the only photo he has left of him as a child with his mother.

▶ Photocopiable Activity 12B p. 193.

See also: *Going for Gold Language Maximiser* Unit 12.

Writing: story (4) p. 105

Aims:
- **to help students edit their writing**
- **to help students use linkers of time in narratives**

1   This task focuses students on typical mistakes. They should work in pairs. Refer them to the Writing reference on p. 155 if they need any help, then check the answers with the whole class.

2 , **3**   Go through the words in the box, and then ask the class to suggest which pairs have similar meaning. Go through the Watch Out box, then ask students to work together to complete Exercise 3.

4   Refer students to the procedure they should follow when they write a story. Remind them that this procedure should be followed with any piece of writing, as it will help them to produce a well-organised text. Remind them to use the checklist in Exercise 1.2 to check their work when they have finished.

ANSWERS

Ex. 1

2
1 Yes.
2 Yes.
3 exited – excited; forgoten – forgotten; enything – anything; stoped – stopped; enormus – enormous; suprise – surprise
4 Yes, e.g. fed up; smart; party hats
5 Yes, e.g. then; eventually
6 Yes, by saving the dramatic part of the story to the end.
7 No. It is about 230 words!

Ex. 2
eventually – finally
as a result – so
firstly – to begin with
just then – at that moment

Watch Out: *at the end* or *in the end*?
In the end means *after a lot of time or discussion*.

Ex. 3
1 eventually   **2** just then   **3** To begin with
4 so   **5** Firstly

Your students are now ready to do Progress test 4 on p. 136.

Units 10–12 Progress check p. 106

ANSWERS

Ex. 1
1 A   **2** B   **3** D   **4** A   **5** C   **6** D   **7** A
8 C

Ex. 2
1 nurse   **2** patient   **3** danger   **4** actor
5 earthquake   **6** poison   **7** frostbite
8 bandage   **9** forget   **10** memory

Ex. 3
1 as sad as   **2** ought   **3** the most   **4** used
5 the best   **6** not/don't you   **7** good as her
8 able

Ex. 4
1 thirty-seven   **2** a (one) hundred and forty-nine   **3** six thousand, nine hundred and sixty-three   **4** seventy-three thousand
5 a quarter   **6** ninety-eight   **7** five point nine six   **8** twelve thousand and fifty-four

Ex. 5
1 unforgettable   **2** reminder   **3** memorise
4 illegible   **5** impatient   **6** unlock
7 unemployed   **8** dangerous   **9** imagination
10 poison

Ex. 6
1 He was finally able *to move* the wardrobe ...
2 My parents *always used to* read ...
3 Why don't you *take* some waterproof ...
4 correct
5 She didn't use to *play* any sport ...
6 This new game *is more exciting* ...
7 You *should have* a holiday ...
8 correct

Ex. 7
1 drop   **2** had   **3** press   **4** had asked
5 says   **6** would   **7** would get   **8** 'll come

UNIT
13 Down under

Reading 1 p. 108

Aims:

- **to remind students of the pre-reading techniques that can help them handle a reading text**
- **to focus on specific vocabulary in the text to work out meaning from context**

Exam information PET FCE CELS

In the Reading paper of the PET and FCE exams, students have to read a passage and choose the correct answer from four options. In the CELS exam, they may have to choose the correct answer from three options. These questions can be about detail, attitude of writer, reference or the meaning of a word. They could also be connected with the writer's intention or the overall purpose of the text.

1 , **2** These two activities remind students of the importance of predicting the content of what they read before they do any reading task. They should work in pairs or small groups.

3 This exercise reminds students that they should always read the text through to get a general idea of what it is about before they do a specific task.

4 Matching the pictures to a particular part of the text reminds students that the text is organised in topics that they can identify (usually by topic sentences). The pictures can help them to identify where the answers to the multiple-choice questions will come.

ANSWERS

Ex. 1
They are all connected to Australia. The pictures show A a kangaroo, B the Great Barrier Reef, C pop singer Kylie Minogue, D Captain Cook arriving in Botany Bay on his

ship *HMS Endeavour* in 1770, E Aborigines on an ocean-going craft.

Ex. 3
c) He is impressed by it.

Ex. 4
Kylie Minogue (Picture C) is not mentioned in the text.
Picture A refers to Paragraph 5 where it says *The most typical of them didn't run but bounced across the landscape.*
Picture B refers to Paragraph 2 where it says *It is the home of the largest living thing on earth, the Great Barrier Reef.*
Picture D refers to Paragraph 4 where it says *the arrival of Captain James Cook and* HMS *Endeavour in Botany Bay in 1770.*
Picture E refers to Paragraph 3 where it says *they could only get there by inventing ocean-going transport – at least 30,000 years before anyone else.*

Ex. 5
1 B   2 D   3 B   4 A   5 A   6 C

Ex. 6
4 Crustaceans are animals with hard shells that mostly live in water, e.g. crabs, lobsters, shrimps.

Vocabulary 1: the physical world
p. 109

Aims:

- **to provide key topic vocabulary**
- **to provide information about the physical world**

1 Ask students to work in groups. They can suggest examples from their own country. Go through the Watch Out box with the whole class. It focuses on words that are often confused. Do choral pronunciation of the words to emphasise the difference.

2 Make sure that students remember the work they've done before on word stress and to think about this when they pronounce the words. If necessary, remind them of the importance of word stress by writing some words from the reading text on the board and asking them to tell you how many syllables each word has and where the stress should be.

➡ Tapescript p. 108

3 This quiz could be done as a game if students work in groups and compete against each other to see who gets the most right.

4 This describe and draw activity should be done in pairs. When the students have finished describing their island, they should compare their partner's drawing with the one in the book. If there are any differences, they should try to work out why. Was it a mistake of grammar, e.g. a wrong preposition, or a pronunciation mistake?

ANSWERS

Ex. 1
Possible answers (students can use examples from their own country)
Continent: Europe
Country: Mexico
Island: Malta
Ocean: the Indian Ocean
Lake: Lake Ontario
River: the Thames
Mountain: Mount Fuji
Forest: the Amazon rainforest
Desert: the Gobi

Watch Out: *desert* or *dessert*?
1 desert. The stress is on the first syllable.
2 dessert. The stress is on the second syllable.

Ex. 3
They are all true.

See also: *Going for Gold Language Maximiser* Unit 13.

Grammar 1: *like* p. 110

Aim:
• **to present and practise the different uses of *like***

1 This matching task focuses on both the use and meaning of *like*.

2 The jumbled sentences provide very controlled practice in using the target structure. Students should work in pairs to put the words in the correct order.

3 This task provides productive controlled practice. When students have completed the dialogue, ask them to read it aloud in pairs to practise pronunciation. Remind them of the language they have learned for:
• suggesting, e.g. *How about ...?*
• asking for opinions, e.g. *What about you?*
• expressing opinions, e.g. *I think ...*
• agreeing, e.g. *That's right.*
• disagreeing, e.g. *I'm sorry, I can't agree.*

4 The discussion personalises the structure for students and allows them to use *like* in a free way. They should do the activity in small groups.

▶ Photocopiable Activities 13A and 13B pp. 194–196.

ANSWERS

Ex. 1
A 2   B 1   C 3

Ex. 2
1 Would you like to visit Australia?
2 People say that I am exactly like my sister.
3 She would like to see Ayers Rock.
4 I don't like getting up early in the morning.
5 What would you like to do tonight?
6 This jacket is like the one in the last shop.
7 She likes going out with her friends at the weekend.
8 This class is not like the one I was in last year.
9 Do you like doing your homework on the computer?

Ex. 3
Fiona: OK, so what would everyone like to do this evening?
Sam: Oh, I don't know. I'd quite like to go bowling. We haven't been for ages!
Jim: I'd prefer to do something else. I've hurt my leg. Anyway, I never like going bowling. It is always too crowded and noisy.
Fiona: How about you, Zoe?
Zoe: I feel like Jim. I'd like to have a quiet evening. How about getting a video and going back to my place?

See also: *Going for Gold Language Maximiser* Unit 13.

Listening 1 p. 111

Aim:
- **to listen for specific information**

Exam information (PET) (FCE) (CELS)

In the Listening papers of the PET, FCE and CELS exams, students have to complete notes based on a listening text, usually a monologue. They may only have to write one or two words.

---

1   Tell students to read the whole text through before they listen to the recording. Remind them that they will only need a word or a short phrase in the gap. Ask them to think about the type of information that is missing before you play the recording.

➡ Tapescript p. 108

2   The discussion allows students to react to the topic.

ANSWERS

Ex. 1

2 comedians   **3** 6 a.m.   **4** 10 a.m.   **5** shops
6 sailing   **7** ferry   **8** Sound City

See also: *Going for Gold Language Maximiser* Unit 13.

Vocabulary 2: tourism p. 111

Aims:
- **to provide key topic vocabulary**
- **to give help with pronunciation of topic vocabulary**
- **to help students with ideas for talking about holidays**

1 , **2**   When students have matched the questions to the answers, they should work in pairs to think of an alternative answer to each question. When they have done this, they could cover both the answers in the book and their own answers, and then ask each other the questions. They should try to remember the answers.

3   This activity focuses on pronunciation of the topic vocabulary and sentence stress. Check students' answers and do pronunciation practice with the whole class.

➡ Tapescript p. 108

4 , **5** , **6**   These activities help students to talk freely about the topic. Remind them to ask each other questions and not just to talk about their own opinions. They can adapt the questions in Exercise 1 to help them with ideas for doing this. As a follow-up to Exercise 6, students could write a paragraph describing either their partner's holiday or their own.

ANSWERS

Ex. 1

1 d)   **2** h)   **3** f)   **4** b)   **5** c)   **6** e)   **7** g)
8 i)   **9** a)

See also: *Going for Gold Language Maximiser* Unit 13.

Speaking p. 112

Aim:
- **to help students organise their ideas when comparing and contrasting pictures**

Exam information (FCE)

In Part 2 of the Speaking paper of the FCE exam, students have to compare and contrast two pictures, and talk about an aspect of the pictures such as how the people are feeling.

---

1   This listening exercise focuses students on the topic of the photographs. Ask them to look at the photographs and think about what the student might say. Then play the recording so that they can check their ideas.

➡ Tapescript p. 108

2   Ask students to work in pairs to complete the text. When they have filled in the missing words, ask them to read through the whole transcript. They could underline words used to:
- compare and contrast, e.g. *on the other hand*
- give reasons, e.g. *because*
- add further information, e.g. *also*.
Play the recording again and check answers.

3   This exercise gives students topic vocabulary for describing the photographs.

4   Ask students to work in pairs to compare and contrast the photographs. Remind them to use some of the phrases they underlined in Exercise 2. Suggest that they highlight, underline or make a note of the three things they should do that are identified in Exercise 4:
- summarise the general content
- say where the photographs were taken
- speculate about what is happening.

> **ANSWERS**
>
> **Ex. 1**
> She talks about 1, 3, 4 and 5.
>
> **Ex. 2**
> **1** show **2** see **3** like **4** remind **5** other
> **6** whereas **7** looks **8** if **9** might
>
> **Ex. 3**
> Useful for Picture A: a museum guide,
>   to listen, a group, an exhibition, to explain
> Useful for Picture B: outdoors, to listen,
>   a group, grass, to explain, a coach

Reading 2 p. 114

Aim:
- **to give students an approach to dealing with multiple-matching tasks**

> **Exam information** PET CELS FCE
>
> In the PET Reading paper, students have to match descriptions of people with summaries of books, videos, holidays, activities and so on. Students have to choose the most appropriate summary for each person described. In the CELS exams, students have to match information to a particular text or piece of information. In the FCE exam, they have to match statements or questions to part of a text or texts and say where the information or statement is mentioned.

1   Remind students to read through all the descriptions and all the extracts before they try to answer any of the questions. Remind them to highlight or underline key words and look for parallel phrases – they must look for more than one key word as there may be more than one extract that seems possible on a

first reading. Only one extract will match all the key words and ideas in each description.

2   After students have discussed the question, you could take feedback from the class and see if there is a favourite book among the class. You could also ask then what their real favourite book is and why.

> **ANSWERS**
> **2** H   **3** C   **4** E   **5** G   **6** B   **7** D   **8** A

Listening 2 p. 115

Aim:
- **to help students with an approach to dealing with true/false statements**

> **Exam information** PET CELS
>
> In the Listening paper of the PET and CELS exams, students have to read a series of statements and listen to a text to decide if the statements are true or false.

1   This pre-listening discussion focuses students on the topic of the listening. Do it with the whole class.

2   This single question allows students to identify the main point of the listening before they focus on the specific information needed for the true/false task. Play the recording and then check the answer with the whole class.

➡ Tapescript p. 108

3   Remind students to read through all the statements before you play the recording. Ask them to check their answers with each other before you check the answers with the whole class. As a follow-up discussion you could ask students if they think that they would like to visit Australia and why or why not. Have they visited any other countries that sound similar to Australia?

> **ANSWERS**
>
> **Ex. 2**
> She talks about space, sport (surfing), being outside, beaches, friendliness and food.
>
> **Ex. 3**
> **1** false **2** true **3** true **4** true **5** false
> **6** false **7** true **8** true

Grammar 2: *so, neither, nor* p. 115

Aim:

- **to present and practise the use of *so, neither* and *nor***

Exam information PET FCE CELS

The phrases examined here are all very useful for the Speaking paper in the PET, FCE and CELS exams.

---

1 , **2** , **3**   Ask students to do these exercises in pairs. They provide controlled practice. Do pronunciation practice of the responses with the whole class so that students learn to use the phrases naturally.

4 , **5**   These exercises allow students to practise using the structures in natural situations. As a follow-up, students could make up more statements and work with a partner to respond to.

ANSWERS

Ex. 1
Situations A, B and C
Ex. 2
1 Nor has Peter.
2 So can I.
3 So is mine.
4 I don't.
5 So did we.
6 Neither will we.
Ex. 3
1 did   2 have   3 can   4 have   5 am
6 does   7 will   8 did

See also: *Going for Gold Language Maximiser* Unit 13.

Writing: article p. 116

Aims:

- **to show students how to organise an article**
- **to do further work on planning and editing written work**

Exam information FCE CELS

In the FCE and vantage and higher CELS exams, students may have to write an article.

Teaching tip

Although the style of an article is different from a letter, the approach to planning and organising information will be similar. Students should always be encouraged to plan and organise their writing.

---

1 , **2**   Ask students to read the task and then look at the example answer. They should work in pairs to find the answers to the questions in Exercise 2. Their answers will provide the basis of a checklist for their own writing.

3   Ask students to do the planning and brainstorming in pairs.

4   Students could write their article for homework. If they do this, then they could show their article to the others at the start of the next lesson. Helping each other edit their work is an important stage in learning how to look for their own mistakes.

ANSWERS
Ex. 2
1 Yes   2 Yes   3 No   4 Yes   5 Yes
6 Informal   7 Yes   8 No   9 Yes

See also: *Going for Gold Language Maximiser* Unit 13.

Your students are now ready to do Unit 13 test on p. 139.

UNIT
14 Elements of nature

Reading p. 118

Aims:
- **to provide a procedure for dealing with the matching task**
- **to provide topic vocabulary**

Exam information FCE

In the Reading paper of the FCE exam, students have to read a text and choose a heading for each paragraph.

Teaching tip

Headings usually give the main idea of a paragraph. Identifying headings is excellent practice for identifying the topic of a paragraph, and discussion of appropriate headings can help students to understand how texts are organised. This understanding helps them with their general reading, and also with their own writing. It can be done with any text whether there is a formal task or not; ask the class what they think the main idea of the paragraph is and discuss it, or ask them to make up their own headings for paragraphs and share their ideas with the class.

1 This discussion prepares students for the topic of the reading text. The pictures show the main idea of some of the paragraphs.

2 Remind students to read the whole text through without worrying about the headings at first. This will help them to understand what the text is about. Then ask them to match the paragraphs to the pictures to identify the main idea of each paragraph. This prepares students for matching the headings.

3 Ask students to read the headings, and to work in pairs to match each heading to the appropriate paragraph. Check the answers with the whole class, and ask students to justify their answers by referring to the clues in the text.

4 This exercise provides topic vocabulary. Ask students to work in pairs.

As a follow-up discussion you could ask students if they feel better when the weather is sunny or cloudy, and why. Does any other type of weather affect their mood?

ANSWERS

Ex. 1

Picture A: The people are on a beach. The woman is putting sun cream on her daughter, as protection from the harmful rays of the sun.

Picture B: This is a procession during the festival of Inti Raymi in Peru. The people are celebrating the beginning of the sun's new year and honouring their sun god.

Picture C: World disasters (e.g. flooding) are sometimes thought to be the result of global warming. Pollution of the atmosphere keeps the sun's rays from being reflected back into space, with the result that the world is becoming warmer. Currents such as El Niño become more powerful and capable of causing disasters such as flooding.

Ex. 2

Picture A: Paragraph 4 refers to sun cream and the need to protect skin from the sun.

Picture B: Paragraph 7 refers to Inti Raymi, the festival of the sun in Peru.

Picture C: Paragraph 6 refers to floods in different parts of the world caused by the warming of the oceans.

Ex. 3

2 D   3 B   4 A   5 E   6 G   7 C   8 F

Ex. 4
1 1 summer   2 sun cream   3 sunny
   4 suntan   5 sunshine   6 solar energy
2
Possible answers
sunburn, sunbathe, sunrise, sunset, sunglasses,
sunhat, sunlight sunshade, Sunday

See also: *Going for Gold Language Maximiser* Unit 14.

Grammar 1: countable and uncountable nouns p. 119

Aims:
- **to show the difference between countable and uncountable nouns**
- **to provide practice in using them**

1   Discuss the picture and the questions with the class. Point out the difference between countable and uncountable nouns. Do Exercise 1.1 with the whole class. Then ask students to complete the sentences in Exercise 1.2 in pairs. Check answers with the class.

2   Ask students to work together to identify the mistakes. They often have difficult with this, so it is worth going through the answers carefully with the whole class.

3   Explain that some nouns can be both countable and uncountable. Ask students to decide which nouns from the box can't be used in both ways. For practice, they could make sentences using the other words as countable and uncountable nouns.

4   Explain that uncountable nouns do not take *a* or *an*. This exercise asks students to identify countable and uncountable nouns by deciding whether they can take an article or not. Students should work in pairs.

5   This exercise puts the grammar into a personal context for students. Ask them to work with a partner to explain their answers.

ANSWERS
Ex. 1
1 1 no (*weather* is uncountable)
  2 yes (*problem* is countable)

2 1 are   2 aren't   3 Is   4 Are
   5 few, many   6 is   7 isn't   8 Is
   9 little, much

Ex. 2
  1 Would you like *some* fruit?
  2 *Is* there any water in the bucket?
  4 I'd like *some* information about the price of computers, please.
  6 There is some *evidence* of crime in the area.
  7 She's got *a* really bad headache.
  9 I can't hear *a* word you're saying.
 10 I really need *some* advice about where to stay.

Ex. 3
1 1 B   2 A
2 *advice* and *work* cannot be countable.

Ex. 4
1 –   2 a   3 –   4 –   5 a   6 a   7 a   8 –
9 an   10 –

See also: *Going for Gold Language Maximiser* Unit 14.

Vocabulary 1: the weather p. 121

Aim:
- **to provide key topic vocabulary**

1, **2**   These exercises can be done in pairs or small groups. As a follow-up, students could choose another country and describe what they think the weather is like there. The others could then agree or disagree, giving their own ideas. Remind students of some of the phrases they have learned for agreeing and disagreeing.

ANSWERS
Ex. 1
hot/cold: it's really hot; it's mild; it's warm and
    pleasant; it's freezing; it's quite cold
sun/cloud: it's sunny with a clear sky; it's sunny;
    it's cloudy
rain/no rain: it's raining very hard; it's a dry
    day; there's a thunderstorm; it's raining a
    little
wind/no wind: there's no wind; there's a
    pleasant breeze; it's very windy

See also: *Going for Gold Language Maximiser* Unit 14.

Listening 1: song p. 121

Aims:

• to revise topic vocabulary (weather)
• to allow students to talk about how the weather makes them feel
• to listen for pleasure

1 , **2** Ask students to do these tasks in pairs. Then play the recording.

➡ Tapescript p. 109

3 Ask students to do the discussion in small groups. They could then compare their answers with the rest of the class and see if everyone feels the same in any particular situation. Extend the discussion by asking whether students think that weather in different countries affects national characteristics.

ANSWERS

Ex. 1
All the lines sound as if the singer is feeling positive.

Ex. 2
1
1 A   2 E   3 D   4 G   5 F   6 B   7 C

Writing: transactional letter (2) p. 122

Aims:

• to help students to organise a transactional letter
• to focus on ways of linking paragraphs together

Exam information FCE CELS

In the Writing paper of the FCE exam, there is a compulsory question. Students are given some information and they have to write a letter in response to this. In their letter they may have to give information, request information, make a complaint, correct some incorrect information or respond to suggestions. There is also a transactional letter in the CELS exam.

---

1 This exercise focuses on the organisation of the letter and on the topics for each paragraph.

2 You could do this with the whole class, as it is important that they all understand how the linking words make the writing easier to follow.

3 One of the problems with a transactional letter is that students often do not complete all of the task because they either forget to include all the information or they have not read the task carefully enough. These questions aim to make students read the task carefully.

4 These questions are to help students to think about planning and organising their ideas.

5 , **6** The letter could be written for homework, or done in class. It is important that students read each other's work.

▶ Photocopiable Activity 14A p. 197.

ANSWERS

Ex. 1
1 He is asking you for information and your suggestions for the weekend plan.
2
Paragraph 2: Going on the London Eye
Paragraph 3: Visiting parks
Paragraph 4: Asking what to do inside

Ex. 2
1 1 first of all   2 parks, outside
2
Using a word (or words) from the last sentence of one paragraph in the first sentence of the next paragraph.

Ex. 3
1 a friend who has written to you (as per the letter in Exercise 1)
2 the weather; information about the London Eye, Hyde Park and the Science Museum
3 yes
4 120–40 words

See also: *Going for Gold Language Maximiser* Unit 14.

Listening 2 p. 123

Aim:
- **to help students to deal with note-taking tasks**

Exam information PET FCE CELS

In the Listening papers of the PET, FCE and CELS exams, students have to complete notes based on a listening text, usually a monologue. They may only have to write one or two words.

1, **2** These pre-listening tasks give students key vocabulary to help them understand the listening more easily.

3, **4** Remind students to read through the sentences before they listen and to try to predict the kind of information they have to listen for. Play the recording and then ask students to compare their answers before you check them with the whole class.

➡ Tapescript p. 109

5 These follow-up questions can be done with the whole class or in small groups.

ANSWERS

Ex. 1
2
cutting down trees; pollution from cars, factories, waste products; litter; over-fishing/hunting; killing animals for pleasure (e.g. sports, fur coats, etc.)

Ex. 3
2 She's not a typical eco-warrior because she's older, quiet and ordinary-looking. The stereotypical image of an eco-warrior is a young man in his early twenties who is loud and rough in his manner.
3 It is spraying crops with chemicals (e.g. DDT).

Ex. 4
1 first **2** quiet **3** Silent Spring **4** humans
5 governments **6** chemical **7** ill
8 Birds and animals

Grammar 2: articles p. 124

Aim:
- **to present and practise the rules for using articles**

1 Ask students to work in pairs to match the rules to the examples. Refer them to the grammar reference on p. 145 if they need help.

2 Remind students to read through the whole text before they try to fill in any of the gaps. If necessary, ask them comprehension questions such as
Which is more important, food or water?
Where is the driest place on Earth?
What are the nets for?
You could also ask them to suggest a possible title for the text. Then ask them to work together to fill in the gaps where necessary.

3 This task gives students more practice in editing their work.

ANSWERS
Ex. 1
1 a **2** c **3** e **4** b **5** f **6** d
Ex. 2
2 X **3** X **4** the **5** X **6** a **7** X **8** The
9 a **10** the **11** a

See also: *Going for Gold Language Maximiser* Unit 14.

Vocabulary 2: phrasal verbs with *take* p. 124

Aim:
- **to present and practise phrasal verbs with *take***

1, **2** Students can work in pairs to complete the matching exercises and the sentences. These provide a clear context for the verbs.

3 These questions allow students to use the phrasal verbs naturally in a personal context. Once they have discussed the questions with a partner, they could change partners and see if they give different answers. They could also think of new questions of their own to ask.

ANSWERS

Ex. 1

1

1 to challenge
2 to like (somebody) when you first meet
3 to understand completely

2

1 to start (a new hobby)
2 to admit that you were wrong
3 to look or behave like an older relative
4 to get control and responsibility (for something)
5 to have a holiday from work

Ex. 2

1 back **2** off **3** up **4** in **5** on **6** after
7 to **8** over

See also: *Going for Gold Language Maximiser* Unit 14.

Speaking p. 125

Aims:

- **to give practice in using phrases for agreeing and disagreeing**
- **to give practice in using phrases for pausing and thinking, and for asking someone else's opinion**

Exam information FCE

In Part 4 of the Speaking paper of the FCE exam, students have to discuss some general questions that are related to the topic they have discussed in Part 3.

Teaching tip

It is helpful to ask one or two general questions that extend the topic of any reading or listening task, as this will broaden students' knowledge and make it easier for them to think of ideas for speaking and writing.

1 Discuss what the connection between the pictures might be with the whole class and then play the recording. Discuss the other questions together.

➡ Tapescript p. 109

2 Ask students to read the phrases listed. Play the recording and ask them to tick the ones used. Practise pronunciation, and then ask students to work in pairs to practise using them.

3 Ask students to read the questions. Then play the recording so that they can mark those that they hear discussed. Ask them to read the phrases and play the recording again so that they can tick the ones that are used. Practise pronunciation. Ask students to complete the dialogue in pairs, and practise reading it.

➡ Tapescript p. 109

4 Ask students to discuss the questions in Exercise 3.1, using the phrases from Exercises 2 and 3.

ANSWERS

Ex. 1

1 They are all things connected with looking after or destroying the environment.
2 Question 1

Ex. 2

1 They use *In my opinion ...*, *That's right, I think ...* and *I don't agree at all!*

Ex. 3

1 Question 3
2 They use *Well, it depends ...*, *What do you think?*, *I'm not sure, but ...* and *Do you agree?*

Ex. 4

1 agree **2** depends **3** think **4** about
5 sure

▶ Photocopiable Activity 14B p. 198.

See also: *Going for Gold Language Maximiser* Unit 14.

Your students are now ready to do Unit 14 test on p. 141.

UNIT
15 The business of food

Reading p. 126

Aim:

- **to practise identifying the main point of a paragraph**

1 This quiz starts students thinking about the topic of the reading text. They could do it in pairs or small groups.

2 Discuss these questions with the whole class. Write any answers they give on the board.

3 Remind students to read the title of the article first, and then ask them to read the text to check whether their answers to Exercise 2 were correct. Ask them if they can identify the main topic of each paragraph. Discuss their ideas with the whole class, then tell them to look at the headings in Exercise 4.

4 Remind students to read all the headings before they try to match them to the paragraphs. Remind them of the techniques they used in Unit 14. Discuss with the whole class why H goes with paragraph 1. Then ask students to work in pairs to match the other headings to the paragraphs.

For follow-up work you could ask the class if anything in the article surprised them.

ANSWERS

Ex. 3
2 mostly man-made

Ex. 4
1 *Thousands of different brands ...*
2 2 F 3 A 4 E 5 C 6 B 7 D 8 G

Grammar 1: passives (past and present) p. 127

Aim:

- **to present and practise the form and uses of the passive**

1, **2** Work through these exercises with the whole class. Refer students to the Grammar reference on p. 146 for more information.

3, **4** Do the example with the whole class. Then ask students to complete the exercises in pairs. Check the answers with the whole class.

5 This task provides free practice of the passive.

ANSWERS

Ex. 1
1 b
2 passive
3 *This house was built in 1960 by my grandfather* is more likely because we only include the agent if it adds interesting information. If there is no extra interesting information about the agent, we would say *This house was built in 1960* (without adding *by someone*).

Ex. 2
Paragraph 1: are available (present simple passive)
Paragraph 2: are told (present simple passive)
Paragraph 3 was obtained (past simple passive); were found (past simple passive)
Paragraph 4: was developed (past simple passive); was discovered (past simple passive)
Paragraph 5: is collected (present simple passive)
Paragraph 6: is heated (present simple passive); is made (present simple passive); are transported (present simple passive)

Paragraph 7: are used (present simple passive)
Paragraph 8: were laid (past simple passive)

Note: there is also an example of the present perfect passive (have been developed) in paragraph 7.

Ex. 3
1 present simple passive   2 past simple passive   3 present simple passive   4 present simple   5 past simple   6 present simple

Ex. 4
1 People in the UK spend £120 million on chewing gum every year.
2 Someone in California blew the biggest gum bubble.
3 People use sugar-free gum to keep teeth healthy.
4 900 million litres of bottled water are consumed in the UK every year.
5 Last year, 25% of the UK's bottles of water were imported from Asia.
6 Square watermelons are grown inside glass boxes.

See also: *Going for Gold Language Maximiser* Unit 15.

Vocabulary 1: buying and selling
p. 128

Aim:
• **to provide key topic vocabulary**

1, **2**   These exercises provide vocabulary and pronunciation practice of key words for talking about buying and selling.

➡ Tapescript p. 109

3   This discussion allows students to use the vocabulary in a personal context.

ANSWERS
Ex. 1
B company   C logo   D consumers
E market   F advertisement   G research
H brand

See also: *Going for Gold Language Maximiser* Unit 15.

Listening   p. 128

Aim:
• **to listen for specific information**

Exam information   FCE
Some of the multiple-choice questions students have to answer in the Listening paper of the FCE exam focus on specific information, but others may focus on the speaker's attitude. Some of the work in this section helps students to identify different types of information.

1   This matching exercise introduces key vocabulary for the listening task.

2   Remind students to read through the words again and then to number them in the order they hear them.

➡ Tapescript p. 109

3   The questions in Exercise 3.1 help students to identify the type of information they are looking for. Ask them to work in pairs, but check the answers with the whole class.

Remind students to read through all the questions before you play the recording. They could mark the questions according to whether they think they are asking for content, relationship or attitude.

▶ Photocopiable Activity 15 pp.199–200.

ANSWERS
Ex. 1
A fizzy drink   B pizza   C vegetables
D meat   E cake   F milkshake
Ex. 2
1 pizza   2 vegetables   3 meat
4 fizzy drink   5 cake   6 milkshake
Ex. 3
1 1 content   2 content   3 relationship
   4 content   5 attitude   6 content
2 1 C   2 B   3 B   4 A   5 C   6 B

See also: *Going for Gold Language Maximiser* Unit 15.

Grammar 2: causative *have* p. 129

Aim:
- **to present and practise the uses of the causative *have***

1   Ask students to discuss the answers in pairs. Then check with the whole class. Remind them that they will find more information in the Grammar reference on p. 146.

2   Ask students to work in pairs to complete the sentences.

3   This personalises the grammar for the students and makes it easier for them to remember. Encourage them to respond to their partner's ideas in an interested way, and to ask for further details.

ANSWERS

Ex. 1

1
Picture A: I'm going to make the cake.
Picture B: I'm going to have the cake made.

2
1 Picture A
2 Picture B
3 past participle

Ex. 2

1
Other services: pizzas and other food delivered; hair cut/dyed, etc.; car washed/repaired/serviced; house repaired/decorated/painted, etc.; photo taken/developed, etc.; clothes made/cleaned/repaired, etc.; machines (e.g. watch, video, computer, etc.) repaired/mended, etc.

2
1 have, prepared   2 had, cut   3 've had, washed   4 have, repaired   5 'm having, taken   6 had, cleaned   7 have, mended   8 're having, painted

---

See also: *Going for Gold Language Maximiser* Unit 15.

Use of English: transformations p. 130

Aims:
- **to raise students' awareness of different ways of saying the same thing**
- **to improve students' ability to paraphrase**

Exam information PET FCE

In the PET and FCE exams, students have to rewrite sentences so that they mean exactly the same as the original sentence, but using different words or structures.

Teaching tip
Paraphrase is a very useful way of extending students' ability to vary the structures they use in speaking and writing. Take some sentences out of a reading passage or a listening tapescript and ask students if they can think of any other way to say the same thing.

---

1   Explain that it is often possible to say the same thing in different ways. Then ask students to do Exercise 1 in pairs. Discuss their answers with the whole class.

2   This allows students to produce sentences that have the same meaning. Remind them that they should not use more than three words in the gaps. Then ask them to complete the sentences in pairs.

ANSWERS

Ex. 1
1 different (in a) I cleaned them myself; in b) someone cleaned them for me   2 same
3 different (in a) Paula runs faster; in b) they run at the same speed   4 same   5 same
6 same   7 same   8 different (in a) eating is prohibited; in b) eating is not necessary, but is allowed   9 same   10 same   11 same
12 different (in a) most students left early; in b) most students stayed late, only a small number left early

Ex. 2

1 I'm going *to have* my computer repaired.
2 My car *was cleaned* yesterday.
3 The film wasn't *as interesting as* the book.
4 The last maths equation was *easier than / less complicated than* this one.
5 He wasn't *near enough / close enough* to hear her.
6 The presentation *is being given* this afternoon.
7 She asked him *if he was* going to the party that night.
8 Simon isn't *allowed to* eat any salt.
9 If *you don't start* working, you will fail the exam.
10 Although *they tried to* help, they couldn't do anything useful.
11 You'd *better* change your job.
12 Nearly *all the teachers* knew her.

4 *savoury* describes food which has a pleasantly sharp taste (not sweet) like crisps; *sweet* describes food which contains sugar or tastes like sugar
5 *fatty* describes food which has a lot of fat in it; *fattening* describes food which makes people fat quickly
6 *to boil* means to cook food in hot water; *to fry* means to cook food in hot oil
7 *to bake* means to cook in the oven without oil (e.g. cakes and bread); *to roast* means to cook in the oven with oil (e.g. meat)

Ex. 3

1 raw   2 vegetarian   3 fatty   4 rare
5 boil   6 cooker, roast   7 bake   8 fry
9 fattening   10 sweet, savoury   11 cook

See also: *Going for Gold Language Maximiser* Unit 15.

Vocabulary 2: food p. 131

Aims:

• to provide key topic vocabulary
• to help students with words that are easily confused

1 , **2**   Ask students to do these exercises in pairs. Do choral pronunciation of the words in Exercise 2 if necessary.

3   Ask students to complete the sentences using the words they have already discussed in Exercise 2. Then check their answers with the class.

ANSWERS

Ex. 1
2
1 Yes, I do.
2 Only brazil nuts, coconuts and oranges.
3 Yes, I do.

Ex. 2
2 a *vegetable* is a type of food like carrots, potatoes, peas, onions, etc.; a *vegetarian* is a person who does not eat meat or fish
3 *rare* describes meat (especially steak) which is cooked very quickly and is still pink; *raw* describes food which is uncooked

Speaking p. 132

Aims:

• to extend the discussion of food and eating
• to provide practice in using the language of making suggestions, asking for suggestions and reaching a decision

Exam information PET FCE

In the Speaking papers of the PET and FCE exams, students have to discuss a situation together and complete a task, which usually involves reaching a decision. This discussion requires them to make and respond to suggestions, agree and disagree.

1   This exercise provides students with the vocabulary they will need to complete the speaking task.

2   Read through the task with the class so that they understand what they have to do. Then ask them to work in small groups.

3   Tell students that when they do similar tasks, they need to ask for opinions, give opinions, agree and disagree. Ask them to read the phrases, put them in the correct order and decide the function of each one. Play the recording so that they can check their answers and then check their pronunciation as they repeat the sentences.

➡ Tapescript p. 110

4   Ask students to discuss the questions in small groups. Tell them to try to use the language they encountered in Exercise 3.

ANSWERS

Ex. 3
1
1 I don't agree at all.
2 I think you're right.
3 Well, it depends on many things.
4 In my opinion, people eat too much.
5 I'm not sure, but you're probably right.
6 I agree up to a point, but fizzy drinks are fattening.

Writing: report (2) p. 133

Aims:
- **to focus on the organisation of a report by providing a paragraph plan**
- **to help students to use the appropriate style of language for a report**

Exam information FCE CELS

In the Writing paper of the FCE and Vantage and Higher CELS exams, students may have to write a report.

1   This exercise asks students to identify the parts of the task so that they cover everything asked for.

2, **3**   These exercises focus on style. Refer students to the Writing reference on p. 151 for examples of formal and informal language.

4   Make sure that students answer the questions correctly as they focus on the main points of the task. Refer them to the Writing reference on p. 157 for more information about reports.

5   The report could be set for homework. Remind students to use the paragraph plan to help them with their planning and organisation.

ANSWERS

Ex. 1
Three things: what food they usually like, what food they usually don't like and typical meal times

Ex. 2
1 informal 2 formal

Ex. 3
1 You could include phrases 1, 2, 4, 6, 7 and 8. Phrases 3, 5 and 9 are not appropriate because they are not formal enough.
2
This report is intended to ... / Linking expressions of consequence: *therefore, so, consequently* / *it's important that ..., I believe we should ...*

Ex. 4
1 three paragraphs   2 yes   3 (1) what young people from your country usually like eating; (2) what they usually don't like; (3) typical meal times

See also: *Going for Gold Language Maximiser* Unit 15.

Your students are now ready to do Progress test 5 on p. 143.

Units 13–15 Progress check p. 134

ANSWERS

Ex. 1
1 Would you like to go to the cinema?
2 Maria's got some jeans just like mine.
3 My sister doesn't like doing her homework.
4 My new teacher isn't like my last one.
5 I asked Aya if she would like to have some dinner.
6 Costas and Yuri like reading magazines about computers.
7 Do you think I look like my brother?
8 I'd like to go on holiday to Majorca next year.
9 I think that the film is very like the book.
10 I don't like waiting for buses or trains.

Ex. 2
1 You're too busy to take on any more work.
2 Why don't you take up jogging?
3 She took three days off.
4 I found it difficult to take in the bad news.
5 She took over the project when her boss left the company.
6 I can't believe how much you take after your father.
7 I hope you will take back what you said.
8 Everyone takes to him immediately.

Ex. 3
1 So can I.   2 Nor will I.   3 So do I.
4 Nor did I.   5 Nor have I.   6 So am I.
7 Nor can I.   8 So will I.   9 So have I.
10 So did I. 11 Nor am I.   12 Nor do I.

Ex. 4
1 sugar   2 a minute   3 meat
4 information   5 blood   6 a supermarket
7 people   8 space   9 photographs
10 a queue   11 evidence   12 a headache

Ex. 5
1 country   2 flight   3 airport   4 ocean
5 continent   6 duty-free   7 souvenirs
8 island   9 mountains   10 sightseeing
11 desert   12 guidebook

Ex. 6
1 are exported   2 they clean   3 my hair cut
4 can I have   5 were transported
6 are having   7 was the telephone
8 to have   9 were invited
10 have my jacket

Ex. 7
1 B   2 C   3 D   4 A   5 D   6 B   7 B   8 A

Recording scripts

UNIT 1
page 6, Grammar 1, Exercise 2

1
A: OK, thank you. So, what's your surname?
B: It's Aitchison.
A: Sorry, how do you spell that?
B: That's A-I-T-C-H-I-S-O-N.
A: A-I-T-C-H-I-S-O-N. Fine, thank you.

2
A: And if I could also just have your surname?
B: Sure. It's Roxburgh.
A: You mean R-O-X-B-O-R-O-U-G-H?
B: Actually no, the spelling is R-O-X-B-U-R-G-H.
A: Oh I see. Got it.

3
A: Did you say Olearski?
B: Yep, that's right.
A: And how exactly do you spell that?
B: Yes, it is a bit unusual! It's O-L-E-A-R-S-K-I.
A: OK. O-L-E-A-R-S-K-Y.
B: No, it's I – the last letter's I, not Y.
A: Oh sorry. Yes, I see.

UNIT 1
page 6, Listening, Exercise 1

Speaker: How big's her family?
Man: So, do you have a large family?
Girl: Well, not really. I mean there's my mum. And then there's Terry, my brother, and Marion and me. We're very close, me and Marion. Probably because we're the two girls.

UNIT 1
page 7, Listening, Exercise 3

Speaker: 1 What's the time?
Man: Excuse me. I'm sorry, but you don't have the time, do you?
Woman: Yes, of course. It's twenty five to nine.

Speaker: 2 What's Sally buying her dad for Christmas?
Man: So what are you going to get Dad for Christmas?
Woman: I really don't know. Maybe a tie or a new shirt?
Man: You must be joking!
Woman: I know. They're not very exciting. How about a new tennis racket?
Man: That's better. He just broke his old one!

Speaker: 3 What are they doing tonight?
Woman: So, what do you feel like doing this evening?
Man: Oh, I don't know. What about seeing a film or getting a video?
Woman: Oh no, I went to the cinema last night. Why don't we go out for a pizza?
Man: Great idea!

Speaker: 4 What does Claire's boyfriend look like?
Man: So, what's he like?
Woman: Well, he's really quite good-looking. He's got great hair – it's quite long – but no beard or moustache! And he wears really cool glasses.
Man: He sounds nice.

Speaker: 5 How does Kevin usually get to school?
Girl: So, do you get the bus to school?
Boy: No, not normally. I'd like my mum to take me in her car but she's always too busy. So most days I end up walking. It's not that far really.

UNIT 1
page 8, Speaking, Exercises 2 and 3

Katia: In my family we have a big meal with everyone together every month. We all go to my parents' house. There are usually about ten of us, all different ages. I love it especially because I can see my niece. She is nearly three years old.
Tomek: We don't have occasions like this very often, but always at Christmas. I quite like them, but my mother gets quite anxious because she wants everything to be perfect!
Katia: My dad and I are very good! We help my mother with all the preparations. I really like that too. It's all good fun.

UNIT 2
page 12, Listening, Exercise 3

This is the Alton Towers Box Office. There is no one here to take your call, but do not hang up, as further information follows.

Alton Towers is Britain's biggest and best known theme park. There are hundreds of rides and attractions for the whole family. You can, for example, choose a thrilling day out on rides like Oblivion, the world's first vertical-drop roller coaster. Or if you'd prefer, take a quiet walk through beautiful gardens. Whatever you want to do, Alton Towers is the place you should be.

Alton Towers occupies a huge area and was once part of the estate of the Earl of Shrewsbury. Even today many of the towers and old walls remain, and a small part of the mansion is used for the gift shop and cafeteria.

Everyone who comes to Alton Towers wants adventure and fun and they certainly will not be disappointed. There are rides suited to all ages. The famous Nemesis and Oblivion rides will give you the thrill of a lifetime. Then there is the ever popular Ug Land. Ug Land is a virtual reality cave game where you race dinosaurs and escape from Ug beasts on the Corkscrew ride, which takes you through rocky swamps.

If you feel you need some relaxation after so much excitement, you can row on the lake, take an aerial cable car ride, or simply enjoy walking in the gardens, which still have many of the plants, ornaments and fountains from the original design.

Alton Towers is open every day from 1st April until 29th October. The park grounds are open from 9.30 a.m., with rides and attractions opening at 10 a.m. Closing times vary depending on the time of year. These are displayed at the main entrance, or you can telephone for details in advance.

Bookings can be made in person (cash, cheque or credit card), by post (cheques only) or by telephone (credit cards only). We also accept credit card bookings by fax on 0285 704 021. For these bookings you need to use our booking form.
Thank you for calling.

UNIT 2
page 15, Speaking, Exercise 3

Sally: I've been doing it seriously for about two years now. In the summer, I play at least three times a week and sometimes more. I play in winter as well, but not as much. The weather can be a problem.

I started playing after my brother asked me to play with him and some friends. He even gave me his old racket. Now I'm a member of a local club, and there are always people at the club who want to play.

Why do I like it so much? Well, I love being outdoors. I really like running around and I think getting exercise is very important. But most of all I love being able to do it with other people. It's such a friendly game!

UNIT 2
page 18, Grammar 2, Exercise 1

Simon: What are you doing?
Katrina: I am reading about a new cinema complex.
S: Are you thinking of going?
K: Yes, maybe this weekend. What are you doing on Saturday? Would you like to come?
S: Yes. Why not? I am not doing anything else!

UNIT 3
page 24, Listening 1, Exercises 2 and 3

Speaker: 1 Which situation is the woman talking about?
Woman: One of the worst things about where I live is the smell of petrol. The pollution is really bad. I was walking along the high street the other day and I couldn't stop coughing. The fumes from all the cars and buses were terrible.

Speaker: 2 What did the woman make?
A: Hi, Bill. Come in.
B: Hello. Oh! What's that lovely smell? It smells like you've been cooking. Mmm ... what is it? Let me guess ... biscuits? Or cake? No, I think it's chocolate mousse.
A: Nearly right. It's a chocolate cake.
B: Mmm ... it smells really delicious!

Speaker: 3 Which does the man say is the biggest problem for him?
Man: I can't smell at all. Having no sense of smell affects different people in different ways. Some people, for example, find that if you can't smell the food you're eating, then it tastes really horrible. I find the worst thing is the danger element. For example, if you can't smell gas, you might not know if there is a problem with a gas pipe in your house.

Speaker: 4 What new products with added smells does the woman say you can buy?

Woman: There are already thousands of deodorants, soaps and washing powders for sale in shops with thousands of different smells. But now there are new products with smells added to them. Imagine wearing socks, for example, which smell of apples!

Speaker: 5 How much does the perfume cost?
Man: The world's most expensive perfume is called V1 and comes in a box made of platinum, gold and diamonds. The company has made five bottles of V1 so far and Michael Jackson is planning to buy two bottles at £47,750 each. The other three are still for sale.

UNIT 3
page 26, Listening 2, Exercises 2, 3 and 4

***Don't say you love me* by The Corrs**
I've seen this place a thousand times
I've felt this all before
And every time you call
I've waited there as though you might not call at all

I know this face I'm wearing now
I've seen this with my eyes
And though it feels so great I'm still afraid
That you'll be leaving anytime

We've done this once and then you closed the door
Don't let me fall again for nothing more

Don't say you love me unless forever
Don't tell me you need me if you're not gonna stay
Don't give me this feeling I'll only believe it
Make it real or take it all away

I've caught myself smiling alone
Just thinking of your voice
And dreaming of your touch is all too much
You know I don't have any choice

UNIT 4
page 32, Listening, Exercises 2 and 3

Daniel: Hi, Maria, have you seen my puzzle magazine? I can't remember where I put it and it's got some really good puzzles in it.
Maria: No, sorry, I haven't seen it.
D: There's something really interesting in it about neurobics as well.
M: What's that? Is it like aerobics?
D: Similar, but it's not about doing exercises for a healthy body, it's about exercises for the mind, to keep your brain healthy and working properly. You can make yourself more intelligent by practising and doing mind exercises.
M: Oh, really? I thought that after the age of about 20, your brain started to 'die'!
D: That's what scientists thought before, but now they say that your brain can develop throughout your life. In my magazine it says that the best way of improving your intelligence is to work your brain hard. And they say that your brain actually functions better at the end of a day's work than at the beginning!
M: Really?! So, how can I make myself more intelligent?
D: Well, basically it's all about exercise. The more you exercise, the more blood goes to your brain, bringing oxygen with it. And, of course, the more oxygen going to your brain the healthier it will be. And the healthier your brain is, the more you can do with it, and the more intelligent you are.

M: What kind of exercises do you do?

D: All kinds of 'mind games', like in my magazine – doing crosswords, mental arithmetic, memorising different things ... learning languages too.

M: It sounds really good. I'd like a healthier brain. One problem though – your memory is so bad you've even forgotten where the magazine is!

UNIT 5
page 38, Listening 1, Exercise 2.1

Woman: 'Masks of the world' is a new exhibition at the Kingsway Centre which opened this week. It is a fantastic opportunity to see some amazing masks from many different countries. The idea of all masks is that they cover the wearer's face. Different cultures, however, make masks for different reasons.

UNIT 5
page 38, Listening 1, Exercises 2.3 and 3

Woman: 'Masks of the world' is a new exhibition at the Kingsway Centre which opened this week. It is a fantastic opportunity to see some amazing masks from many different countries. The idea of all masks is that they cover the wearer's face. Different cultures, however, make masks for different reasons.

The ancient Egyptians made masks of people who had died. One of the most beautiful Egyptian masks was made in the year 1350 BC for the Pharaoh Tutankhamen when he died. Masks that look like particular people can also be a way of remembering dead relatives.

In some countries, masks are used in connection with health and food. In Indonesia, the medicine man called the 'shaman' has a very powerful mask. People believe it has magic powers and that it can help people get over serious diseases. American Indians believe that masks have special powers too, especially for giving them the right weather to grow sufficient food. During special ceremonies, their dancers wear masks showing the earth, clouds and rain.

In some places it is traditional to wear masks not only for ceremonies, but also for parties and festivals, like Hallowe'en and Carnival. In the theatre, people use masks to get round the problem of playing different characters. The audience then don't see the actor's face, but the face of a character in the story. The traditional theatres of both Italy and Japan use masks for this reason.

A selection of all these different types of masks can be seen in the exhibition, which will be open for the next two months. For more information on opening times, call our box office on 01865 298772.

UNIT 5
page 42, Listening 2, Exercises 2 and 3

Interviewer: Hello. Today we've got Lara Jackson here. She's fashion editor for *His 'n' Hers* magazine. Lara, hello.

Lara: Hi. Great to be here.

I: So, we're talking about beautiful people. What do you think, Lara? Do people always agree about who is good-looking? Is it a personal opinion?

L: I think that people will always argue about whether Julia Roberts is more attractive than Anna Kournikova, for example. Or whether Brad Pitt is better looking than Ben Affleck. Who do you like best? I must say, I like Brad Pitt!

I: Oh, I don't really agree. I prefer Ben Affleck.

L: Well, there you are! We all have our personal tastes ...

I: But what things do beautiful people have in common?

L: Well, actually there is quite a lot of agreement about what is good-looking. In 1993, there was some research done to explore how much people agree about beauty.

I: Oh, really?

L: Researchers showed photos of women to people in Russia, South America and the USA and asked them to put them in order of beauty! The results showed that people in all those countries liked women with small chins and large eyes.

I: That's interesting. Do you agree with that opinion?

L: Well, I agree up to a point. But don't forget, although we may agree on who is beautiful now, things were different 30 or 40 years ago.

I: Mmm ... many female models and actors nowadays think it's attractive and fashionable to be really slim, don't they?

L: That's right. Actually, some of them are really thin. I mean, think about Kate Moss. In my opinion she's skinny; she looks unhealthy. But if we go back to the 1950s, women like Marilyn Monroe were more popular. And she certainly wasn't skinny!

I: No, and further back in history too, I suppose.

L: Yes, things have changed a lot. For example, 300 years ago, people thought large, fat chins were very attractive!

I: Oh no! I don't agree at all! That's awful!

UNIT 5
page 45, Speaking, Exercise 1

A: I think Brad Pitt is better looking than Ben Affleck.

B: Oh, I don't really agree. I like Ben Affleck!

A: Well, in my opinion it's a matter of personal taste. Do you agree?

B: I agree up to a point, but it depends on when you're talking about. Fashions change, don't they?

A: That's right. Three hundred years ago, fat chins were considered very attractive!

B: Oh no! I don't agree at all!

UNIT 6
page 46, Listening 1, Exercises 2 and 3

Tom: Hey, Paola, listen to this.

Paola: What is it? What are you reading?

T: It's an article about the Internet. You know, when the Internet first started ... when it first became possible to move information electronically from one computer to another. Do you know when that was?

P: Umm, it must be ... oh, about 30 years ago, was it?

T: More or less, yes, it was on the 20th of October 1969 in California. And what about the first email – when do you think they sent the first email?

P: More recently, I think. About the mid-seventies? 1975 or 76?

T: Well, nearly, it was in 1972. Oh, and this is interesting ... when could you order the first pizza on the Internet?

P: In the eighties? I'm not sure.

T: No, it was in 1994. It says here that Pizza Hut started its first website in 1994. That's not very long ago really, is it?

P: No, it isn't. And now there are millions of websites. You can buy almost everything over the Internet. I think I'd prefer to go to the shops and really see what I'm buying.

T: I know what you mean, but actually e-shopping is very easy. Oh, and listen to this. It says there's someone who was called Mitch Maddox. Then he changed his name to DotComGuy!

P: What? DotComGuy? Why did he do that?

T: Well, it says that he wanted to try to live by only using the Internet. He spent one year living in an empty house, with only his computer, a laptop, oh, and his cat!

P: Really? What about people? Did he see his friends?

T: Umm, it says he had visitors but he didn't go out. He ordered everything he needed online. Or sometimes he emailed his friends to bring things to the house: food, medicine, entertainment, everything. And there was a digital camera in every room filming him. People could watch everything he did on his personal website.

P: Oh, I think that's stupid! How boring to watch someone in an empty house. Some people watch real rubbish!

UNIT 6

page 50, Speaking, Exercises 1 and 2

Elena: Wojtek, it's nearly the summer holidays – two more days to go! Have you got any plans for the holidays? What are you going to do?

Wojtek: Well, I'd like to see a film this weekend. My friend told me about a new science fiction film and I love that kind of film. We're probably going to see it on Saturday. And then, I'm not sure, but I think we'll go and have a pizza on Sunday. After that, well, basically I'm just going to relax for the first week.

E: Yes, that sounds good. And what about the rest of the holidays?

W: I'm going to go camping with my family. We haven't decided exactly where yet. One idea is to go to France, but it depends on the weather really.

E: Anything else?

W: Yes, I'm thinking about getting a holiday job, just for a couple of weeks. I'm going to ask in some local cafés and shops. I'd like to earn some extra money. There are loads of things I want to buy ...

UNIT 6

page 50, Speaking, Exercise 3

1 I'd like to go to university.
2 I'm thinking about having a party.
3 It depends on my exam results.
4 I'm probably going to go travelling.
5 One idea is to buy a new computer.
6 I'm not sure but I think I'll get a job.

UNIT 6

page 51, Listening 2, Exercises 2 and 3

This is the Computer Games Festival box office. There is no one here to take your call, but do not hang up, as further information follows.

The festival begins on the 12th of June and continues to the 28th. Many of Europe's leading computer games designers are in the New Media Centre from the 12th to the 15th. There are demonstrations of the newest games from top British and other European companies such as Codemasters, Rebellion and Lionhead. For fans of Japanese and American games, there are plenty of those to try as well.

If you're worried about the effect of computer games on health or education, there's plenty for you too. We have a Health and Education Capsule, from the 16th to the 22nd, which offers information and advice. Over 75% of children aged between seven and 14 now have a games console, like Playstation or Dreamcast. On average, children play computer games for 45 minutes a day. Sometimes their hands and arms become painful and they may have difficulties concentrating. However, there is also other research which shows that children who become addicted to computer games may actually be more intelligent than average. Come to the Capsule, talk to our experts and find out more.

One of the special attractions at this year's festival is our computer games competition 'Zapdome'. The final of the competition takes place on the last day of the festival, the 28th of June. This year we also have a guest star player, Sujoy Roy. Sujoy is a champion computer games player in his mid twenties. He earns over $200,000 a year competing in computer games competitions. You are advised to get your entry forms in early for the competition, as it is always very popular.

For more information, visit the Box Office from 10.00 a.m. to 8.00 p.m. Mondays to Fridays, or 12.00 to 6.00 p.m. on Saturdays. Bookings can be made in person (cash, cheque or credit card), by post (cheques only) or by telephone (credit cards only) on 01279 393782. Thank you for calling.

UNIT 6

page 52, Grammar 2, Exercise 1

A: Have you been to the computer games festival? It finishes on Saturday, you know.

B: I know, I really want to go.

A: Thierry and I are going to the final of the competition on Saturday morning. Would you like to come with us?

B: Oh, yes, great. I'd love to!

A: Well, I'm meeting Thierry there on Saturday at 10.30 and the game starts at 11.00.

B: Fantastic. See you on Saturday!

UNIT 7

page 57, Speaking, Exercises 2 and 3

Gerhard: So, Carla, what kinds of exercise do you like doing?

Carla: Well, I like going to the gym because it's near to my home and I can watch MTV while I do my exercise. What about you?

Gerhard: Yes, I like going to the gym too because I go with my friends and then we go for a coffee after. But I also like going jogging. It's very peaceful in the morning. I think it's relaxing, don't you?

Carla: No I don't. I think jogging is really boring. I hate it. Also sometimes the weather is bad and I definitely don't want to go jogging then!

Gerhard: That's a good point. It's not much fun when it's raining. So what other kinds of exercise do you like?

Carla: I quite like playing tennis in the summer ...

UNIT 7

page 60, Listening, Exercises 2 and 3

Presenter: So Martin, could you tell us just how you got into this rather unusual job?

Martin: I suppose I've liked tattoos ever since I was little. I got my first one done on my back when I was about 16. It was a birthday present. My mum was really great. I thought she'd try to stop me, but she came along, helped me choose the design and everything!

Now I have my own shop where I do tattoos. Sometimes clients are very particular and bring me drawings to work from.

More often though people want the same kind of quite simple things: birds, stars, names, hearts or oriental symbols.

Presenter: So how does your day start, then?

Martin: Well, I've just bought a stupid alarm clock which looks like a monkey, so I usually start laughing when I look at it in the morning. I'm a very happy person and normally walk around all day with a big smile on my face!

I get questions about my tattoos from all over the world, so first thing in the morning I switch on my computer to see if there's any email. Then I have toast and coffee before getting into a nice hot bath. It really relaxes me.

I cycle to work or get the bus if it's raining. I love what I do. I think it's really creative. And I really like all the different people I meet. You'd be amazed at the variety of people who come in – housewives, lawyers, teachers, all sorts.

People often ask me if it hurts to get a tattoo done. Well, it really depends on where you have it done. Basically, it hurts less where you have more flesh and hurts more if it's near bone. People have tattoos done on all parts of their body but most common I think are shoulders and arms.

Another big question is always 'Can you remove a tattoo?' Of course, it is possible but it's not easy and it's very expensive, so I always tell people to think long and hard before deciding to get one done.

UNIT 7
page 61, Grammar 2, Exercise 2

1
A: Could you turn the music down a bit, please?
B: Sorry, I couldn't hear what you said.

2
A: Can you lend me your tennis racket?
B: Sorry, but I'm playing Tim at 11 o'clock.

3
A: Would you fill out this form, please?
B: Sure, but can I borrow a pen?

4
A: Can I have a cheeseburger, please?
B: OK. With or without French fries?

5
A: Could I try on these jeans, please?
B: Yes, of course. The changing room is over there.

6
A: Would you open the window, please?
B: Of course. It is quite hot in here.

7
A: Can you clean the table, please?
B: No problem. I'll just get a cloth.

UNIT 8
page 66, Vocabulary 1, Exercise 3

Katia: Hello?
Pietro: Oh, hello, Katia. Have you finished your packing yet?
K: Oh, not yet. There's so much to do.
P: You sound tired. How are you feeling about moving house?
K: Well, I live in a really small village in the country at the moment. It's nice in some ways, but ...
P: What do you like about living in the country?
K: Well, there aren't many people – it isn't too crowded. It's very peaceful actually, and I really like living in a place that has

plenty of open space. You know, it isn't too built up. It's great being able to breathe really fresh air too! There isn't much traffic and it's really not polluted at all.

P: So, are you upset about moving away?
K: Umm, no, because it's really boring! There aren't many facilities. I mean, you have to travel a long way to go to things like the swimming pool, or shopping centres, you know. And the public transport isn't very frequent either, so you have to use a car a lot. My parents always have to take me to places.
P: What are you going to like about the city most, do you think?
K: Well, the place we're moving to has really good nightlife, so I'm really looking forward to going out to the cinema and clubs.

UNIT 8
page 69, Listening, Exercises 2 and 4

Anna: This article is about a man ... it's really interesting ... do you know, he's been on holiday in room 23, the same room, at Pine de Plage hotel, the same hotel, in St Tropez for the past nine years! That's amazing!

Oliver: Do you think so? I think that's really boring. I think it's much more interesting to go to different places for your holiday.

A: But some people like things to be the same. Some people like a regular routine. You know, then they know what they're getting – no surprises. Look! Here's another one ... a married couple, George and Diana, they've had breakfast in the same café, The Railway Café, every day for 30 years! Thirty years! I can't believe it!

O: They must be so bored! What do they eat? Do they have the same things to eat every day?

A: Umm, it says that the menu in the café hasn't changed at all since the café first opened. And for breakfast, Diana always has a sandwich and George always has a big breakfast of eggs, bacon and tomatoes. The same – they've eaten the same breakfast since they were young people in their mid 20s ... now they're about 50!

O: I think it's really depressing. It's awful. They haven't had many different experiences in life!

A: Oh, I don't agree. I think it's OK. They obviously enjoy it and they know what they're going to get.

O: Yes, that's true but I wouldn't like it.

UNIT 9
page 74, Vocabulary 1, Exercise 1

Sound effects:
1 someone whispering
2 a loud crash of a vase breaking on the floor
3 a ring on a front door bell
4 someone yawning
5 a door banging
6 a woman's scream
7 someone whistling
8 someone sneezing

UNIT 9
page 74, Listening 1, Exercises 3 and 4

***When you say nothing at all* by Ronan Keating**
It's amazing how you can speak right to my heart
Without saying a word, you can light up the dark
Try as I may, I can never explain
What I hear when you don't say a thing

The smile on your face lets me know that you need me
There's a truth in your eyes saying you'll never leave me
The touch of your hand says you'll catch me wherever I fall
You say it best, when you say nothing at all

All day long I can hear people talking out loud
But when you hold me near, you drown out the crowd
Try as they may, they can never define
What's been said between your heart and mine

The smile on your face lets me know that you need me
There's a truth in your eyes saying you'll never leave me
The touch of your hand says you'll catch me wherever I fall
You say it best, when you say nothing at all

UNIT 9
page 76, Speaking, Exercises 2 and 3

A: So, what on earth are we going to get Emma when she goes off to Italy?

B: Well, how about some kind of Italian language learning course? You know, with CDs and books and stuff.

C: Yes, that's an interesting suggestion, but do you know how expensive they are? And anyway, Emma doesn't like sitting at computers ... she'd prefer to study in class with other people.

A: OK, well, in that case, what about a new CD Walkman? Then she can listen to all her favourite music on the plane over and when she's in her new place.

B: Yeah, that's not a bad idea, but I'd like to get her something to do with Italy. Surely there must be something else.

C: I know. Why don't we get her some nice travel books about Italy? She loves travelling and this will help her know where to go!

A: Excellent! That's a really good idea ... and hopefully she'll ask us to go along too!

UNIT 9
page 77, Listening 2, Exercises 2 and 3

Julian: I didn't know your mum was Spanish!

Natalia: Yeah, apparently my dad was in Spain, in Alicante, on holiday one summer and met my mum, who was brought up there, in a club. They stayed in touch, and a couple of years later they got married and she moved to London.

J: Wow ... So, do you speak Spanish?

N: Hmmm, not really, not very well. You see, I've got two older sisters, Isabella and Christina. When Isabella was growing up, my mum really wanted her to be bilingual, so she would only speak to her in Spanish. My dad just spoke to her in English (his Spanish isn't too good actually) but mum was very strict about only speaking Spanish. And, as well as that, they always went, every summer, to stay with my mum's family in Alicante.

J: So, Isabella's Spanish is pretty good.

N: It's perfect really. You see, Isabella, who studied Spanish at university, now lives in Barcelona and has even got a Spanish boyfriend. So, nowadays, people can't tell if she's Spanish or English!

J: And what about your other sister, Christina?

N: Well, Christina's not bad. I mean, I think she can get her message across most of the time and understand most things, but she's certainly not completely fluent. I think Mum was pretty busy when Christina was born and so was more relaxed about speaking English some of the time.

J: And so what about you? How good's your Spanish?

N: Yes, well, that's a bit of a disaster really. Not great at all. I mean, in my school holidays I was doing a lot of horse-riding, which I really loved. So that meant I didn't often go to Spain in the summer – and Mum had more or less stopped speaking Spanish at home, so ... It's all a bit embarrassing. I really wish I was better at it. Actually, I'm thinking of spending some time in Barcelona with Isabella next year before I go to college so I can get some practice. Maybe that will help a bit.

UNIT 10
page 83, Vocabulary 1, Exercise 1

54 mph
86.9 km/h
2.75 seconds
183 and 274 m
100-metre
9.85 seconds
1994
80
150
1/4 mile
0.4 km
56 hours
86,000
7 lb
3.175 kg
273 tons
1,087,146
20 ft
6.096 m
1958
34.5 mph
55.5 km/h
55.5%

UNIT 10
page 85, Speaking, Exercises 2 and 3

Conversation 1

Karen: So, what are we going to do tonight?

Andrew: Why don't we go to the Rainforest Café, you know, in the centre of town. It's supposed to feel like you really are in the rainforest with tropical birds, huge fishtanks, waterfalls ...

Tania: Oh no, I've just eaten ... not a café.

Simon: I'm not hungry either.

Andrew: Well, what about a film? How about the new Matt Damon then?

Karen: Yes, that's a good idea. I agree. Tania and Simon aren't hungry so let's go and see a film.

Conversation 2

Tom: So, what are we going to do tonight?

Rob: Well, we could go round to Sarah's ...

Paula: All I know is that I'm hungry!

Kate: Me too!

Rob: And me!

Paula: So why don't we go for a pizza?

Tom: I think you're right. We're all hungry so going for a pizza is the best idea!

UNIT 10
page 86, Listening, Exercise 3

1

Well, me and my friend, Caroline, were on holiday in Australia. It was really hot and we'd been lying on this beautiful sandy beach for ages … well, *anyway*, then we decided to go for a swim … *So*, we're walking into the water … there are lots of other people around Then, *just as* the water's about up to the top of my legs, I hear this screaming 'Shark! Shark!' Well, I can tell you, everyone just started screaming and running for the beach! *Honestly*, I've never been so frightened in all my life. *In the end*, it turns out it was just a kid playing a joke … *can you believe it!*?

2

Have I told you about our cat, Twix? She's really funny. Just yesterday, I was sitting doing my homework in my dad's study with the door open … *you know*, it goes out into the garden and the pond. *Anyway*, Twix was out in the garden and was sitting on the edge of the pond. *Well*, you know there are fish in the pond, *well*, so does Twix and she loves to watch them. *So*, there she is … sitting, looking to see where the fish are. *Suddenly*, there's this great 'splosh' and this ball of wet fur flies past me and back into the house. She'd got just a bit **too** interested in the fish and fallen right in the pond. *Really, you know*, I just couldn't stop laughing!

3

OK well, I've got an even better horror story for you. *You see*, I was camping for the weekend with some friends. I'd woken up quite early and, *you know*, I was half asleep. *Anyway*, I was just about to put on my shoes before going off for a shower when I saw – in my shoe – the most **enormous** spider you have EVER seen. It was huge ... and furry ... I nearly fainted. I was in a complete panic. Just thinking about what would have happened if I hadn't been paying attention, it's too ... brrgghghh!

4

It was some time last year, I think. I was going for a walk with my dad. We'd cut across some fields and got a bit lost. … *Anyway, suddenly*, there in this field, we found ourselves staring into the eyes of this very very big, black bull. I'd never been quite so close to one before. I could feel myself go white with fear. I was paralysed. I couldn't move a muscle. *Eventually*, the bull seemed to lose interest and wandered off. *You cannot believe* how relieved we were!

UNIT 10
Page 88, Grammar 2, Exercise 3

1 If I'd known you were in hospital, I would have visited you.
2 I would have helped them if they had asked.
3 If I hadn't gone to the party, I wouldn't have seen Antonia.
4 I would have sent you a postcard if I had had time.
5 If the weather hadn't been so bad we would have gone out.
6 I would have missed tennis practice if you hadn't woken me up.

UNIT 11
page 94, Listening, Exercises 2 and 3

A: Wasn't it a lucky escape for that father and son, trapped in the mountains? Did you read about it?
B: Yes, I did. It was all over the papers. It just makes me think how careful you have to be when you go up in the mountains. Did you see that other article about things you should and shouldn't do to prepare properly before you go?

A: No, I must have missed that. What did it say?
B: Well, first of all, apparently, you should make sure you dress properly. Ideally you ought to wear three different layers, which basically keeps you warm and dry. They say that once you are wet, it is very difficult to get dry.
A: Yes, I can imagine that. And then what does it say?
B: Well then it's really about what you carry with you. Firstly, you ought to take some kind of source of heat, like matches or a lighter. Then they suggest you take one of those space blanket type things – you know, with the sort of foil outside which is supposed to be amazing for keeping you warm. Next on the list is something to signal with, like a mirror or a whistle. And then finally it's about the kind of food you carry.
A: Let me guess … plenty of chocolate!
B: I wish! Actually, not so much chocolate as carbohydrates. They say you should take foods which are high in carbohydrates like bread and potatoes because proteins, for example, need heat to break them down and require more water for digestion.

UNIT 11
page 95, Vocabulary 2, Exercise 3

1 The nurse put a clean bandage on his leg.
2 I'm going on a first aid course at the local hospital.
3 The room shook and pictures fell off the walls during the earthquake.
4 I cut my finger and got blood on my shirt.
5 It was so cold they were worried about getting frostbite.
6 He waved to signal that he was ready to start.
7 He was attacked by a lion when he was in Africa.
8 Sandy can't play basketball because of a knee injury.
9 Factory waste has poisoned many rivers in this area.
10 He escaped from prison by digging a tunnel.

UNIT 12
page 102, Listening, Exercise 2

A: Hmmmm, that's a hard one but I actually have really strong memories of us all packing our suitcases, choosing what we could and couldn't take with us, filling up our old car and then driving off on a hot August day. Hours later, hot and tired, we'd arrive at this little place that we went to every year. We'd be greeted by Mrs Jenkins who ran it … and then go up to our rooms. Straightaway, I used to unpack my case, put on my swimming costume and run down to the beach. The water used to be freezing but I didn't care. I loved it!

UNIT 12
page 102, Listening, Exercise 3

B: What I particularly remember is the times when there'd be delicious smells coming out of the kitchen. I can remember going along to investigate and there'd be all sorts of spoons and bowls and ingredients everywhere. I was terribly impatient for the baking to be done, but if I was lucky, Mum would give me the mixing bowl to clean out while I was waiting. Then I'd get to have the cake mixture which got left behind … yum!

C: What made it really magical was that Mum and Dad used to spend all of one night putting up the tree and covering it with all sorts of wonderful decorations. There'd be lights and coloured glass balls and lots of little ornaments. And my favourite was little chocolate snowmen, which we'd get to eat later. Anyway, I'd come down one morning and there it would be … all done. Magic! After that, each day, a few presents would be added to the bottom of the tree and the pile would grow bigger and bigger ...

D: He's actually a lot older than me, 13 years in fact. So, he was a teenager when I was born. You'd think he wouldn't have been interested in a baby at that age, but I know from all the photos – and from a few memories – that he actually spent a lot of time with me. The worst thing though was that he used to love tickling me! Unfortunately, I am very very ticklish, especially my feet – I used to almost cry with laughter!

UNIT 12
page 104, Speaking, Exercise 4

... and this is one of my favourite photos. It was taken years ago. We were on holiday in the south-west of England. We were spending the day on the beach, and I remember really wanting to make a sandcastle. My mother said she'd help me and we spent hours building this huge sandcastle. In the picture you can see me with my bucket running off to get more dry sand, I think. I remember having so much fun. This photo's quite special for me because a few years ago I lost all my family photo albums in a fire ... and this is the only one I have left of me as a child with my mother.

UNIT 13
page 110, Vocabulary 1, Exercise 2

continent   country   island   ocean   lake   river   mountain forest   desert

UNIT 13
page 111, Listening 1, Exercise 1

Well, now everyone's here, let me just start by saying a very big and warm Welcome to Sydney, Australia's premier city and the oldest settlement in Australia.
Now, I know you're all getting hungry, so I'm sure you'll be interested to hear that shortly we'll be having a barbecue at the top of the hotel, overlooking the harbour. Then there'll be a show from two of Sydney's funniest comedians. Their introduction to life here in the city is guaranteed to have you crying with laughter, I promise!
Tomorrow please make sure you've tried our excellent buffet breakfast (which opens at 6 a.m.) before meeting in reception at 10 a.m. We'll leave the hotel at 10.15 and during the first part of the day we'll be having a good look around 'The Rocks'. This is the oldest part of Sydney and is a great area to walk around. It's got various interesting old buildings and art galleries, plus wonderful shopping opportunities!
In the afternoon, there is a choice. For the more adventurous, it's back to the harbour to try your hand at some sailing with our experienced guide, Daniel. Or, alternatively, you can join us for a somewhat less energetic but equally scenic ferry ride on the Manly ferry.
Following that, after a bit of time to relax and change, there's another choice to be made. That is either firstly to visit the Sydney Opera House with a highly recommended performance of Mozart's *Don Giovanni*. Or, alternatively, a group will be going along to Sound City, one of Sydney's most famous nightclubs, which always provides an opportunity for celebrity spotting!
All right, now, would anyone like to ask any questions at this stage ...

UNIT 13
page 112, Vocabulary 2, Exercise 3

1 Was it a long flight?
2 Did you buy anything in duty-free?
3 What did you think of London?
4 Have you taken many photos?
5 How did you get here from the airport?
6 Would you like to do a bit of sightseeing today?
7 Are you going to buy a guidebook?
8 Have you bought many souvenirs?
9 Did you have a look round the shops?

UNIT 13
page 112, Speaking, Exercises 1 and 2

Well, both pictures show young people on holiday maybe and travelling, but in very different ways! In picture A I can see two young people carrying, what's the word, oh yes, rucksacks. They look like they're in the middle of a city. The buildings remind me of Spain or Italy but I'm not sure. On the other hand, picture B seems to be in the country.
The first couple probably don't have much money whereas the people in picture B must be quite well off because the car looks quite expensive! Also, the people in the second picture look quite relaxed but the first couple look hot and tired as if they've been walking around for a long time. I think they might be looking for somewhere to stay.

UNIT 13
page 115, Listening 2, Exercises 2 and 3

Sally: Yes, that's right. My whole family had to leave Australia when my dad's company sent him to Britain. And, well, we've been here ever since.
Michael: So, what is it you miss most about Australia, Sally?
S: Well, I suppose a sense of space is the first thing ... and maybe the main thing. I don't just mean out in the countryside, or 'the bush' as we often call it, but even in Australian cities you feel that, well, that there's more room to move. The streets are wider than they are in Europe, and most houses have gardens around them and of course there are fewer people – under 20 million in the whole big, beautiful country.
M: That sounds really great.
S: Yes, and another thing I missed a lot, especially at the beginning, was spending a lot of time out of the house. Australians love to be outside – at the beach or out in the bush or even in parks in the cities, playing sport or just having a barbecue with friends.
M: Hey, so do I! It's not just Australians, you know!
S: No, I know! But of course the Australian beaches are absolutely amazing – long stretches of golden and even pure white sand, often without another person anywhere in sight. I missed them a lot, especially when I lived in London. I never learnt to surf myself, but I had friends who were almost obsessed with it and spent every weekend looking for the perfect wave.
M: And what about your friends and family?
S: Yes, well, I missed all my friends terribly the first couple of years I was away from home and I still do really. I now think that Australians behave quite differently to people in Europe. We're much friendlier and less formal. It's not unusual for total strangers to start a conversation at a bus stop or even while

waiting to cross the road. Australians generally know their neighbours and socialise with them, often inviting them to eat in their homes. Mmm, that's another thing I miss, come to think of it ... being able to go out to eat almost any kind of food from almost any country on Earth, often within a very small area of the city. Oh yes, and some of the best coffee I've ever had anywhere – but then I haven't been to Brazil!

UNIT 14

page 121, Listening 1, Exercise 2

Feelin' so good by Jennifer Lopez

When I opened up my eyes today – (I) felt the sun shining on my face.
It became so clear to me that everything is going my way.
I feel like there's no limit to what I can see – (I) got rid of fears that were holding me.
My endless possibilities – has the whole world opened up for me?
That's why I'm feeling ...

I'm feeling so good – I knew I would.
Been taking care of myself – like I should.
'Cause not one thing can bring me down.
Nothing in this world's going to turn me around.

Now the day is turning into night and everything is still going right.
There's no way you can stop me this time – or break this spirit of mine.
Like the stars above, I'm going to shine – anything I want will be mine.
Tonight I'm going to have a good time – call a few friends of mine.
'Cause I'm loving life and tonight's for feeling ...

I'm feeling so good – I knew I would.
Been taking care of myself – like I should.
'Cause not one thing can bring me down.
Nothing in this world's going to turn me around.

UNIT 14

page 123, Listening 2, Exercises 3 and 4

Hello and welcome to this week's edition of *People who changed the world*. This week we're talking about someone who you have probably never heard of. But every single one of us has been affected by her work. She was an extraordinary woman. Her name was Rachel Carson and she took on governments and companies in her fight to save the environment.
Rachel Carson was an eco-warrior: probably the world's first eco-warrior. But she didn't look like most people's idea of an eco-warrior. She was in her mid fifties and looked like anyone's mother or grandmother. People who met her took to her quiet manner immediately. She was also a highly qualified scientist and a very good writer. In the early 1960s, she wrote a book about her work, called *Silent Spring*. The book was more than just a best seller. It was, and is, one of the most important books of all time.
Why is it so important? What's the message of Rachel's book? Well, its message to the public was, and still is, that when humans damage one part of the environment, we damage everything. The whole world is affected. At the time she wrote the book, it was hard for people to take in how important this was. Governments and big multinational companies didn't want to know about the damage they were causing.

The most important thing she wrote about was the use of DDT, a chemical used in agriculture. Farmers spray their crops with it. Aeroplanes fly over fields killing the insects that damage plants. But Rachel found that DDT was not only killing insects. It was killing other things – a lot of other things. Sometimes, farm workers became ill immediately after spraying. Birds and animals also died because the food they ate had been sprayed ...

UNIT 14

page 125, Speaking, Exercises 1 and 2

Pablo: Well, in my town there are a lot of cars. In my opinion, too many people use cars and there are always traffic jams.
Erica: That's right. It's the same in my town. The pollution is awful and it always takes a long time to get anywhere. The trouble is that the buses aren't very good so people need their cars. Ummm, is there much litter in your town?
P: No, not really. Most people do use the litter bins and it isn't really a problem.
E: My town is quite clean too. I hate it when people throw their rubbish on the streets. I think it's really selfish.
P: And graffiti – some people think that graffiti is like art.
E: Oh, I don't agree at all!
P: No, I think it is vandalism. There isn't much graffiti in my area. In fact, my town is very beautiful and there are some lovely places. You know, quiet streets with trees and places to sit ...

UNIT 14

page 125, Speaking, Exercise 3

P: ... Well, it depends ... I think that cars are a big problem in cities. Yes, I think that if people had to pay every time they used their car in the city, then they might leave their car at home sometimes. What do you think?
E: I'm not sure, but in my opinion, the bus service should be better. If the public transport system was better, people wouldn't need their cars so much. Do you agree?
P: I agree up to a point, but sometimes people really need to use their cars ...

UNIT 15

page 128, Vocabulary 1, Exercise 2

1 What is your favourite brand of sports clothes?
2 Can you describe the logo of that brand?
3 Can you remember a good advertisement you've seen recently on TV?
4 What product is it advertising?
5 Which company produces it?
6 Which market do you think it is for?
7 Which do you think consumers prefer: cheap goods with little packaging, or more expensive goods with more attractive packaging? Why?
8 Research shows that people don't like eating blue food. Why do you think this is?

UNIT 15

page 128, Listening, Exercises 2 and 3

1
Assistant: Dominion Pizzas. Can I help you?
Customer: Oh hello. I'd like to have a pizza delivered, please.
A: OK.
C: I'd like the Hawaiian pizza, please – with ham and pineapple.
A: What size? Small, medium, large or extra large?

C: Extra large.
A: Fine. What's the address, please?
C: It's 24 Alexandra Avenue.
A: 24 Alexandra Avenue. We'll be with you in 15 minutes.
C: Thank you.

2

Teacher: OK, everybody. Great to see you. I'll start by saying what we're going to do today. First I'll show you some of the machines and equipment in the kitchen. Then we'll see some basic techniques, including a simple way of doing vegetables. Before we start, I'd like to ask ...

3

Teacher: Right, it's very important that you complete the section where it asks if you have any special dietary requirements. The school needs to know if anyone is allergic to certain foods, if you don't eat meat or if you can't eat certain foods for religious reasons. If you need any help with this section, please ask me.

4

Announcer: Don't miss this week's bargains! Two for the price of one! Buy two packets of chewing gum for the price of one, two packets of cereal for the price of one, and many more. Special deal on take-away lunches! Buy a sandwich, a packet of crisps and a chocolate bar and you get a fizzy drink absolutely free!

5

Woman: I've got so much to prepare for this party.
Man: Calm down. What have you done already?
W: Well, I'm having the food prepared in advance. It's coming on Saturday morning.
M: That's done then. Have you made the cake yet?
W: No, I'm going to have the cake made too. It's a really good company who make cakes to order ...
M: Well, you don't need to worry ...

6

Researcher: Hello. I wonder if I could ask you a few questions. I work for a market research company and we're asking people what they think of our new range of milkshakes. We are changing a lot of our products and we would value your opinions. It won't take more than five minutes ...

UNIT 15
page 133, Speaking, Exercise 3

1 I don't agree at all.
2 I think you're right.
3 Well, it depends on many things.
4 In my opinion, people eat too much.
5 I'm not sure, but you're probably right.
6 I agree up to a point, but fizzy drinks are fattening.

Unit 1 test

1 Look at the answers a student gave in an interview. Write the questions.   (10 marks)

Interviewer *What's your name?* ....

Student Sophie Grosjean.

Interviewer (1) ....

Student G-R-O-S-J-E-A-N.

Interviewer (2) ....

Student I'm from Montpellier in France.

Interviewer (3) ....

Student Here in London. I'm sharing a flat with some other students.

Interviewer (4) ....

Student About three months. I arrived here in September.

Interviewer (5) ....

Student I like the theatres and the parks. I think the shops are wonderful too.

Interviewer (6) ....

Student I need it for my job. I'm a hotel receptionist.

Interviewer (7) ....

Student Well, French, of course, and some Spanish. I'm also studying Italian.

Interviewer (8) ....

Student I like going out with my friends to the cinema or for a meal. I also like
listening to music and shopping.

Interviewer (9) ....

Student I'm going back in a few days for the Christmas holidays, but I'm coming
back here in January to finish my English course.

Interviewer (10) ....

Student It finishes in June, just after we do our exams.

2 Write definitions for these names of family members.   (10 marks)

father-in-law   *the father of your husband or wife* ....

sister-in-law   (1) ....   stepfather (6) ....

daughter-in-law (2) ....   aunt (7) ....

grandmother   (3) ....   uncle (8) ....

grandson   (4) ....   cousin (9) ....

stepsister   (5) ....   nephew (10) ....

3   Choose the best alternative to fill in the answers to this questionnaire.   (10 marks)

Full name and title: (1) ....

Home address (including post code): (2) ....

Telephone number: (3) ....

Nationality: (4) ....

Date of birth: (5) ....

Present occupation (if you are a student, say what you are studying): (6) ....

How many brothers and sisters do you have? (7) ....

Do you still live with your parents? (8) ....

Which members of your family are you closest to? (9) ....

Are you closer to your family or your friends? (10) ....

1	A Simon Barnett, Mr	B Mr Simon		C Mr Barnett
2	A London, NW5	B 6 Crawley Gardens, London NW5		C 6 Crawley Gardens
3	A Yes	B No		C (020) 7624 4216
4	A Ireland	B Irish		C Yes
5	A September	B 1st September		C 21/9/80
6	A Student at Roehampton Institute	B No		C Student. Computer Science
7	A One	B One sister		C Yes
8	A No	B For three years		C 1998
9	A Yes	B All		C My father and my sister
10	A To my friends	B No		C Both

4   Change the questions in the questionnaire in Exercise 3 into indirect questions.
Use the words in brackets to start your questions.   (10 marks)

Example: What are your plans for the future? (I'd like to know …)
I'd like to know what your plans for the future are. ....

1 (Could you tell me what …)   ....

2 (I'd like to know where …)   ....

3 (I'd also like to know what …)   ....

4 (Could you also tell me what …)   ....

5 (And could you tell me what …)   ....

6 (I'd like to know what …)   ....

7 (Another thing I'd like to know is how many …)   ....

8 (Could you tell me if …)   ....

9 (And could you also tell me which …)   ....

10 (Finally, I'd like to know if …)   ....

5   Punctuate these sentences.   (2 marks each = 10 marks)

1 is margarets appointment on thursday or friday
2 i want to learn italian spanish and portuguese
3 whats your name asked the boy
4 she eats fish but she wont eat chicken
5 ill let you know what time shes arriving

Unit 2 test

1   Match the first parts of these sentences (1–5) to the second parts (a–g). There are two second parts that you do not need to use.   (5 marks)

1 'Grumpy'
2 Cats
3 Water
4 Cigarettes
5 The library

a) damage your health.
b) like fish.
c) is bad for you.
d) isn't open on Sundays.
e) boils at a lower temperature at the top of Mount Everest.
f) means slightly angry or annoyed.
g) freeze at zero degrees.

2   There are mistakes with verbs that are not used in continuous tenses in five of these sentences. Find the mistakes and correct them.   (5 marks)

1 I'm enjoying my new English course.
2 Tim's not liking spaghetti.
3 'Sympathetic' doesn't mean 'sympathique'.
4 I can't speak French, but I am understanding it.
5 You are seeming familiar. Have I met you before?
6 Mike is wanting some new trainers for his birthday.
7 Clara is getting tired of going to the gym.
8 Are you needing any help?
9 No, thank you. I'm just looking.
10 These jeans don't fit me.

3   Fill in the gaps in the following sentences with the correct present simple or present continuous form of the verbs in brackets. Put the adverbs of frequency in the correct position.   (20 marks)

1 I .... getting up early in the morning because everything .... so quiet and peaceful. (love/seem)

2 I .... before everyone else in the family. I .... in the garden and I .... the sun rise. (get up/often sit/watch)

3 I .... get up so early because school .... until eight thirty. (not have to/not start)

4 My parents and my brothers and I .... breakfast together at about seven. I .... really hungry so I .... a really big breakfast. (have/always be/usually eat)

5 Mum .... us to school and we .... a lift home in the afternoon with my friend Paula. (always drive/usually get)

6 On Tuesdays I .... to a theatre club after school. (go)

7 We .... a play which we .... at the end of the year. (write/perform)

8 I .... acting to writing, but this time I .... writing the play. (usually prefer/enjoy)

9 My friend Susanna .... the costumes for the play. She .... how to use a sewing machine so another friend, Carla .... them. (design/not know/ make)

10 My cousin Stephanie .... from France to see the play. She .... to be an actor in France. (come/study)

4 Make questions from these prompts. Use the verbs in the box. You will need to use some of them more than once.   (10 marks)

| go   play   collect   take |

1 how many times a week/you/jogging? ....

2 tennis/Saturdays or Sundays? ....

3 how often/cinema? ....

4 you usually/many photographs/when/on holiday? (two verbs) ....

5 your brother/chess? ....

6 you/stamps? ....

7 how long/you/guitar? ....

8 you/ever/horse riding? ....

9 your parents/exhibitions/at the weekends? ....

10 any of your friends/records from the 1960s? ....

5 Divide this letter into paragraphs.   (10 marks)

915 Downing Drive
Toronto
Canada 308-To

12th September 2003

Dear Marcia, It was really good to get your letter and to learn something about you.
You said you would like to get to know me a bit, so here goes! As you can see, I live in Toronto, Canada. It's a really lovely city, though it can be very cold in winter. I'm 16, so like you, I still live at home with my parents and my two brothers. My daily routine is quite similar to yours. I don't get up as early as you and I sometimes don't eat breakfast. I sometimes get the bus to school if my dad can't drive me. We finish school a bit later than you, at around four in the afternoon. I've just started going to a gym in the evenings. It's really good fun. I go with a group of friends from school. We're trying to get fit because we spend so much time studying that we sometimes don't get as much exercise as we need. On the days I go to the gym I don't get home till about 7 p.m. That's when we usually have dinner and then I study for an hour or so. What do you usually do at the weekends? Write back soon and tell me all about a typical weekend.
All the best,
Eva

Progress test 1 (Units 1–3)

Part 1

1 Choose the best alternative to fill in the gaps. There is an example (0) which has been done for you.

(10 marks)

I had a very strange dream last night. I was in a village. I know I've actually (0) _seen_... that village in real life but I can't remember where. I was walking along the street in the dream when I (1) .... a very (2) .... noise coming from a little white house with a blue door. I pushed the door open but it was very dark inside. I had a strange (3) .... something was going to happen. I lit a match and then I (4) .... a very strange sight. There was a little old man sitting at a table (5) .... to a cat playing a violin. The old man was (6) .... a big, red apple. He (7) .... me very carefully as I walked into the room. I (8) .... something cold and wet (9) .... my ear and I screamed. I think it was the (10) .... of my own scream that woke me up. My cat, Thomas, was on the bed next to me sniffing my ear.

0	A	watched	B	seen
1	A	heard	B	listened
2	A	strong	B	loud
3	A	feel	B	feeling
4	A	looked	B	saw
5	A	hearing	B	listening
6	A	eating	B	drinking
7	A	watched	B	looked
8	A	touched	B	felt
9	A	touch	B	feel
10	A	sight	B	sound

2 There are spelling mistakes in seven of these sentences. Find them and correct them.   (10 marks)

1 There's been a big improvment in Tania's English.
2 Wearing black gives some people a feeling of security.
3 What was your impresion of the film *Amélie*?
4 How long will the alterrations at the bank take?
5 There's been a lot of excitment about the new gallery.
6 He's very intelligent but sometimes his lazyness stops him doing well.
7 Doing yoga exercises helps you improve your flexiblty.
8 Don't ruin other people's enjoyment by smoking. Some of us hate the smell!
9 Could you give me some information about French classes?
10 Chocolate is one of my big weaknesses.

3 Complete the second sentence of each pair so that it has a similar meaning to the first sentence.

(10 marks)

1 You can express yourself very easily through colour.
   Colour is a very easy way ....

2 She has to travel by plane and it's making her very nervous.
   She is very nervous ....

3 I've been waiting for Nigel for too long.
   I'm tired ....

4 I really want to learn how to cook Turkish food.
   I'm really interested ....

5 They said they were sorry that they had arrived so late.
   They apologised ....

6 My father can cook Italian food really well.
   My father is really good ....

7 I'll be glad when I finish my exams.
   I'm looking forward ....

8 I might go over to Tony's tomorrow evening.
   I'm thinking ....

9 Driving a car without a licence is illegal.
   It's illegal ....

10 Buying CDs is a waste of money.
    It's a waste of money ....

4 Fill in the gaps in this letter with the correct form of the verbs in brackets. (15 marks)

Dear Isabel,

I'm sorry I haven't been in touch for such a long time but this is the first time in weeks I've managed (1) .... (find) some time to write. I've got a lot to tell you.

Do you remember Sophie from our class at the Cambridge School? Well, a couple of weeks ago she phoned me and suggested (2) .... (organise) a party for all the people from our old class. I thought this sounded like a really great idea and I agreed (3) .... (help) her.

Since we didn't know where everyone was, we decided (4) .... (get in touch) with the school. They were very nice and offered (5) .... (contact) everyone. This involved (6) .... (send) lots of email messages and (7) .... (make) some international phone calls. It must have been quite expensive.

We had planned (8) .... (meet up) at a restaurant, but the school director said we could use a room at the school and we thought it would be more fun too. It also meant that we could avoid (9) .... (share) a space with a lot of strangers.

It was a real success. We all had a great time. I really enjoyed (10) .... (see) everyone again and so did Sophie. Imagine twenty ex-classmates and their boyfriends and girlfriends (11) .... (dance) to fantastic music and (12) .... (eat) delicious food, and you've got some idea how much fun it was. There were typical dishes from ten different countries and the room was decorated with coloured balloons. We didn't finish (13) .... (clean up) until 2 a.m.!

The only disappointing thing was that you couldn't be there with us. Everyone missed you a lot! We're hoping (14) .... (do) it again next year and we want you (15) .... (promise) to come. OK?

Write soon and tell me all your news.

Love,

Francesca

5 Choose the best alternative to complete these sentences. (5 marks)

1 He looks ...
   A friendly person.　　　B friendly.

2 It looks as if ...
   A rainy.　　　B it's going to rain.

3 She looks like ...
   A she's very fit.　　　B fit.

4 They look ...
   A they are a bit bored.　　　B a bit bored.

5 It looks like ...
   A an interesting place.　　　B interesting.

Part 2

1 Use the information in this text to complete the form. (10 marks)

My name is Lucca Di Pasquale and I was born on the 15th of February 1987. My mother's name is Roberta and my father is called Gianfranco. My mother is a doctor and my father is a teacher. I've got two brothers. Tomaso, who is two years younger than me and Francesco, who is a year older. We are all studying at the same secondary school here in Rome, where we live. My favourite subject is science. I spend a lot of my free time using the Internet. I use it mainly for chatting to friends, downloading music and looking up information about my favourite groups. I suppose I spend about two hours a day using it.

Full name: (1) ....

Date of birth: (2) ....

Number of brothers and sisters (3) ....

Mother's first name: (4) ....

Father's first name: (5) ....

Parents' occupations: (6) ....

Your occupation (if you are a school student, say what your favourite subject is): (7) ....

City: (8) ....

How much time do you spend using the Internet each day? (9) ....

What do you mainly use the Internet for? (10) ....

2   Choose the best alternative to complete these sentences.   (10 marks)

1   One of my .... points is getting up very late on Sundays.
    A weak   B weakness

2   I'd like some .... about learning to sail.
    A informing   B information

3   I can be a bit .... sometimes.
    A laziness   B lazy

4   I get a lot of .... from reading.
    A enjoyment   B enjoying

5   She didn't make a very good .... in the interview.
    A impress   B impression

6   Fitting a car alarm makes some people feel more ....
    A secure   B security

7   There's been a big .... in the number of road accidents.
    A reduce   B reduction

8   I sometimes wonder if my Spanish will ever ....
    A improve   B improvement

9   The .... of being away from home for the first time was almost too much.
    A exciting   B excitement

10 You have to be very .... if you want to work for this company.
    A flexible   B flexibility

3   Complete the second sentence of each pair so that it has a similar meaning to the first sentence.
                                    (2 marks each = 10 marks)

1   Tim is taking me to the cinema on Friday.
    I am going ....

2   Could you tell me your address?
    I'd like to know where ....

3   I was able to see Mount Teide when I visited Tenerife.
    I managed ....

4   You'll have to study maths if you want to do architecture.
    Doing architecture involves ....

5   Why don't we buy Carlos a watch for his birthday?
    I suggest ....

4   Decide which form of the verb is possible in these sentences. Sometimes both forms are possible.
                                    (10 marks)

1   I *am enjoying/enjoy* my English classes.
2   I *am liking/like* most of the other students in my class.
3   I *am knowing/know* some of them from the course I did last year.
4   One of the boys in my class *is looking/looks* like Johnnie Depp.
5   In class we *are often listening to/often listen to* cassettes of people speaking English.
6   I *am understanding/understand* more and more every time.
7   I *am loving/love* it when we *listen/are listening* to songs in class.   (2 marks)
8   Sometimes the teacher *is letting/lets* us bring our favourite CDs.
9   Next week my brother *is lending/lends* me his new Red Hot Chillie Peppers CD.

5   Five of the adverbs of frequency in these sentences are not in the normal position. Find the adverbs and change their position.   (10 marks)

1   I go often to the cinema.
2   I never drink tea.
3   I have always a glass of milk for breakfast.
4   Do you usually get the bus to the centre of town?
5   My friend gives me occasionally a lift.
6   Sometimes I ride my bike.
7   I play usually tennis on Saturday afternoon.
8   Does Juan always play too?
9   He often is late.
10 He doesn't usually win.

Unit 4 test

1 There are mistakes with verb tenses in this story. Correct the mistakes.   (10 marks)

was
Anita Sabatini ~~had been~~ the most forgetful fifteen year old any of her friends had ever met. She was forgetting her books, her sports things and even what day of the week it was.

One day when she got to school her classmates talked nervously outside the classroom. They told her there had been a French test that morning. At first Anita wasn't worried because she was forgetting that she was doing French that year. Then the teacher told her that she had to do the test.

She couldn't answer any of the questions because she hadn't known any French. After a while she was falling asleep. She was sleeping peacefully when she had heard someone calling her name. She woke up and her mother stood next to the bed. It had all been a dream.

2 Fill in the gaps in these sentences.   (10 marks)

1 Most of my classmates went to university, but a few of them .... school at 16 and got jobs.

2 Small children whose parents both work often have to go to .... school.

3 In my country we start .... school when we are six and .... school when we are twelve.   (2 marks)

4 Some degree .... take three years to complete but others take four, five or even six years.

5 I met my boyfriend at the beginning of the first .... in 2003. We were both studying the same ....: physics, chemistry, biology and maths.   (2 marks)

6 We don't have the same ...., though. Paul has maths and biology on Tuesday morning and I have them on Friday afternoon.

7 My cousin Kamil did computer science at university. He wants to do a postgraduate .... in Australia next year.

8 The academic .... starts in March and finishes in November in Australia.

3 Choose the best alternative to fill in the gaps in this story.   (10 marks)

Max had slept very (1) .... He woke up and heard his two brothers shouting
(2) .... at each other in the next room. He banged (3) .... on the wall and called
out to them. 'Be (4) ....! I'm trying to get some sleep.' They didn't answer so he got
out of bed as (5) .... as he could and ran into the next room. 'What's going on?' he
said. 'Sam gave my personal stereo to his new girlfriend!' said Andy, the younger one. 'Is
this true?' asked Max in a very (6) .... voice. Sam, Max's other brother, was looking
very (7) .... at the floor. 'Well, is it true or not. Speak up!' 'I only said she could borrow
it for a few days.' Sam answered very (8) .... 'What a stupid thing to do! You'll have

to ask her to give it back,' said Max and walked out of the room shutting the door (9) .... behind him. It looked as if today was not going to be a very (10) .... day.

1	A bad	B badly	6 A angry	B angrily
2	A nervously	B angrily	7 A nervously	B nervous
3	A hard	B loud	8 A quiet	B quietly
4	A quietly	B quiet	9 A hard	B hardly
5	A fastly	B fast	10 A well	B good

4 Complete the second sentence of each pair so that it has a similar meaning to the first sentence.   (2 marks each = 10 marks)

1 First I finished my homework and then I went out for a walk.
   After I ....

2 He phoned Jenny and then he went out.
   As soon as he ....

3 We all went home before Claudia got to the beach.
   By the time Claudia ....

4 Sven finished his homework and went to bed.
   As soon as Sven ....

5 Clara went to bed before I phoned her.
   I tried to phone Clara but she ....

5 Choose the best alternative to complete these sentences.   (10 marks)

1 I .... you every success in the future.
   A hope   B want   C wish   D make

2 You should see that new film .... yourself.
   A in   B for   C with   D to

3 Her Italian is .... but she makes quite a lot of mistakes.
   A fluidly   B fluid   C fluent   D fluently

4 'I'm trying to improve my grammar,' she .... me.
   A told   B said   C spoke   D talked

5 She reads grammar books, does exercises, keeps a record of her errors and .... on.
   A more   B further   C later   D so

6 She is bilingual and can switch from one language to .... without any difficulty.
   A other   B the other   C another   D each other

7 He immediately made all the new students feel .... ease.
   A on   B at   C in   D for

8 My parents are celebrating their 25th wedding .... next week.
   A party   B ceremony   C anniversary   D event

9 Did you .... how like David that boy was?
   A watch   B remind   C notice   D look

10 How many languages can you ....?
   A talk   B pronounce   C speak   D tell

Unit 5 test

1 Rewrite these direct speech sentences in reported speech.

(2 marks each = 20 marks)

Example: 'I won't be home tomorrow evening,' she said.

She said (that) she wouldn't be home the following evening.

1 'Where are you going?' he asked her.

  ....

2 'I am going to the theatre with Eva,' she said.

  ....

3 'Why didn't you get me a ticket too?' he asked.

  ....

4 'I forgot!' she said.

  ....

5 'I can phone the theatre and see if there are any left,' she said.

  ....

6 'I don't really like the theatre very much anyway,' he said.

  ....

7 'Are you sure you don't want to come?' she asked.

  ....

8 'Can I think about it and phone you tomorrow morning?' he asked.

  ....

9 'You promised to do that last time and then you forgot,' she said.

  ....

10 'Do you mean last month when Diana came to visit?' he asked.

  ....

2 Rewrite the sentences in Exercise 1 with *said* using *told*.   (5 marks)

Example: *She told him (that) she wouldn't be home the following evening.*

  ....

  ....

  ....

  ....

  ....

3 Put the words in order to make sentences. (5 marks)

1 through Carlos to on his mobile get can't I
  I can't get through to Carlos on his mobile.

2 on get we well really together

....

3 old people to over get sometimes a long time take an illness

....

4 teachers to the away with gets often rude being Tina

....

5 difficult by get it's to because expensive food is so

....

6 did get round you how problem the Spanish not speaking of?

....

4 Now match the sentences in Exercise 3 to these responses. (5 marks)

a) I'm sure she'll be better soon, though. ...*3*....
b) Would you like to borrow some money? ....
c) They shouldn't let her! ....
d) Why don't you send him a message? ....
e) I spoke Portuguese and people seemed to understand me. ....
f) Are you thinking of getting married? ....

5 Rewrite these sentences using the words in bold. (2 marks each = 10 marks)

1 Her grandmother hadn't answered the door so Little Red Riding Hood let herself in.
                                                                    because

....

2 Her grandmother was wearing her normal clothes, but she looked very different.
                                                                    although

....

3 She had very big ears as well as a very big mouth.   **and**

....

4 Although Little Red Riding Hood knew something was wrong, she didn't want to
  be rude.   **but**

....

5 Because she was a bit suspicious she didn't stand too close to the bed.   **so**

....

6 Complete these questions about physical appearance. (5 marks)

1 How tall .... he?   4 .... does he .... like?
2 .... he .... a moustache?   5 .... he very overweight?
3 .... colour .... his hair?

Progress test 2 (Units 4–6)

Part 1

1   Match the first parts (1–6) with the second parts (a–f).   (5 marks)

1   You should open .....*f*....

2   You don't need to type that out again. ....

3   Make sure you save that document ....

4   When I checked my email after being away for a week ....

5   I realised I had a virus ....

6   I lost most of what I'd done ....

a)   when my computer kept crashing for no reason.
b)   because I hadn't made a back-up copy.
c)   before you try to print it.
d)   I had received 150 messages!
e)   Just cut and paste it into the new document.
f)   a new document if you're going to start writing that essay.

2   Fill in the gaps with *going to* or *will*.
                                                                                        (10 marks)

1   I think I .... phone Celia. She'll know what to do.

2   We .... buy a new computer. The one we've got is really slow.

3   Marcos can't help us paint the flat. He .... have lunch with his parents.

4   There's someone at the door. I .... phone you back later.

5   It's suddenly turned very cold. I think I .... wear my overcoat.

6   That maths homework looks really complicated. I .... help you if you like.

7   What .... buy Tina for her birthday?

8   I'm not sure. Perhaps I .... buy her a CD.

9   .... Tina .... have a birthday party?

10 Yes. I'm sure you .... get your invitation in the next few days.

3   Match the first parts (1–6) to the second parts (a–f).   (5 marks)

1   Tania's a very good student. ....*f*....

2   Watch out! ....

3   It's already very warm outside. ....

4   It's our end-of-year dance next Saturday. ....

5   I haven't seen my cousin Marek since I was seven. ....

6   You and Alberto have been seeing a lot of each other. ....

a)   You're going to spill that drink if you're not careful.
b)   I'm sure he'll invite you to the dance.
c)   It's going to be a really hot day.
d)   I wonder if he'll recognise me.
e)   It's going to be absolutely fantastic!
f)   I'm sure she'll do well in the test.

4   Choose the correct prepositions.   (10 marks)

I've always been really interested (1) *in/on* everything to do with technology. I'm quite good (2) *for/at* maths and science but I'm also very keen (3) *at/on* electronic music. I'd like to study music and electronics when I finish school and then make records. My parents are a bit worried (4) *for/about* this idea because they say it's not very practical. I don't think they're aware (5) *about/of* all the fantastic computer music that's coming out now and how popular it is. Some people don't like it, of course, because they say that music should be produced by people and not by machines. Personally, I don't think there's anything wrong (6) *with/at* computers producing music. I suppose many of us are afraid (7) *about/of* machines. It's a bit similar (8) *to/at* the reactions a lot of people have to robots. I think we're often nervous (9) *about/for* machines that imitate things that humans can do and that's why we have such strong reactions (10) *to/at* them.

5 Fill in the gaps in these conversations. Use the verbs in the box in the present simple, present continuous, *going to* future or *will* + infinitive. You will need to use some verbs more than once. (10 marks)

> be   come   leave   meet
> start   do   pick up   spend

Yourgos I'm going to Athens tomorrow morning. Do you think you could give me a lift to the airport?

Tatiana What time (1) .... your plane ....?

Yourgos At 11.30 but I have to be at the airport by 10.

Tatiana Fine. I (2) .... you .... at 9.

Stefano (3) .... you .... anything special this Friday evening?

Rafaella No. Why?

Stefano I wondered if you'd like to see the film that they're showing at the Social Centre.

Rafaella What time (4) .... it ....?

Stefano 9 o'clock, I think.

Rafaella Great. I (5) .... you there at 8.30 and we can have a coffee first.

Nuria Hurry up! We (6) .... late! Our train (7) .... at 10.30.

Pau I (8) .... not .... I don't feel very well.

Nuria But Claudia and Roger (9) .... really disappointed!

Pau I know but I've made up my mind. I (10) .... the day in bed.

6 Choose the best alternative to complete these sentences. (5 marks)

1 We're .... going to Barcelona in November.
   A could   B maybe   C probably

2 I'm not ...., but I think we're leaving on a Saturday morning.
   A sure   B know   C surely

3 One .... is to visit the Picasso Museum.
   A fact   B idea   C opinion

4 It depends .... how much time we have.
   A of   B on   C for

5 I'm thinking .... inviting Lucy to come too.
   A to   B of   C for

7 Write what these abbreviations mean. (5 marks)

1 p.m. ....
2 tel. no. ....
3 NB ....
4 e.g. ....
5 asap ....

Part 2

1 Choose the best alternative to complete these sentences. (10 marks)

1 You're getting too .... You should eat more!
   A slim   B skinny   C short

2 He decided to grow a .... while he was on holiday.
   A hair   B beard   C curl

3 Celia has got long, ... red hair.
   A wavy   B waved   C wave

4 Tina is .... but her sister is very tall.
   A middle height   B medium high
   C medium height

5 Tony goes to a gym so he's very ....
   A well-build   B well-built   C good-built

6 A lot of girls think he's very ....
   A good-looks   B well-looking   C good-looking

7 His sister is very .... too.
   A attractive   B attracting   C attracted

8 They have another sister who is rather ...., unfortunately.
   A straight   B flat   C plain

9 Sonia would be beautiful if she wasn't so ....
   A overheavy   B overweight   C overweighed

10 Julian has got short dark hair .... a moustache.
   A with   B but   C and

2 Put the verbs in brackets into the correct tenses. (10 marks)

1 He had an accident while he .... home from work. (drive)

2 Have you decided what you .... Helen for her birthday? (buy)

3 Hurry up! The taxi .... outside. (wait)

4 What time .... your plane ....? (leave)

5 I .... my husband when I was travelling in Europe a few years ago. (meet)

6 I don't think I .... to the cinema tonight after all. (come)

7 Lucca and Sandro .... a dinner party next week. (have)

8 Lucca told me that he .... anyone yet, though. (not invite)

9 He said he .... rap music. (not like)

10 I told the person who interviewed me that I .... four languages. (speak)

3 A student has done these sentence transformations but there are mistakes in five of them. Find the mistakes and correct them.

(2 marks each = 20 marks)

1 'I went to the cinema last night,' she said.
She told me that she has been to the cinema the night before.

....

2 'Do you want me to give you a lift to college tomorrow?' she asked.
She asked me if I wanted her to give me a lift to college the next day.

....

3 'I won't be able to come to Gloria's party next week,' she said.
She said that she won't be able to come to Gloria's party the following week.

....

4 'I had a lot of trouble getting to sleep last night,' she said.
She said that she had a lot of trouble getting to sleep the night before.

....

5 'Where did you buy your trainers?' he asked.
He asked me where had I bought my trainers.

....

6 'Can you speak any other languages?' she asked.
She asked if I could speak any other languages.

....

7 I met Johannes two years ago.
She said that she had met Johannes two years before.

....

8 I didn't finish painting my house.
He told me that he hadn't finished painting his house.

....

9 'Did they see you?' he asked.
He asked if they had seen us.

....

10 'Where were you last night?' he asked.
He asked us where we had been the last night.

....

4 Complete the second sentence of each pair so that it has a similar meaning to the first sentence.

(2 marks each = 10 marks)

1 Susanna has a beautiful singing voice.
Susanna sings ....

2 Tomasso speaks English very well now.
Tomasso's English ....

3 I play tennis quite well.
I'm quite good ....

4 Be careful when you lift that statue.
Please lift that statue ....

5 I want to go to university when I finish school.
I would ....

Unit 7 test

1 Fill in the gaps in these conversations.   (10 marks)

Tim   Are there any tennis (1) ..*courts*........ near here?

Greg   Yes, there are. They're next to the swimming (2) ....

Tim   Great. I want to start playing tennis again.

Greg   You can borrow my (3) .... if you like.

Tim   Thanks. I've broken the handle of mine.

Mikka   Did you watch the motor racing on TV on Sunday?

Ralph   No. Why?

Mikka   Well, they were all going round the (4) .... when suddenly the wheel on one of the cars came off.

Ralph   What happened?

Mikka   The car went straight into a wall. It was a good thing the driver was wearing a (5) ....

David   Did your team (6) .... last week?

Roberto No. They lost 5–0.

David   How did the (7) .... react?

Roberto They were furious. They even threw things onto the (8) .... Some people blame the
             (9) .... They say he isn't a good leader. Personally, I think it was the (10) .... 's fault.
             He gave the other team three penalty kicks.

David   That's terrible. When's the next match?

Roberto Next Sunday. We're playing one of the top teams. They'll probably (11) .... us too.

2 Complete this conversation. Use *must, mustn't, have to/has to* or *don't/doesn't have to* and the verbs in the
box. You will need to use some verbs more than once.   (10 marks)

| go | remember | forget | let | give | take | collect | stay | finish |

Soraya   I (1) ..*must remember* to get tickets for the concert next Saturday.

Angelou I don't think I'll be able to go. My grandmother has come down with very bad flu and my mother says we
             all (2) .... and visit her.

Soraya   You (3) .... me a definite answer until tomorrow. I'm not going to get the tickets until then.
             Perhaps your grandmother will be better by Saturday and you'll be able to come after all.

Angelou I don't think so. I had the flu myself a few weeks ago and I took about a week to get over it completely.
             My mother keeps telling my grandmother that she (4) .... in bed and drink plenty of water and
             orange juice and that she (5) .... herself get cold.

Soraya   (6) .... any medicine?

Angelou That reminds me. I (7) .... to go to the chemist's. I (8) .... my grandmother's pills for
             her. The doctor says she (9) .... them three times a day.

Soraya   Don't worry. I (10) .... too. I'm meeting Carla at the library. We (11) .... a project we're
             doing together.

3 Match the requests (1–6) to the responses (a–g). There is an extra response you do not need to use.

(5 marks)

1 Could you speak up a bit? ..*b*......
2 Can you lend me five euros until tomorrow?
3 Would you bring us another coffee and some biscuits, please?
4 Could I have a stamp for this letter to Italy?
5 Would you take us to Mercer Road, please?
6 Can you phone me back?

a) No problem. Is it the top or bottom of the road?
b) Sorry. I'm afraid it's a very bad line.
c) OK. What's your number?
d) No, you can't.
e) Yes, of course. That's 65p.
f) Sorry. I haven't got any money with me.
g) Yes, of course. What kind of coffee would you like?

4 Fill in the gaps in these sentences. Use the words in the box.   (5 marks)

out   over   down

1 Is there something getting you ..*down*..........? You seem a bit depressed.
2 I'm just worn .... I've been working very hard lately.
3 Are you sure you're not coming .... with something. There is a virus around at the moment.
4 I know. Sonia had a very high fever and then she came .... in a really horrible rash.
5 Has she got .... it yet or is she still not well?
6 Well, she came to college but she nearly passed .... on the bus she felt so ill.

5 Fill in the gaps with the words in the box. There is one word you don't need to use.   (10 marks)

shoulders   teeth   toes   thumb   skin   ankle   eyebrows   neck   tongue   nose   knees

1 Angela had such a bad cold she couldn't breathe through her .... at all.
2 If you don't brush your .... properly, they'll fall out.
3 Most swimmers have broad ....
4 Can you touch your .... without bending your ....?   (2 marks)
5 He cut his .... so badly he couldn't hold a pen or pencil.
6 People with pale .... should avoid being in the sun between 10 a.m. and 4 p.m.
7 Eating that pistachio ice-cream has made your .... turn green.
8 My grandfather has thick, bushy .... and sparkling blue eyes.
9 Tania was wearing such high heels she fell and twisted her .... quite badly.

6 Complete the second sentence of each pair so that it has a similar meaning to the first sentence.

(2 marks each = 10 marks)

1 Help me move these boxes, please.
   Could ....

2 Andrea is not allowed to eat peanuts because she's allergic to them.
   Andrea mustn't ....

3 Would you lend me a red pen?
   Can I ....

4 What's your opinion about tattoos?
   How do you ....?

5 It's not necessary to pay to use these tennis courts.
   You ....

Unit 8 test

1 Look at this list Gustavo made of things he needed to do. Complete the paragraph about the things Gustavo has and hasn't done. (10 marks)

- finish essay ✓
- write to Bea ✗
- send email message to Kamil ✓
- phone Marina ✓
- choose colour to paint kitchen ✗

- buy paint ✗
- paint kitchen ✗
- study for maths test ✓
- record *Operation success* ✓
- watch *Operation success* ✗

Gustavo has had a very busy day. He (1) ..*has already*. (2) ..*finished*...... his essay but he

(3) .... to Bea (4) .... He (5) .... to Kamil and

(6) .... Marina, but he (7) .... the kitchen or (8) .... the paint,

so obviously he (9) .... the kitchen either. He (10) .... for his maths test

and (11) .... the TV programme *Operation success* but he (12) .... it

(13) ....

2 Put the words in order to make sentences. (5 marks)

1 been you ever have Cairo to?

...*Have you ever been to Cairo?*...

2 decided already we to buy have a new computer

....

3 yet he been to the shops has?

....

4 just he come back has

....

5 liked chicken have I never very much

....

6 he been surfing never before has

....

3 Choose between the past simple and the present perfect to complete these sentences. (10 marks)

1 I *have been/went* to Egypt for the first time in 1995.
2 I *have been/went* all over the country since then.
3 I *have met/met* a lot of really interesting people.
4 I *have learnt/learnt* quite a lot of Arabic too.
5 I *have had/had* some private lessons the first time I went there.
6 Last time I was there I *have been/went* to a language school.
7 The classes *have been/were* very good.

8 My Arabic *has really improved/really improved* since then.

9 I *haven't been/didn't go* back this summer.

10 I *have just written/just wrote* to my friends there telling them I would come next year.

11 They *haven't replied/didn't reply* yet.

4 Choose the best alternative to complete these sentences.   (5 marks)

1 We were surprised the area was so ....
   A built-over   **B** built-on   **C** built-up

2 There was a lot more .... last time we were there.
   A open space   **B** open place   **C** green zone

3 There's a lot of .... along the main avenue.
   A night time   **B** night life   **C** night action

4 Unfortunately most of the bars and discotheques there are very ....
   A crowd   **B** crowded   **C** crowding

5 There are still good .... for people living aboard boats, though.
   A service   **B** installations   **C** facilities

5 Complete the second sentence of each pair so that it has a similar meaning to the first sentence.

(2 marks each = 20 marks)

1 I was really excited about going sailing.

The idea .... for me.

2 It was annoying that Peter arrived so late.

I was .... Peter arriving so late.

3 He was actually a bit frightened as he was getting on the boat.

He found getting on the boat ...., actually.

4 We were amazed to see some dolphins following us.

It .... to see some dolphins following us.

5 It was fascinating to watch them swim along behind us.

I .... to watch them swim along behind us.

6 I felt quite tired after being aboard for so long, though.

Being aboard for so long ...., though.

7 My life had seemed a bit depressing until that day I saw the dolphins.

I .... until the day I saw the dolphins.

8 I suppose I was just bored with my job.

I suppose I was just finding my job ....

9 I was surprised how much better I felt.

It .... how much better I felt.

10 I think studying marine biology would be really interesting.

I'm very .... marine biology.

Progress test 3 (Units 7–9)

Part 1

1 Complete each of these definitions with one of the relative pronouns from the box. (10 marks)

> who   when   which   where   whose

1 A bus stop is the place at the side of the road .... buses stop for passengers.

2 A conductor is someone .... works on a bus or train.

3 A ticket is a piece of paper .... you buy in order to travel somewhere or go to an event.

4 A car park is a large area .... people can park their cars.

5 A bee is a yellow and black insect .... makes honey.

6 A butterfly is an insect .... wings are large and brightly coloured.

7 Dawn is the time of day .... light first appears.

8 A cow is an animal .... milk is used as a food.

9 Spring is the season .... all the flowers bloom again.

10 Domestic animals are animals .... live with people.

2 In which of the sentences in Exercise 1 could you use *that*? (10 marks)

3 The relative pronoun has been left out of all of these sentences. In some cases the sentence is correct, but in others it is wrong. If there is no mistake, put a tick (✓). If there is a mistake, correct it. (5 marks)

1 Where is the magazine I bought yesterday? ✓
2 Is this the one you were looking for?
3 No. It's the one has a photo of Antarctica on the cover.
4 I'm afraid I lent it to the girl lives next door.
5 But it was the only thing I had to read!
6 And I am the kind of person hates having nothing to read.

4 Choose the best alternative to complete these sentences. (10 marks)

1 She was so sleepy that she couldn't stop ....
   A snoring   B nodding   C yawning

2 Someone was .... the doorbell.
   A ringing   B sounding   C banging

3 The girls in the front row at the rock concert were all .... in excitement.
   A streaming   B seeming   C screaming

4 When he dropped the glass vase it .... into hundreds of pieces.
   A mattered   B shattered   C scattered

5 She told him to leave her alone and .... the door in his face.
   A slapped   B slanted   C slammed

6 He walked along the beach .... his favourite tune.
   A whispering   B whining   C whistling

7 He was allergic to cats and couldn't stop ....
   A sneezing   B sneaking   C snoozing

8 She heard the screech of brakes before the two cars .... into one another.
   A crashed   B mashed   C cracked

9 He heard someone .... 'Hey, Sam!' from a window in the tall building.
   A whisper   B shout   C tell

10 It was so quiet I could hear the clock ....
   A clicking   B sticking   C ticking

5 Combine these sentences with a non-defining relative clause. (10 marks)

1 Parrots can live for over a hundred years. They are very intelligent animals.

   Parrots, which are very intelligent animals, can live
   for over a hundred years.

2 They can learn three or four hundred words. They can even use these words in sentences.

....

3 One famous parrot had a vocabulary of nearly five hundred words. His owner was a famous writer.

....

4 The writer often left the radio on in the kitchen. The parrot's cage was there.

....

5 One night the parrot started singing a famous song. The writer was resting.

....

6 The writer was very surprised. He had heard the song many times before.

....

7 The next day he tried to get the parrot to sing the song again. The writer's friend came to visit then.

....

8 The parrot would not sing or say a word. He did not like the writer's friend.

....

9 After a while the parrot started singing again. The writer's friend was just about to leave.

....

10 The writer was very proud and happy. He loved the parrot.

....

11 The parrot was happy too. He loved his owner very much.

....

6 Match the first parts (1–6) to the second parts (a–f). (5 marks)

1 I sometimes tell people ..*d*......
2 A boy in my class told the girl sitting next to him to shut ....
3 No one believed the complicated story Alicia made ....
4 I don't usually have to look ....
5 Would you mind speaking ....
6 Simon told a very funny joke but Anna didn't catch ....

a) on at all and she thought it was a true story.
b) up because she kept talking to her friend.
c) up about having met one of the Backstreet Boys.
d) off for dropping litter in the street.
e) up many words in my dictionary when I read a newspaper.
f) up a bit. We can't hear you at the back of the room.

Part 2

1 **Open cloze**

Use one word to fill in the gaps in this text. There is an example (0) that has been done for you. (10 marks)

She learned to read at 85

When Gregoria Alonso was a child, it took her and her brothers four hours to walk to and (0) ..*from*.......... school every day. When it rained they couldn't get there (1) .... all. Eventually her brothers started working and Gregoria stopped (2) .... to school altogether. Unfortunately, by the time she left school she (3) .... not learned to read. This didn't matter very much in a small village on an island, (4) .... it did when she emigrated to Canada in the 1960s. She found that there was writing everywhere and it seemed as if everyone could read it (5) .... her. Gregoria learned to recognise the things she wanted to buy in the supermarket and, after hours of (6) ...., she could also sign her name, but that was all.

Over the years in Canada, Gregoria had received nearly one hundred letters. The trouble was she couldn't read them. This was so frustrating for her that at the age of 85 she decided she (7) .... learn to read. She asked a neighbour (8) .... he knew anyone who could teach her and a few weeks later she went to her first class at the local community centre.

It took a year before Gregoria could read her letters, but now she writes them herself and (9) .... even used email. 'It's opened up a whole new world to me,' she said. 'I don't know why I (10) .... so long.'

2 Complete the second sentence using the word in bold so that it has a similar meaning to the first sentence. (2 marks each = 10 marks)

1 I came to live here 18 years ago.   **since**

I .... 1986.

2 This is the first time I've been skiing.   **never**

I .... before.

3 Paulo arrived a few minutes ago.   **just**

Paulo .... arrived.

4 It's been ages since I last saw Mikka.   **for**

I .... ages.

5 I saw the film *Signs* last week.   **already**

I .... the film *Signs*.

3 Fill in the gaps in these sentences. (5 marks)

1 I've known Sandra .... I first came to live here.

2 Haven't you finished your homework ....?

3 I've .... fed the dog so don't give him any more.

4 .... your sister ever played badminton before?

5 Sam and Max .... just come back from Madrid.

4 Choose the best alternative to complete these sentences. (15 marks)

1 I need a new tennis .... because my old one is broken.
A bat   B racket   C ball

2 The .... said the ball was out but one of the players didn't agree.
A captain   B leader   C umpire

3 It's illegal to ride a motorcycle without wearing a crash ....
A helmet   B hat   C cap

4 When she scored the winning goal the .... in the stadium cheered loudly.
A competitors   B spectators   C viewers

5 Two girls in the back row were .... to each other.
A whistling   B whispering   C whining

6 Taxi drivers usually get angry if you .... the car doors.
A slant   B slap   C slam

7 We heard a loud .... from the chemistry laboratory as if something had exploded.
A ring   B bang   C bark

8 Some fans managed to get onto the .... during the cup final match.
A track   B court   C pitch

9 Do you like motor ....?
A career   B chasing   C racing

10 I like .... and field sports like athletics.
A track   B trail   C train

11 I don't like going to the supermarket when it's very ....
A crowds   B crowded   C crowding

12 Last night's concert was really ....
A amazing   B amazed   C amaze

13 I'm too .... to go out tonight.
A tiring   B tired   C tire

14 This city is getting more .... all the time.
A contaminated   B corrupted   C polluted

15 There should be better .... for young people.
A faculties   B facilities   C installations

5 There are mistakes in five of these sentences. Find the mistakes and correct them. (10 marks)

1 I like to try on these jeans.

....

2 Can you lend me a blue pen?

....

3 Could you to turn the music down a bit, please?

....

4 I've no ever been to Australia.

....

5 She's finished already making the dinner.

....

6 Who's the most interesting person you've ever met?

....

7 I've just washed the floor so don't walk on it.

....

8 You don't have to help me with the dishes tonight.

....

9 I must to get to bed.

....

10 I have to get up early tomorrow.

....

Unit 10 test

1 Match the first parts (1–10) to the second parts (a–j). (10 marks)

1 42% of British families ....
2 Crocodiles can grow to ....
3 Elephants can walk at ....
4 Tigers sometimes travel ....
5 Pandas need to eat about ....
6 A giraffe's neck can be as much as ....
7 The population of koalas in Australia has fallen ....
8 Domestic cats can weigh as much as ....
9 Polar bears can live comfortably in ....
10 You should not feed a goldfish more than ....

a) 35 kilos of bamboo every day.
b) have at least one pet.
c) lengths of up to 6 metres.
d) 17 kilos.
e) once a day.
f) 80 to 90 kilometres a day in search of food.
g) to below 40,000.
h) 1.8 metres long.
i) temperatures below zero.
j) speeds of up to 30 kph.

2 Choose the best alternative to complete these conditional sentences. (10 marks)

1 If cats eat some types of house plant, they *get/would get* ill.
2 If Max is still not well tomorrow morning I *take/'ll take* him to the vet.
3 If I have to take him to the vet, I *always feel/'ll always feel* very anxious.
4 If he has to have an injection tomorrow, I *am not/won't be* able to look.
5 If Max sees me get the catbox out, he *knows/would know* I'm going to take him to the vet.
6 If he realises that I'm going to take him to the vet, he *runs/would run* and *hides/would hide*.
7 But tomorrow if I remember to put some of his favourite food in first, perhaps he *is/will be* more cooperative.
8 If he's a good boy, I *would/will* buy him a tin of sardines on the way home.
9 My other cat will eat the sardines if Max *isn't/won't be* feeling hungry.
10 If I *buy/bought* them sardines every day, they would refuse to eat normal cat food.

3 Match the first parts (1–10) to the second parts (a–j). (10 marks)

1 If I earn more money in my next job ....
2 If I won £50,000 ....
3 If I could introduce one new law ....
4 If they win the next election ....
5 If I could have a holiday in any country in the world ....
6 If I can get away on holiday this summer ....
7 If I could learn any musical instrument ....
8 If my parents let me ....
9 If I could take only one CD to a desert island ....
10 If we buy Liam a CD for his birthday ....

a) I would give half of it to the World Wildlife Fund.
b) it would be the piano.
c) they'll abolish military service.
d) I'd go to India.
e) I'll save up and buy a house.
f) I'd ban experiments on animals.
g) I'm going to buy an electric guitar.
h) I'll go to France.
i) it will probably be a world music CD of some kind.
j) it would be Badly Drawn Boy's 'About a boy'.

4 One of the words in the box is missing from each of these third conditional sentences. Work out which word is missing and write the sentences out again.

(2 marks each = 10 marks)

~~had~~ if would have not have

1 If we been living in a bigger flat, we would have got a dog.

..*If we had been living in a bigger flat, we would have got a dog.*..

2 If I had learnt to ride when I was a child, I have bought a horse.

....

3 If we had found a kitten in the street, we wouldn't have thought of getting a cat.

....

4 If we had realised how friendly birds can be, we would got a bird years ago.

....

5 She would have taken him to the vet she had realised he was so ill.

....

6 My grandmother would enjoyed having a dog if she had lived in a house rather than a flat.

....

5 Rewrite these sentences using the words in brackets.

(2 marks each = 10 marks)

1 I couldn't go to the concert because I hadn't finished my homework.

I hadn't finished my homework *so I couldn't go to the concert.*.................... (so)

2 The reason I couldn't finish my homework was that my arm was really hurting all day.

My arm was really hurting all day. ....

.... (Consequently)

3 I played tennis for three hours the day before and my arm was very stiff.

I played tennis for three hours the day before. ....

.... (Therefore)

4 I won't be able to play in the tournament because the doctor told me to rest for two months.

The doctor told me to rest for two months ....

.... (so)

5 I use all the same muscles when I work on the computer and my arm gets stiffer and stiffer.

I use all the same muscles when I work on the computer. ....

.... (Therefore)

6 Because I am making the same movements all the time the muscles get tired.

I am making the same movements all the time. ....

.... (Consequently)

Unit 11 test

1 Fill in the gaps in these sentences. (5 marks)

1 Charlotte was stronger .... her brothers.

2 Swimming at night is .... dangerous than swimming during the day.

3 Alligators are not .... big as crocodiles.

4 Most humans can't move as fast .... elephants.

5 Susanna is less intelligent .... Martina.

2 Rewrite the sentences from Exercise 1 using the words in bold. (5 marks)

1 Her brothers weren't .... Charlotte. **as**

2 Swimming during the day .... at night. **less**

3 Crocodiles are .... alligators. **than**

4 Elephants can move .... humans. **than**

5 Martina is .... Susanna. **more**

3 Complete the questions using superlative forms of the adjectives in the box.
(10 marks)

bad   exciting   good   far   terrifying

1 A What's .... experience you've ever had?
  B When I was attacked by an alligator in a lake in Florida.

2 A What's your .... friend's name?
  B Edna.

3 A What's .... holiday you've ever had?
  B When my parents took us to Disneyland Paris.

4 A What's .... mark you've ever got in a test?
  B I once got 0 in a maths test.

5 A What's .... distance you've run without stopping?
  B Seven kilometres.

4 There are mistakes in some of these sentences about jobs and qualities needed for
jobs. If there is no mistake, put a tick (✓). If there is a mistake, correct it. (10 marks)

1 Firefighting often have to be extremely brave.

2 Journalists need to be quite curious.

3 Working as a police officers is sometimes dangerous.

4 Journalists are sometimes dangerous as well.

5 Teachers can be stressful.

6 Nurses need to be good with people.

7 Acting needs to be imaginative and fit too.

8 Until you become famous, acting isn't usually very well-paid.
9 Most well-paid jobs are also stressful.
10 Accounting should be good with numbers.

5 Put the words in order to make sentences giving advice. (5 marks)

1 eat chocolate shouldn't you much so
2 ought go to doctor the you to
3 why bed earlier go to you don't?
4 shouldn't so hard work they
5 get you a dictionary should

6 Match the advice in Exercise 5 to these problems. (5 marks)

a) My parents are always really tired.
b) I'm putting on quite a lot of weight.
c) I can't get up in time for school.
d) I don't know what a lot of these words mean.
e) I haven't been feeling very well lately.

7 Choose the best alternative to complete these sentences about survival. (10 marks)

1 You can use a cigarette lighter or a mirror to .... to rescuers if you are lost in the mountains.
   A sign   B signal   C indicate
2 There was an .... on the village during the night.
   A attack   B attract   C attic
3 She got .... because she wasn't wearing gloves.
   A iceburn   B frostbite   C coldhurt
4 He got quite a serious knee .... during the match.
   A damage   B hurt   C injury
5 You should put a .... on your arm if it's sore.
   A bandage   B cloth   C band
6 A lot of cleaning products contain ....
   A venom   B poison   C toxin
7 How did the girls .... from the alligator?
   A evade   B avoid   C escape
8 No one knew anything about .... so we had to call a doctor.
   A first care   B first help   C first aid
9 Some buildings fell down during the ....
   A earthquake   B terraquake   C earthshake
10 Is that .... on your lip?
   A bleed   B bled   C blood

Progress test 4 (Units 10–12)

Part 1

1   Here is what a student said about her progress in English. Complete these sentences with *can* and *couldn't* and the verbs in the box.   (10 marks)

describe   understand   pronounce
read   write   express

1 I .... the news on the radio now but I .... even .... the recordings in this book a few months ago.

2 I .... short books in English now but I .... even .... a simple text at the beginning of the course.

3 I .... stories, reports and articles in English now but I .... even .... an informal letter when we started using this book.

4 I .... my opinion in English now but I .... even .... a photo properly last September.

5 I .... most words quite well but I .... even .... the pronunciation symbols in the dictionary at the beginning of the course.

2   Write questions about the past to go with the answers in Exercise 1. Use the verbs in the box.   (10 marks)

understand   fill in   read   repeat   talk about

1 But .... the teacher?

2 But .... the texts in this book?

3 But .... an application form?

4 But .... your daily routine?

5 But .... words after listening to the people on the recording?

3   Use *could* or *was/were able to* to complete these sentences. In some of the sentences only *was/were able to* is possible.   (10 marks)

1 I .... get an appointment to see the doctor the same day.

2 He .... see immediately that my problem was quite serious.

3 He asked me if I .... touch my toes.

4 I explained that I .... but that it hurt.

5 He said he .... see me again the following week.

6 I asked him if he .... write me a medical certificate.

7 Luckily I .... get some time off work.

8 After a week I .... touch my toes easily without it hurting.

9 I still .... lift heavy things or stretch.

10 Still, I .... sleep at night and go back to work.

4   There are spelling mistakes in some of these sentences. Find and correct them.   (5 marks)

1 Do you have a good memory for figures?

2 My friend Sam does. He has managed to memmorise the car registration numbers of all his friends.

3 He's hopeless with other things, though. You always have to remind him about birthdays and anniversaries.

4 It's strange that he should be so good at remmembering some things and so forgettful about others.

5 There are also things we've done together that have been really unforgetable experiences for me, but Sam doesn't remember them at all.

5 Fill in the gaps in this conversation. Use the verbs in the box. (10 marks)

remind   remember   leave   forget

Lucy Why do I have to (1) .... you about our wedding anniversary every year?

Luke I (2) .... it last year!

Lucy Well, you (3) .... the week before, but by the time the actual day came round you'd (4) .... all about it.

Luke I suppose I'm just a rather forgetful person. I (5) .... my car keys in the car again this morning.

Lucy I hope you (6) .... to lock it though.

Luke Well, I wouldn't (7) .... something like that.

Lucy I thought some kind of alarm went off to (8) .... you to take the keys out of the ignition before you locked the doors.

Luke They must have (9) .... to install it in our car! By the way, (10) .... me to phone the mechanic tomorrow. The car is due for a service.

6 Complete these sentences. The first one has been done for you as an example. (10 marks)

1 A I think Sonia's a very responsible girl, don't you?
  B No, I don't. I think she's extremely _irresponsible_ !

2 A The people in the hotel were really friendly, weren't they?
  B I found them rather .... , actually.

3 A I hear the comet is going to be visible from here.
  B Only with a telescope. It will be completely .... without one.

4 A I voted for him because he looked honest.
  B And he's turned out to be one of the most .... politicians we've ever had!

5 A Do you like chocolate mousse?
  B I certainly couldn't say that I .... it.

6 A Would you say you were a lucky person?
  B Definitely not! I've always thought of myself as rather ....

Part 2

1 **Key word transformations**

Complete the second sentence using the word in bold so that it has a similar meaning to the first sentence.
(2 marks each = 20 marks)

1 He managed to get the piano up the stairs.   **able**
  He ....
  .... the piano up the stairs.

2 Today is hotter than yesterday.   **as**
  Yesterday was ....
  .... today.

3 You should take a few days off.   **don't**
  Why ....
  .... a few days off?

4 Don't speak to me like that or I'll hang up.   **if**
  I'll hang up ....
  .... to me like that.

5 Bungee jumping isn't as dangerous as rock climbing.   **less**
  Bungee jumping ....
  .... rock climbing.

6 I've never read such a terrifying book.   **most**
  This is ....
  .... I have ever read.

7 Harry is the best guitarist in the group.   **as**
  Nobody else in the group plays the guitar ....
  .... Harry.

8 I didn't study so I failed the test.   **if**
  I wouldn't have failed the test ....
  .... studied.

9 You should wear a hat in this hot sunshine.   **idea**
  It's ....
  .... a hat in this hot sunshine.

10 I knew how to swim when I was three.   **could**
  I ....
  .... when I was three.

2 Multiple-choice cloze

Choose the correct word for each space from the alternatives below.   (10 marks)

A BRAVE WOMAN

Lillie Hitchcock-Coit lived (0) ..*at*.... a time when women didn't wear trousers and they certainly didn't fight fires. Nevertheless, Lillie admired the firefighters in her city and wanted to help them in whatever (1) .... she could.

    In the early days fire engines were made to be pulled by (2) .... The men of San Francisco's Knickerbocker Company Engine Number 5 used to line up along a rope and literally pull the engine to a fire. One day in 1858 the men were finding this more (3) .... than usual. Some of the firefighters were not there that day and the (4) .... of the rest of the men was not enough to move the engine.

    There were a number of men just standing in the street (5) .... the firefighters but fifteen-year-old Lillie stepped (6) ...., took her place on the rope and pulled. She called out to the others in the street, (7) .... them to help: 'Come on you men! Everyone pull and we'll get there.' Because of her, the engine got up the hill and was the (8) .... to the fire.

    After that, Lillie used to go to every fire that the Knickerbocker company attended. Although she could never (9) .... the fire brigade officially, the Company made her an honorary member and gave her a gold badge, which she (10) .... proudly whenever she went to help at a fire.

0 A at   **B** on   **C** for   **D** with

1	A	place	B	time	C	way	D	form
2	A	hand	B	arm	C	foot	D	leg
3	A	hard	B	easy	C	difficult	D	exciting
4	A	strength	B	energy	C	control	D	fitness
5	A	seeing	B	looking	C	viewing	D	watching
6	A	back	B	forward	C	behind	D	under
7	A	encouraging	B	shouting	C	pushing	D	making
8	A	worst	B	last	C	first	D	best
9	A	link	B	unite	C	fix	D	join
10	A	wore	B	had	C	put	D	fixed

3 Error correction

Some of the numbered lines in this text are correct but in others there is an extra and unnecessary word. Underline the word that should not be there and put a tick (✓) next to the lines that are correct. There is an example in line 0.

(15 marks)

 0 Is it true that an elephant never <u>does</u> forgets? It seems to be.
 1 In the wild they are able to remember of their relationships with
 2 hundreds of an other elephants, even if they only see them
 3 occasionally. They also have an excellent memory for places
 4 to drink and find food. This information is passed on from
 5 one generation to another. Scientists would have seen elephants
 6 expressing great sadness over the death of a loved ones.
 7 They will often go back to the place in where a relative died
 8 as if they were visiting its grave. Because of they are so intelligent
 9 elephants can learn to perform complicated tasks. Kindness is
10 the most best approach to training an elephant. You should never
11 deliberately hurt an elephant. If you were do, you may have to face
12 the consequences many years more later. Sometimes an
13 elephant attacks to a zoo keeper for no obvious reason. Then
14 someone mentions a past incident when the keeper who hurt the
15 elephant in some way. Everyone else may have forgotten about, but not the elephant. You can be sure of that.

Unit 13 test

1 Here are some definitions of words about the physical world. Write the words next to the definitions.   (10 marks)

1 a fairly large area of water that is surrounded by land ....

2 a long area of water that flows into the sea ....

3 a very large area of water, separating two or more continents ....

4 a large area of land covered with trees ....

5 a piece of land that is completely surrounded by water ....

6 a large area of very hot dry land where few plants grow ....

7 a very high hill ....

8 one of the large areas of land in the world such as Europe, Africa or Asia ....

9 an area of land that has its own government and people ....

10 a mountain that sometimes explodes sending out fire and hot rocks ....

2 Fill in the gaps in this conversation with *like* or an expression with *like*.   (10 marks)

Pavlos What country (1) .... you most .... to visit?

Maria That's a really difficult question. There are so many places I (2) .... to go, but if I had to choose I think I'd probably say New Zealand.

Pavlos Why?

Maria Well, as you know, I (3) .... doing all sorts of outdoor activities (4) .... trekking and mountain biking and so on and it (5) .... New Zealand is really great for that sort of thing.

Pavlos (6) .... you .... to try bungee jumping as well? I hear that was invented in New Zealand.

Maria I think it (7) .... fun, don't you? Imagine how exciting it must be. It must be a bit (8) .... flying.

Pavlos Maybe, but I don't (9) .... dangerous things like that very much. I (10) .... to try kayaking, though, and I suppose that's quite dangerous.

3 Choose the best alternative to complete these sentences.   (10 marks)

1 The .... to Melbourne took more than twenty hours so we were very tired.
   A fly **B** flew **C** flight

2 One thing that surprised us is that there is a .... for people who have just arrived.
   A free tax shop **B** duty free shop **C** money free shop

3 Melbourne .... is quite a long way from the centre of the city.
   A airport **B** airdrome **C** aircentre

4 We spent the first couple of days ....
   A sightviewing **B** sightseeing **C** sightlooking

5 The public transport system is really good. There are buses, trams, trains and even a small .... called 'The Loop'.
A subground B underway C underground

6 We went out almost every night. The .... in Melbourne is really amazing.
A night-time B nightlife C nightfun

7 We had a really good .... It was actually published in Melbourne itself.
A guidebook B advicebook C planbook

8 There are lots of fantastic shops at Melbourne Central. We did a lot of .... there.
A shopped B shopper C shopping

9 We all bought toy Australian animals as .... of our visit.
A remembers B souvenirs C remembrances

10 We took hundreds of photos. I haven't had mine .... yet.
A revealed B produced C developed

4 One of the responses to each of these comments is wrong. Put a tick (✔) next to the correct responses and a cross (✗) next to the one that is wrong.
(2 marks each = 10 marks)

1 I love to be outside.
A So do I. ✔ B I don't. ✔ C I love too. ✗

2 I don't like doing dangerous things like bungee jumping.
A I like. B Nor do I. C Neither do I.

3 I have never been kayaking.
A I have. B Neither have I. C I have been.

4 My boyfriend has been kayaking several times.
A So has mine. B So does mine. C Mine hasn't.

5 He tried bungee jumping when he went to New Zealand.
A Nor did I. B So did I. C So did my brother.

6 He won't be able to try it again here, though.
A Yes, he will. B Nor will my brother.
C My brother will try.

5 Multiple-choice cloze

Choose the best alternative to fill each gap.
(10 marks)

Tasmania

Tasmania is an island 250 kilometres south (0) ..*of*..... the Australian continent. It has perfect beaches, ancient rainforests and snow-capped mountains. All this (1) .... it a wonderful place to visit if you enjoy the outdoors, but Tasmania also has a (2) .... history. The capital city, Hobart, has some of the (3) .... buildings in Australia. The harbour is always full of boats as well as the ships (4) .... take scientists down to Antarctica. South-east of Hobart is Port Arthur. Port Arthur was built in the 1840s as a prison. Prisoners (5) .... were considered especially dangerous were sent there. More than 30 historic buildings are still there and you can easily (6) .... a day exploring. If you are brave enough, you (7) .... take the night 'ghost tour' instead. It is a four-hour drive to Freycinet National Park on Tasmania's east coast. Here you can kayak, swim, walk (8) .... the eucalyptus forests or go mountain-biking. Don't (9) .... to try some of the local produce. Tasmania is (10) .... for its cheeses, seafood and apples.

0 A to B of C for D at
1 A makes B does C has
  D goes
2 A fascinate B fascinated C fascinating
  D fascinates
3 A old B older C less old
  D oldest
4 A that B who C where
  D whose
5 A whom B who C where
  D whose
6 A pass B use C spend
  D make
7 A can B would C have
  D had
8 A over B for C through
  D under
9 A remind B remember C leave
  D forget
10 A famous B noticed C special
  D proud

Unit 14 test

1   Put the words in the box in the correct columns. The first one has been done for you as an example.   (half a point each = 15 points)

chair glass furniture iron people coffee accommodation rice chocolate advice sandwich luggage suitcase Greek milk book chicken hair travel trip apple fruit corn ravioli plate information pencil salt letter English fish		

Countable	Uncountable	Countable and uncountable
chair		

2   Circle the alternative that is not possible in these sentences.   (10 marks)

1 Can you close the window? It's *really/bit* freezing in here.
2 It had been *hot/heat* all day but in the evening there was a very pleasant *blow/breeze*.
   (2 marks)
3 I don't think I could bear to live in a place where there was no *sun/thunderstorm* for three months of the year.
4 There's been no *wind/cloud* for days so we haven't been able to go windsurfing.
5 It's only 5°C outside but it's sunny with a *dry/clear* sky.
6 It rained very *hard/strong* during the night but it's *warm/freezing* and pleasant now.
   (2 marks)
7 If we don't get a *dry/rainy* day soon we won't ever be able to play our tennis match.
8 At the top of that mountain it is almost always very *windy/freezing*.

3   Here is part of a text a student has written. There are mistakes with articles. Look at the underlined words and correct the mistakes.   (10 marks)

Jane Goodall is (1) ∕ ^a scientist and eco-warrior. She works with (2) the chimpanzees in (3) the Africa. She wants to persuade (4) the people to preserve (5) forest. Her message is that (6) forest is (7) only one we've got and once it has gone we will not be able to get it back. She says everyone should have (8) opportunity to experience (9) the silence and that this is something we never have in cities. In the forest, however, all (10) the human beings can find (11) the peace.

4   Match the first parts (1–6) to the second parts (a–f).   (5 marks)

1 I was so shocked that I couldn't take ..*d*......
2 I'm the only one in our family who takes ....
3 The boss keeps trying to get me to take ....
4 I only met her once but we took ....
5 I want to lose weight so I've decided to take ....
6 She said some terrible things but she took ....

a) to each other immediately.
b) after Uncle Nigel.
c) on more work but I've got too much to do already.
d) in what she said.
e) them all back the next day.
f) up swimming.

5   Use a word or phrase with *sun* or *solar* to complete these sentences.   (10 marks)

1 I wasn't wearing any .... when I went to the beach, so I had terrible .... on my back and legs.   (2 marks)
2 If it's a .... day tomorrow, why don't we have a picnic in the country?
3 Nicole and Marc went to Greece for their holiday and they both came back with lovely ....
4 I don't really enjoy .... so I usually go to the mountains for my holidays.
5 Do you use .... to heat the water in your house? Yes, we've got .... on the roof.   (2 marks)
6 People who live in countries where there isn't much .... sometimes get depressed.
7 I must buy some new .... The pair I've got are badly scratched.
8 Last night there was the most amazing .... The clouds were pink and orange and violet.

Progress test 5 (Units 13–15)

Part 1

1   Make these sentences passive if appropriate. Put a tick (✓) next to the sentence if it is better as an active sentence.   (20 marks)

1   People speak French and Arabic in Morocco.
   French and Arabic are spoken in Morocco.

2   Nourredin, the Moroccan boy in our class, speaks English as well. ✓

   ....

3   Scientists are discovering new ways of growing crops.

   ....

4   People are growing genetically-modified corn in some countries.

   ....

5   The government in my country has banned genetically-modified crops.

   ....

6   People did not eat potatoes in Europe until the 17th century.

   ....

7   I ate a huge serving of chips with my hamburger.

   ....

8   In the 19th century a disease destroyed the Irish potato crop completely.

   ....

9   While the cook was preparing our hamburgers we had a coke.

   ....

10   My mother makes the most delicious chocolate cakes.

   ....

11   People make chocolate from cocoa beans.

   ....

12   Almost everyone I know likes chocolate.

   ....

2   Choose the best alternative to complete these sentences.   (5 marks)

1   Nike, Adidas and Reebok are all popular *companies/ brands* of sports shoe.
2   The Nike *logo/brand* is a tick.
3   The sports shoe *market/consumers* is growing.
4   All the shoe *companies/brands* bring out new *products/research* every year.
5   *Advertisements/Research* is done to find out what *consumers/the market* want.
6   Nike, Adidas and Reebok are all famous for their television *advertisements/market*.

3   Complete these questions.   (10 marks)

1   Do you do your own hair or do you ..*have it done*..?
2   Do you go out and get the newspaper every

   morning or ....?
3   Does he wash and iron his own shirts or does he

   .... at a laundry?
4   Does Sonia repair her own computer or ....

   ....?
5   Are you making the birthday cake yourself or ....

   ....?
6   Did you paint the house yourself or ....

   ....?

4   Choose the best alternative to complete these sentences.   (10 marks)

1   I'm thinking of .... a cake for Sofia's birthday.
   A roasting   B baking   C cooking

2   Cakes and pastries are very ....
   A fattening   B fatty   C fatting

3   Sam's a .... so we can't have meat or fish for dinner.
   A vegetal   B vegetable   C vegetarian

4   I don't really like very .... drinks.
   A sweety   B sweet   C sugared

5 I try to eat quite a lot of .... vegetables in salads.

   A rare   B rear   C raw

6 We had .... beef for dinner one night.

   A baked   B cooked   C roast

7 I like the .... taste of lemons.

   A sour   B sore   C sear

8 We bought a new .... to go in our new kitchen.

   A cook   B cooker   C cookie

9 .... the potatoes and let them cool.

   A peel   B pale   C boil

10 .... foods are very fatty.

   A boiled   B fried   C baked

5   Key word transformations

Complete the second sentence using the word in bold so that it has a similar meaning to the first sentence.

                        (2 marks each = 20 marks)

1 Someone stole their car while they were away. **had**

   They ....

   .... while they were away.

2 Sam is friendlier than Max.   **not**

   Max is .... Sam.

3 The print is too small for her to read.   **big**

   The print is .... for her to read.

4 Early farmers ate corn more than 5,000 years ago.

                             was

   Corn ....

   .... more than 5,000 years ago.

5 Peter's doctor told him not to eat dairy products.

                            must

   Peter's doctor told him that ....

   .... dairy products.

6 Stop eating so much chocolate or you'll get really fat.   **not**

   If you ....

   .... so much chocolate, you'll get really fat.

7 Most of her classmates liked her.   **by**

   She .... most of her classmates.

8 Because she was late for work she lost her job. **so**

   She was late for work, ...

   .... her job.

9 'Where can I buy a bus pass?' he asked her. **where**

   He asked her .... a bus pass.

10 Silvia can understand German, but she won't speak it.   **although**

   Silvia can understand German, ...

   .... it.

Part 2

1   Reading

(Question 1 = 12 marks; Question 2 = 8 marks; Total = 20 marks)

1 Read this article on the history of popcorn and choose the most suitable heading (A–H) for each paragraph (1–6) of the article.

   A How was the first popcorn prepared?

   B It took over from other popular foods

   C The first breakfast cereal

   D Street food

   E Other uses of popcorn

   F The corn is still popping at home

   G A very ancient food

THE HISTORY OF POPCORN

0 ..G....

When we think of popcorn we think of colourful striped cartons, huge paper cups of soft drink and, of course, movies. It seems a very modern kind of food. In fact, it is one of the earliest. Popcorn over 5,600 years old has been found in caves in New Mexico. It is believed by archaeologists to be the oldest of five varieties of sweet corn. Grains of popcorn that are more than 1,000 years old are sometimes so well preserved they can still be popped today.

1 A......

Originally popcorn was popped by throwing it on very hot stones placed on top of a fire. Naturally, as it popped it flew off in all directions. The game was to catch the popcorn and eat it. Clay pots used for popping corn have been found throughout southern and northern America.

2 E......

But it wasn't only a food. Christopher Columbus, in 1492, observed girls wearing popcorn in their hair. Cortez, another European explorer, wrote in his diaries that for the Aztecs it was a symbol of peace. They also decorated statues of their gods with necklaces made of popcorn.

3 .C...
When the first British colonists arrived in Massachusetts, the native Americans brought popcorn as a gift. The colonists liked it so much that they ate it with sugar and milk in the morning.

4 .D......
After the invention of the first corn poppers in 1885, it became even more popular. Popcorn carts were seen everywhere in the United States. They could easily be pushed through parks, fairs and carnivals.

5 .A......
During the Great Depression of the 1930s, popcorn was one of the few luxuries families could afford. Its popularity grew during World War II when sugar was sent overseas to soldiers and there weren't many sweet things to eat in the United States. As a result, Americans ate three times more popcorn than usual.

6 .F......
After the invention of television in the 1940s, people didn't go out to see movies so often and less popcorn was sold. Now that it can be popped in the bag in a microwave oven, sales have risen again because more and more people are eating it while they watch TV. Today the American public eats nearly one billion kilos of popcorn per year.

2 Find words in the article to match these definitions. The definitions are in the same order as the words in the text.

  1 very large
  2 the seeds of crops that we grow for food
  3 a type of heavy soil used for making things
  4 something that shows or represents something else
  5 people who settle in a new colony
  6 things that you don't really need but that you buy because you will enjoy them
  7 to a foreign country that is over the sea
  8 a machine that cooks food very quickly using electric waves instead of heat

3 In some of the numbered lines of this text there is an extra unnecessary word. Find the word and cross it out. If the line is correct, put a tick (✓). (15 marks)

  0   People are often surprised when they learn that ✓
00 the restaurant is ~~being~~ quite a recent idea. It
  1 seems be so normal today to go and sit at a table
  2 in a room full of strangers and eat a meal. In fact
  3 until in the eighteenth century it was not the normal
  4 thing to do at all. Of course, there were the inns,
  5 but they mainly were provided travellers with a place
  6 to stay. The restaurant as we know it today was
  7 invented in France. During the French Revolution,
  8 people began to make a healthy vegetable soups to
  9 serve to their family and friends. These soups, which they
10 were supposed to restore energy, became so popular
11 that the most successful cooks had attracted customers
12 who were willing to pay for to eat in their houses.
13 Gradually, other dishes were added to the menu
14 and the long kitchen table was replaced by smaller tables
15 where small groups of customers could to eat together.
     That is how the restaurant was born.

Test keys

Unit 1 test

1 1 How do you spell 'Grosjean'?   2 Where are you from?
3 Where do you live?/Where are you living (at the moment)?
4 How long have you been here?   5 What do you think of
London?/What do you like about (living in) London?   6 Why are
you studying English?   7 What other languages do you speak?
8 What do you like doing in your free time?   9 When are you
going back to France?   10 When does your course finish?

2 1 the wife of your brother / the sister of your husband
2 the wife of your son   3 the mother of your father or mother
4 the son of your daughter or son   5 the daughter of your
stepfather or stepmother   6 the husband of your mother, who is
not your father   7 the sister of your father or mother
8 the brother of your father or mother   9 the child of your uncle
and aunt   10 the son of your brother or sister

3 1 A   2 B   3 C   4 B   5 C   6 C   7 B   8 A   9 C   10 A

4
1 Could you tell me what your full name and title are?
2 I'd like to know where you live.
3 I'd also like to know what your telephone number is.
4 Could you also tell me what your nationality is/what nationality
   you are?
5 And could you tell me what your date of birth is?
6 I'd like to know what your present occupation is, and if you are a
   student, what you are studying.
7 Another thing I'd like to know is how many brothers and sisters
   you have.
8 Could you tell me if you still live with your parents?
9 And could you also tell me which members of your family you
   are closest to?
10 Finally, I'd like to know if you are closer to your family or your
   friends.

5
1 Is Margaret's appointment on Thursday or Friday?
2 I want to learn Italian, Spanish and Portuguese.
3 'What's your name?' asked the boy.
4 She eats fish but she won't eat chicken.
5 I'll let you know what time she's arriving.

Unit 2 test

1 1 f   2 b   3 e   4 a   5 d

2 1 correct   2 Tim doesn't like spaghetti.   3 correct   4 I can't
speak French, but I understand it.   5 You seem familiar. Have I
met you before?   6 Mike wants some new trainers for his
birthday.   7 correct   8 Do you need any help?   9 correct
10 correct

3
1 I love getting up early in the morning because everything seems
   so quiet and peaceful.
2 I get up before everyone else in the family. I often sit in the
   garden and I watch the sun rise.
3 I don't have to get up so early because school doesn't start until
   eight thirty.
4 My parents and my brothers and I have breakfast together at
   about seven. I am always really hungry so I usually eat a really big
   breakfast.

5 Mum always drives us to school and we usually get a lift home in
   the afternoon with my friend Paula.
6 On Tuesdays I go to a theatre club after school.
7 We are writing a play which we are performing at the end of the
   year.
8 I usually prefer acting to writing, but this time I am enjoying
   writing the play.
9 My friend Susanna is designing the costumes for the play. She
   doesn't know how to use a sewing machine so another friend,
   Carla is making them.
10 My cousin Stephanie is coming from France to see the play. She
   is studying to be an actor in France.

4
1 How many times a week do you go jogging?
2 Do you play tennis on Saturdays or Sundays?
3 How often do you go to the cinema?
4 Do you usually take many photographs when you go on holiday?
5 Does your brother play chess?
6 Do you collect stamps?
7 How long have you been playing guitar?
8 Have you ever gone/been horse riding?
9 Do your parents go to exhibitions at the weekends?
10 Do any of your friends collect records from the 1960s?

5
(Half a mark each for separating the beginning and the end, plus
three marks for each paragraph division)
Dear Marcia,
It was really good ...
My daily routine is ....
I've just started going to a gym ...
What do you usually do ...
All the best,
Eva

Progress test 1 (Units 1–3)

Part 1

1 1 A   2 B   3 B   4 B   5 B   6 A   7 A   8 B   9 A   10 B

2 1 improvement   2 correct   3 impression   4 alterations
5 excitement   6 laziness   7 flexibility   8 correct   9 correct
10 weaknesses

3
1 Colour is a very easy way to express/of expressing yourself.
2 She is very nervous about travelling by plane.
3 I'm tired of waiting for Nigel.
4 I'm really interested in learning how to cook Turkish food.
5 They apologised for arriving so late.
6 My father is really good at cooking Italian food.
7 I'm looking forward to finishing my exams.
8 I'm thinking of going over to Tony's tomorrow evening.
9 It's illegal to drive a car without a licence.
10 It's a waste of money to buy CDs.

4 1 to find   2 organising   3 to help   4 to get in touch
5 to contact   6 sending   7 making   8 to meet up   9 sharing
10 seeing   11 dancing   12 eating   13 cleaning up   14 to do
15 to promise

5 1 B   2 B   3 A   4 B   5 A

Part 2

1 1 Lucca Di Pasquale   2 15/2/87   3 Two brothers   4 Roberta
   5 Gianfranco   6 mother – doctor; father – teacher   7 secondary
   school student; science   8 Rome   9 about two hours a day
   10 chatting to friends, downloading music, looking up information
   about groups

2 1 A   2 B   3 B   4 A   5 B   6 A   7 B   8 A   9 B   10 A

3
1 I am going to the cinema with Tim on Friday.
2 I'd like to know where you live.
3 I managed to see Mount Teide when I visited Tenerife.
4 Doing architecture involves studying maths.
5 I suggest buying/we buy Carlos a watch for his birthday.

4 1 both are possible   2 like   3 know   4 looks   5 often listen to
   6 understand   7 love, listen   8 lets   9 is lending

5 1 I often go ...   2 correct   3 I always have ...   4 correct
   5 My friend occasionally gives ...   6 correct   7 I usually play ...
   8 correct   9 He is often ...   10 correct

Unit 4 test

1
(1 mark for correcting each mistake plus two marks for not changing
any of the correct verbs)
She forgot her books ...   ... her classmates were talking nervously ...
They told her there was ...   ... because she had forgotten ...
... because she didn't know any ....   she fell asleep   ... sleeping
peacefully when she heard someone ...   her mother was standing ...

2 1 left   2 nursery   3 primary, secondary   4 courses
   5 term, subjects   6 timetable   7 degree/course   8 year

3 1 B   2 B   3 A   4 B   5 B   6 A   7 A   8 B   9 A   10 B

4
1 After I had finished my homework, I went out for a walk.
2 As soon as he had phoned Jenny, he went out.
3 By the time Claudia got to the beach, we had all gone home.
4 As soon as Sven had finished his homework, he went to bed.
5 I tried to phone Clara but she had already gone to bed.

5 1 C   2 B   3 C   4 A   5 D   6 B   7 B   8 C   9 C   10 C

Unit 5 test

1
1 He asked her where she was going.
2 She said she was going to the theatre with Eva.
3 He asked her why she hadn't got him a ticket too.
4 She said that she had forgotten.
5 She said that she could phone the theatre and see if there were
  any left.
6 He said that he didn't really like the theatre very much anyway.
7 She asked him if he was sure he didn't want to go.
8 He asked if he could think about it and phone her the following
  morning.
9 She said that he had promised to do that the previous time/the
  time before and then he had forgotten.
10 He asked if she meant the previous month/the month before
   when Diana had come to visit.

2
2 She told him (that) she was going to the theatre with Eva.
4 She told him (that) she had forgotten.
5 She told him (that) she could phone the theatre and see if there
  were any left.
6 He told her (that) he didn't really like the theatre very much
  anyway.
9 She told him (that) he had promised to do that the previous time
  and then he had forgotten.

3
2 We get on really well together.
3 Old people sometimes take a long time to get over an illness.
4 Tina often gets away with being rude to the teachers.
5 It's difficult to get by because food is so expensive.
6 How did you get round the problem of not speaking Spanish?

4 b 5   c 4   d 1   e 6   f 2

5
1 Little Red Riding Hood let herself in because her grandmother
  hadn't answered the door.
2 Although her grandmother was wearing her normal clothes, she
  looked very different.
3 She had very big ears and a very big mouth.
4 Little Red Riding Hood knew something was wrong, but she didn't
  want to be rude.
5 She was a bit suspicious so she didn't stand too close to the bed.

6 1 is   2 Does ... have/Has ... got   3 What ... is   4 What ... look
   5 Is

Progress test 2 (Units 4–6)

Part 1

1 2 e   3 c   4 d   5 a   6 b

2 1 'll   2 are going to   3 is going to   4 'll   5 'll   6 'll
   7 are you going to   8 'll   9 Is ... going to   10 'll

3 2 a   3 c   4 e   5 d   6 b

4 1 in   2 at   3 on   4 about   5 of   6 with   7 of   8 to
   9 about   10 to

5 1 does ... leave   2 'll pick ... up   3 Are ... doing   4 does ... start
   5 'll meet   6 're going to be   7 leaves   8 'm ... coming
   9 will be   10 'm going to spend

6 1 C   2 A   3 B   4 B   5 B

7 1 afternoon/evening   2 telephone number   3 take note
   4 for example   5 as soon as possible

Part 2

1 1 B   2 B   3 A   4 C   5 B   6 C   7 A   8 C   9 B   10 C

2 1 was driving   2 are going to buy   3 is waiting   4 does ... leave
   5 met   6 'll come   7 are having/are going to have
   8 hadn't invited   9 didn't like   10 spoke

3
1 She told me that she had been to the cinema the night before.
2 correct
3 She said that she wouldn't be able to come to Gloria's party the
  following week.
4 She said that she had had a lot of trouble getting to sleep the
  night before.
5 He asked me where I had bought my trainers.
6, 7, 8 and 9 correct
10 He asked us where we had been the night before/the previous
   night.

4
1 Susanna sings beautifully.
2 Tomasso's English is very good now.
3 I'm quite good at playing tennis.
4 Please lift that statue carefully.
5 I would like to go to university when I finish school.

Unit 7 test

1 2 pool   3 racket   4 track/circuit   5 helmet/seatbelt   6 win
   7 spectators/crowd/fans   8 pitch   9 captain   10 referee
   11 beat

2 2 have to go   3 don't have to give   4 must stay   5 mustn't let
6 Does she have to take   7 mustn't forget   8 have to collect
9 has to take   10 have to go   11 have to finish

3 2 f   3 g   4 e   5 a   6 c

4 2 out   3 down   4 out   5 over   6 out

5 1 nose   2 teeth   3 shoulders   4 toes, knees   5 thumb   6 skin
7 tongue   8 eyebrows   9 ankle

6
1 Could you help me move these boxes, please?
2 Andrea mustn't eat peanuts because she's allergic to them.
3 Can I borrow a red pen?
4 How do you feel about tattoos?
5 You can use these tennis courts for free./You don't have to pay to use these tennis courts.

Unit 8 test

1 3 hasn't written   4 yet   5 has sent an email message
6 (has) phoned   7 hasn't chosen the colour to paint   8 bought
9 hasn't painted   10 has studied   11 (has) recorded
12 hasn't watched   13 yet

2
2 We have already decided to buy a new computer.
3 Has he been to the shops yet?
4 He has just come back.
5 I have never liked chicken very much.
6 He has never been surfing before.

3 2 have been   3 have met   4 have learnt   5 had   6 went
7 were   8 has really improved   9 didn't go   10 have just written
11 haven't replied

4 1 C   2 A   3 B   4 B   5 C

5
1 The idea of going sailing was really exciting for me.
2 I was annoyed about Peter arriving so late.
3 He found getting on the boat a bit frightening, actually.
4 It was amazing to see some dolphins following us.
5 I was fascinated to watch them swim along behind us.
6 Being aboard for so long was quite tiring for me, though.
7 I had been a bit depressed until the day I saw the dolphins.
8 I suppose I was just finding my job boring.
9 It was surprising how much better I felt.
10 I'm very interested in studying marine biology.

Progress test 3 (Units 7–9)

Part 1

1 1 where   2 who   3 which   4 where   5 which   6 whose
7 when   8 whose   9 when   10 which

2 One mark for identifying that sentences 2, 3, 5 and 10 can use *that* and one mark for not putting *that* in each of the others

3 2 ✓   3 It's the one which/that has ....   4 the girl who lives ...
5 ✓   6 the kind of person who hates ...

4 1 C   2 A   3 C   4 B   5 C   6 C   7 A   8 A   9 B   10 C

5
2 They can learn three or four hundred words, which they can even use in sentences.
3 One famous parrot, whose owner was a famous writer, had a vocabulary of nearly five hundred words.
4 The writer often left the radio on in the kitchen, where the parrot's cage was.
5 One night, when the writer was resting, the parrot started singing a famous song.
6 The writer, who had heard the song many times before, was very surprised./The writer, who was very surprised, had heard the song many times before.

7 The next day, when the writer's friend came to visit, he tried to get the parrot to sing the song again.
8 The parrot, who did not like the writer's friend, would not sing or say a word.
9 After a while, when the writer's friend was just about to leave, the parrot started singing again.
10 The writer, who loved the parrot, was very proud and happy.
11 The parrot, who loved his owner very much, was happy too.

6 2 b   3 c   4 e   5 f   6 a

Part 2

1 1 at   2 going   3 had   4 but   5 but/except   6 practice
7 would/must/should   8 if   9 has   10 took

2
1 I have lived here since 1986.
2 I have never been skiing before.
3 Paulo has just arrived.
4 I haven't seen Mikka for ages.
5 I have already seen the film *Signs*.

3 1 since   2 yet   3 already   4 Has   5 have

4 1 B   2 C   3 A   4 B   5 B   6 C   7 B   8 C   9 C   10 A   11 B
12 A   13 B   14 C   15 B

5
1 I would like to try on these jeans.
2 correct
3 Could you turn the music down a bit, please?
4 I've never been to Australia.
5 She's already finished making the dinner.
6, 7 and 8 correct
9 I must get to bed.
10 correct

Unit 10 test

1 1 b   2 c   3 j   4 f   5 a   6 h   7 g   8 d   9 i   10 e

2 1 get   2 'll take   3 always feel   4 won't be   5 knows
6 runs, hides   7 will be   8 will   9 isn't   10 bought

3 1 e   2 a   3 f   4 c   5 d   6 h   7 b   8 g   9 j   10 i

4
2 If I had learnt to ride when I was a child, I would have bought a horse.
3 If we had not found a kitten in the street, we wouldn't have thought of getting a cat.
4 If we had realised how friendly birds can be, we would have got a bird years ago.
5 She would have taken him to the vet if she had realised he was so ill.
6 My grandmother would have enjoyed having a dog if she had lived in a house rather than a flat.

5
2 My arm was really hurting all day. Consequently, I couldn't finish my homework.
3 I played tennis for three hours the day before. Therefore, my arm was very stiff.
4 The doctor told me to rest for two months so I won't be able to play in the tournament.
5 I use all the same muscles when I work on the computer. Therefore, my arm gets stiffer and stiffer.
6 I am making the same movements all the time. Consequently, the muscles get tired.

Unit 11 test

1 1 than   2 more   3 as   4 as   5 than

2
1 Her brothers weren't as strong as Charlotte.

2 Swimming during the day is less dangerous than swimming at night.
3 Crocodiles are bigger than alligators.
4 Elephants can move faster than humans.
5 Martina is more intelligent than Susanna.

3 1 the most terrifying   2 best   3 the most exciting   4 the worst
5 the farthest/furthest

4
1 Firefighters often have to be extremely brave.
2 correct
3 Working as a police officer is sometimes dangerous.
4 Journalism is sometimes dangerous as well.
5 Teaching can be stressful.
6 correct
7 Actors need to be imaginative and fit too.
8 and 9 correct
10 Accountants should be good with numbers.

5
1 You shouldn't eat so much chocolate.
2 You ought to go to the doctor.
3 Why don't you go to bed earlier?
4 They shouldn't work so hard.
5 You should get a dictionary.

6 a 4   b 1   c 3   d 5   e 2

7 1 B   2 A   3 B   4 C   5 A   6 B   7 C   8 C   9 A   10 C

Progress test 4 (Units 10–12)

Part 1

1 1 can understand; couldn't … understand   2 can read; couldn't … read   3 can write; couldn't … write   4 can express; couldn't … describe   5 can pronounce; couldn't … pronounce

2 1 could you understand   2 could you read   3 could you fill in   4 could you talk about   5 could you repeat

3 1 was able to   2 could/was able to   3 was able to   4 could   5 could   6 could   7 was able to   8 was able to/could   9 couldn't/wasn't able to   10 was able to

4 1 correct   2 memorise   3 correct   4 remembering, forgetful   5 unforgettable

5 1 remind   2 remembered   3 remembered   4 forgotten   5 left   6 didn't forget/remembered   7 forget   8 remind   9 forgotten   10 remind

6 2 unfriendly   3 invisible   4 dishonest   5 disliked   6 unlucky

Part 2

1
1 He was able to get the piano up the stairs.
2 Yesterday was not as hot as today.
3 Why don't you take a few days off?
4 I'll hang up if you speak to me like that.
5 Bungee jumping is less dangerous than rock climbing.
6 This is the most terrifying book I have ever read.
7 Nobody else in the group plays the guitar as well as Harry.
8 I wouldn't have failed the test if I had studied.
9 It's a good idea to wear a hat in this hot sunshine.
10 I could swim when I was three.

2 1 C   2 A   3 C   4 A   5 D   6 B   7 A   8 C   9 D   10 A

3 1 of   2 an   3 ✓   4 ✓   5 would   6 a   7 in   8 of   9 ✓
10 most   11 were   12 more   13 to   14 who   15 about

Unit 13 test

1 1 lake   2 river   3 ocean   4 forest   5 island   6 desert
7 mountain   8 continent   9 country   10 volcano

2 1 would … like   2 would like   3 like   4 like   5 looks like
6 Would … like   7 looks like   8 like   9 like   10 would like

3 1 C   2 B   3 A   4 B   5 C   6 B   7 A   8 C   9 B   10 C

4 2 A ✗ B ✓ C ✓   3 A ✓ B ✓ C ✗   4 A ✓ B ✗ C ✓
5 A ✗ B ✓ C ✓   6 A ✓ B ✓ C ✗

5 1 A   2 C   3 D   4 A   5 B   6 C   7 A   8 C   9 D   10 A

Unit 14 test

1 Countable: *chair*, people, sandwich, suitcase, book, trip, apple, plate, pencil, letter
Uncountable: furniture, accommodation, rice, advice, luggage, milk, travel, corn, ravioli, information, salt, English
Countable and uncountable: glass, iron, coffee, chocolate, Greek, chicken, hair, fruit, fish

2 1 bit   2 heat, blow   3 thunderstorm   4 cloud   5 dry
6 strong, freezing   7 rainy   8 freezing

3 2 no article   3 no article   4 no article   5 the forest
6 the forest   7 the only one   8 an/the opportunity   9 no article
10 no article   11 no article

4 2 b   3 c   4 a   5 f   6 e

5 1 sun cream/sunscreen, sunburn   2 sunny   3 suntans
4 sunbathing   5 solar energy/solar power, solar panels
6 sunshine/sunlight   7 sunglasses   8 sunset

Progress test 5 (Units 13–15)

Part 1

1
3 New ways of growing crops are being discovered (by scientists).
4 Genetically-modified corn is being grown in some countries.
5 Genetically-modified crops have been banned in my country.
6 Potatoes were not eaten in Europe until the 17th century.
7 ✓
8 In the 19th century the Irish potato crop was completely destroyed by a disease.
9 We had a coke while our hamburgers were being prepared (by the cook).
10 ✓
11 Chocolate is made from cocoa beans.
12 ✓

2 2 logo   3 market   4 companies, products
5 Research, consumers   6 advertisements

3 2 do you have it delivered   3 have them washed and ironed/done
4 does she have it repaired   5 are you having it made
6 did you have it painted

4 1 B   2 A   3 C   4 B   5 C   6 C   7 A   8 B   9 C   10 B

5
1 They had their car stolen while they were away.
2 Max is not as friendly as Sam.
3 The print is not big enough for her to read.
4 Corn was eaten by early farmers more than 5,000 years ago.
5 Peter's doctor told him that he must not eat dairy products.
6 If you don't stop eating so much chocolate, you'll get really fat.
7 She was liked by most of her classmates.
8 She was late for work, so she lost her job.
9 He asked her where he could buy a bus pass.
10 Silvia can understand German, although she won't speak it.

Part 2

1
1 1 A   2 E   3 C   4 D   5 B   6 F

2 1 huge   2 grains   3 clay   4 symbol   5 colonists   6 luxuries
7 overseas   8 microwave oven

2
1 be   2 ✓   3 in   4 the   5 were   6 ✓   7 ✓   8 a   9 they
10 ✓   11 had   12 for   13 ✓   14 ✓   15 to

Teacher's notes for photocopiable activities

1A What's the word? (p. 168)

Aim
- to recycle vocabulary
- to practise reading skills (guessing unknown words from context)

Rationale
Students at this level often rely on their dictionaries too much. They need to realise that they don't have to understand every word in a reading text, and that they can often work out the meaning of important words through their context. They need to develop confidence in reading texts without using a dictionary as they have to do this in the PET and FCE exams (they can use a monolingual dictionary in the CELS exams).

Time
15 minutes

Preparation
Make a copy of worksheet 1A for every student.

Procedure
1 Give out the copies of worksheet 1A. Ask students to work in pairs to do activity 1. They should choose the right words to fill in the gaps and complete the sentences, giving reasons for their choice. They can then check their answers with another pair and compare their reasons.
2 Explain that the dialogue in activity 2 contains nonsense words. They should work in pairs to decide what the nonsense words mean. They should then complete the key below the dialogue, thinking about their reasons.
3 Ask students to practise reading their dialogues to the rest of the class to check their answers. Discuss the reasons for the answers with the class.
4 If time, continue the activity by giving students an example of a two-line dialogue with one word replaced by a nonsense word, e.g.
   A *I love going to the* **caddler** *– you can see such exciting films now.*
   B *Yes, and the screens are so big. It's great fun!*

Ask students to work in pairs to make up a nonsense word and write their own two-line dialogue using it. They should read their dialogue to the class to see if the others can guess what the nonsense word means.

Note: Stage 4 could also be set for homework. In this case, ask students to read their dialogues at the start of the next lesson. This would provide useful revision.

ANSWERS

1

1 The answer is a) because it is delivered by the postman. A bag is not delivered and a carton is something that contains milk or juice.
2 The answer is b) because neither a wardrobe nor a desk contain food. A wardrobe contains clothes and a desk usually has papers.
3 The answer is b) because you don't drive a bicycle, you ride it. We wouldn't say *her bus* because a bus is public.
4 The answer is c) because you don't have a holiday or do a hobby in an office.
5 The answer is b) because you don't *take some diet*, you *go on a diet*, and you don't get fat if you have no food.

2

pobbles = people (it is followed by *brothers*, *sisters*, *mother* and *father*)
retart = relationship (*we have a good* followed by this noun means *get on well with*)
aggle = argue (a verb which is connected to *disagree*)
cuffy = city/town (a place to live; you can be *in the middle* of it and it's *noisy*)
bart = bus (a noun which is something you *catch* and that uses the roads)
frudge = flat (a place to live which is on the *tenth floor* of an *apartment block*)
hanter = house (a place to live which is *detached* and has a *garden*)

1B The blip game (p. 169)

Aim
- to recycle vocabulary
- to practise speaking and listening skills (guessing unknown words from context)

Rationale
Students may have to deal with speaking situations where they don't understand every word. This activity will show them how they can use the context to guess the meaning of new words, and will also help them to remember words they have been taught in the unit.

Time
10 minutes

Preparation
Make one copy of worksheet 1B for each group of four students and cut it into cards.

Procedure
1 Ask students to work in groups of four. Give each group a set of cards which they place face down on the table.
2 Explain that students will have to take turns to pick up a card, which they **mustn't** show to the group. They will then have to make up and say a sentence which brings out the meaning of the word on their card. They must not actually say the word; they should say *blip* instead of it. The others have to guess the meaning of the word *blip* in their sentence.
3 Give students an example before they start playing the game, e.g.
*I went up to my **blip** early last night, but I couldn't sleep because there was too much noise from next door.*
Ask students what they think *blip* means here, and why, e.g.
A blip is a bedroom because you went there last night to sleep and it's upstairs.
4 Students then play the game.

2A My ideal summer job (p. 170)

Aim
- to give further practice in the skill of prediction in reading
- to help students to deal with cloze passages by asking them to think what the missing words might be before they fill in the spaces

- to improve students' pronunciation and spelling by asking them to dictate phrases to each other

Rationale
Students have to complete cloze passages in the PET and FCE exams. In the PET Speaking paper they also have to spell a word. This activity motivates them to complete the gapped text and at the same time focuses them on any problems they may have with either pronunciation or spelling.

Time
20 minutes

Preparation
Make one copy of worksheet 2A for each pair of students and cut it in half.

Procedure
1 Tell students they will be given a text but that there are words missing. Give the Student A text to half the class and the Student B text to the other half.
2 Ask them to work in pairs (AA and BB). They should read through their worksheets. Remind them to read the title. Ask them to guess what the text is about and what any of the missing words might be.
3 Then regroup them into AB pairs. Tell them they **mustn't** show their worksheets to each other. Ask students what they can say if they don't understand what their partner says. Write their suggestions on the board, e.g.
Can you repeat that, please?
Sorry – what did you say?
Could you spell that, please?
4 They then take turns to read their worksheets aloud, filling in the missing words as they go. Student A should start. When A reaches a gap, B reads the missing words so that A can write them down. When B reaches a gap, A takes over reading again and B writes down the missing words. (There is a space for each missing word in the texts.)
5 When students have completed all the missing words, tell them to show each other their texts so that they can check for spelling mistakes and accuracy. If they made any mistakes, ask them to think about why each mistake was made – was it because:
- they didn't know the word?
- they couldn't understand what their partner said?
- they were careless?

Discuss how they can help themselves in future, e.g. they can:

- do work on pronunciation of difficult sounds
- check in a dictionary and make a note of words they spelled wrong

6 To finish the activity, focus on comprehension of the whole text. Ask students to read through their completed texts and then ask them the following comprehension questions orally.

1 Where does the writer live? (*near a theme park*)
2 What kind of ticket does he have? (*a lifetime pass*)
3 How often does he visit the park? (*every weekend*)
4 Does he like going alone? (*no, he prefers going with friends*)
5 How does he feel when he doesn't go? (*he misses it*)
6 What does his brother enjoy? (*playing football*)
7 What does the writer want to do next summer? (*work in the park*)

7 As a final discussion question, ask students what they think of the idea of working in a theme park. Would they like it? Why/Why not?

Note: In a large class it may be difficult to regroup the pairs for stages 2 and 3. In this case, give out the worksheets in AB pairs. Ask students to read their own worksheet through and think about the missing words by themselves, without showing their worksheet to their partner. Then move on to stage 3.

ANSWERS

I am a very lucky person because I live just up the road from an amazing theme park. I have a lifetime pass so I can go there whenever I want. I usually go every weekend. I never get tired of it! There are always new things to do and when I go with friends we have a wonderful time. I think it's always more fun when you share things with other people. When I have too much homework, I don't go, but then I miss it! My brother doesn't enjoy it as much as me – he's usually too busy playing football to come with me. I want to work there next summer – there are always jobs when there are a lot of people visiting the park. Then I can enjoy myself and earn money at the same time!

2B Snap (holidays and leisure activities) (p. 171)

Aim

- to recycle vocabulary around holidays and leisure activities

Rationale

The aim of this game is to finish with pairs of words + definitions. It employs vocabulary which will be useful for the PET and FCE Speaking papers. It is easier for students to learn vocabulary if it is presented in a fun context.

Time

10 minutes

Preparation

Make one copy of worksheet 2B for each group of four students and cut it into cards.

Procedure

1 Ask students to work in groups of four. Explain that they are going to play a game in which they match words and phrases connected with holidays and free time with their definitions. Shuffle the cards in each set.

2 Give a set of cards to each group and ask them to divide the cards equally between them (eight cards each). They should not show the others their cards. Ask them to look at the cards in their hand.

3 The first student should put one card face up in the middle of the table. The student who has the matching card should put it next to the first card and say *Snap*! If all students agree that the cards match, then the second student picks up both cards. If they disagree, then the student should take back the card and another student should try to match the original card.

4 When the match has been made, the next student then puts down a different card, the matching card is found, and so on. The game finishes when all the cards have been matched.

5 At the end, ask the students to lay all the pairs down on the table so that they can check that they are all correct.

ANSWERS

See worksheet. The correct definition is to the right of each word/phrase.

3A Noun, verb or adjective?

(pp. 172–3)

Aim

• to extend students' awareness of different forms of words
• to help them with fast recognition of words

Rationale

Students often know the right word but use the wrong form in a sentence, e.g.
*I am learning **England** language.*
In the FCE exam there is an exercise on word formation in the Use of English paper. If students are made aware of the different forms of words early then they will find this part of the exam easier when they come to do it.

Time

20 minutes, or two ten-minute activities (1 + 2 and 3 + 4)

Preparation

Make a copy of worksheet 3A (both pages) for every student.

Procedure

1 Put the word *decide* on the board. Ask students whether it is a noun, a verb or an adjective. (It is a verb.) Ask them what the other forms of the word are and write them on the board:
Noun – *decision*   Adjective – *decisive*
2 Remind students of the suffixes they learned in the unit. Explain that they need to know the different forms of words and that it is a good idea to make a note of them all in the same place in their vocabulary books.
3 Give out the first worksheet. Ask students to work in pairs to complete the table in activity 1. They can use a dictionary if they want to. Check the answers by drawing the table on the board and asking students to come and write up their answers.
4 Practise pronunciation of the different words with the class.
5 Ask students to do activity 2 in pairs. Check the answers orally.
6 Now give students the second worksheet. Ask them to complete the activity 3 wordsquare in pairs by circling the words. They then complete the sentences in activity 4. Do this as a speed game. The first pair to finish will be the winners.

Note: If students find it hard to find the words in the wordsquare, suggest they try to guess the missing words in activity 4 first. They will then know which words they are looking for.

ANSWERS

1

Noun	Verb	Adjective
apology	*apologise*	*apologetic*
smoke	smoke	*smoky*
excitement	*excite*	exciting
impression	*impress*	*impressive*
management	manage	*managing*
description	*describe*	*descriptive*
improvement	*improve*	improved
information	*inform*	informative
enjoyment	*enjoy*	*enjoyable*
waste	waste	*wasteful*

2

1 ~~smoke~~ smoky   2 ~~impression~~ impressive
3 ~~describe~~ description   4 ~~information~~ informative   5 ~~improvement~~ improve
6 ~~enjoyable~~ enjoy

3

c	f	g	h	l	m	g	k	v	c	b
s	u	c	c	e	s	s	f	u	l	f
t	p	a	c	h	m	l	d	t	e	p
a	j	r	e	p	e	a	t	b	s	a
t	s	e	n	d	x	s	s	d	s	i
i	n	f	o	r	m	a	t	i	o	n
o	s	u	k	i	y	p	r	o	n	f
n	f	l	j	t	i	k	q	g	v	u
z	g	f	m	e	x	c	i	t	e	l

4

1 successful   2 excites   3 information
4 station   5 send   6 careful   7 repeat
8 painful   9 lesson

3B A street scene (p. 174)

Aim
• to help students describe a single picture

Rationale
In Part 3 of the Speaking paper of the PET exam, students have to speak by themselves for about a minute and describe a picture. They often find it difficult to do this because they run out of things to say. This activity will provide a framework to help them, as well as giving them practice in doing the task.
Note: In the actual exam, students will describe a photograph, not a line drawing.

Time
10 minutes

Preparation
Make a copy of worksheet 3B for every student.

Procedure
1 Tell students that they are going to describe a picture. Explain that they need to talk about three things:
  1 what the picture is and what they can see
  2 what the people are doing and wearing
  3 how the people are feeling
  Write these on the board. Students should use this framework every time they describe a picture.
2 Give out the worksheets. Ask students to work in pairs. They should look at the picture and decide how they can use the words in the box to describe it. They should then complete the sentences below the picture.
3 Ask students to cover the sentences and practise describing the picture to each other, using the framework on the board. They can add any ideas of their own if they want to.
4 For further practice in other lessons, students could each bring in a picture and give it to a partner to describe in the same way.

ANSWERS

1

The picture is in the city.
There are lots of shops on each side of the street.
In the middle of the picture there are two people.
On the right I can see a woman.
The weather is hot and sunny.

2

The two people in the middle of the picture are talking together.
The man is wearing jeans and a T-shirt and the woman is wearing a summer dress.
The woman behind them is wearing a skirt and a short-sleeved blouse.
She is carrying a lot of bags.

3

The two people in the middle of the picture look relaxed and happy but the other woman looks stressed because she is in a hurry.

---

4 Picture story (p. 175)

Aim
• to practise forms of past tenses in a narrative

Rationale
Students find it very difficult to distinguish between the past forms of a verb and often misuse them. This activity allows students to use narrative tenses naturally. It will also help them with describing a picture.

Time
15 minutes

Preparation
Make one copy of worksheet 4 for each pair of students and cut it in half so that the pictures are on one half and the text on the other.

Procedure
1 Ask students to work in pairs. Hand out the top half of the worksheet. Tell them that the pictures can be combined in different ways to tell a story; they can use a picture more than once.

2 Ask them to decide on the order and then plan their story. They should think about the vocabulary they will need, and the form of the verbs (past tenses). Ask them to make up their own ending. They should not write their story down, but just discuss it.

3 They then tell their stories to a new partner. They could decide which story has the best ending.

4 Finally, hand out the second part of the worksheet. Ask students to work with their original partner and to choose the best form of each verb to complete the version of the story.

> **ANSWERS**
>
> **1** were driving (or drove) **2** was
> **3** were feeling (or felt) **4** were driving
> **5** were singing (or sang) **6** (were) laughing
> (or laughed) **7** were looking **8** arrived
> **9** put up **10** went **11** had **12** went
> **13** were feeling (or felt) **14** woke
> **15** was raining **16** tried **17** was raining
> **18** decided **19** arrived **20** came

5A Phrasal verbs with *get* (p. 176)

Aim
- to recycle phrasal verbs with *get* from the unit
- to introduce two new phrasal verbs with *get*

Rationale
Phrasal verbs are difficult for students to remember. This activity will help them to remember the verb and preposition together. A good knowledge of phrasal verbs is very important for students taking the FCE exam.

Time
10 minutes

Preparation
Make a copy of worksheet 5A for every student.

Procedure
1 Tell students that there are parts of six phrasal verbs with *get* hidden in the wordsquare. Four of them have been taught in the unit and two are new.

2 Ask them to work in pairs to try to find the missing parts of the phrasal verbs, by moving around the wordsquare letter by letter. Draw their attention to the example. Each letter must be in an adjacent square. They can use a letter more than once, and they can move in any direction.

3 They should then use the verbs to complete the sentences in activity 2. Tell students that they may need to change the form of the verb to fit the sentences.

Note: If they can't find the verbs in activity 1, suggest that they try to complete the sentences in activity 2 first and then find the verbs in the wordsquare. Alternatively, write the meanings of the phrasal verbs on the board to help them look for them.

> **ANSWERS**
>
> **1**
> get about, get over, get through, get away with, get up to, get on with
>
> **2**
> **1** get about
> **2** get away with
> **3** get through
> **4** get over
> **5** getting up to
> **6** get on with

5B What did she say? (p. 177)

Aim
- to practise controlled speaking
- to practise functions of language

Rationale
In the PET and FCE exams, students will need to complete a Speaking task. This will involve making suggestions, giving opinions, agreeing, disagreeing and reaching decisions. The worksheet focuses on these everyday functions of language.

Time
20 minutes

Preparation
Make a copy of worksheet 5B for every student.

Procedure
1 Revise ways of agreeing, suggesting and giving opinions from the unit by writing an example of each on the board, e.g.
I agree with you, Let's ..., I think ...

2 Tell the students that the conversation in activity 1 is between two friends who are trying to decide what to do for the evening. They are talking about another friend, Sue, and wondering whether to invite her to come with them or not. The lines of the conversation are mixed up. Ask students to work in pairs to decide on the correct order.

3 Check answers. Then ask students to practise reading the conversation in pairs. You could ask different pairs to read the conversation in front of the class.

4 Ask students to work in pairs again and to underline the functions from activity 2 in the conversation.

5 Go through the chart in activity 3 and ask students to make up their own conversation in pairs, following the suggested order. They can write it down.

6 When they have practised reading it together in their pairs, ask them to cover their writing and try to remember their conversation. You could choose pairs to act out their conversation in front of the class.

ANSWERS

1

A <u>Let's</u> go out tonight – <u>we could</u> go bowling.

B <u>That's a good idea</u> – but what about Sue? Do you think we should invite her?

A Oh, I phoned her last night and I think she's already doing something else.

B What did she say?

A I think she said last night that she planned to go to the cinema with some friends.

B Really? She told me last week that she wanted to go out with us tonight.

A Oh, well, maybe I misunderstood her.

B Anyway – you think she doesn't want to come with us, <u>is that right?</u>

A <u>That's right</u>. So <u>I think</u> we should go bowling without her.

B <u>Right</u>. We can go out with Sue another day.

2

Making a suggestion: Let's ..., we could ...

Agreeing: That's a good idea, That's right, Right

Giving your opinion: I think ...

Checking if you understand something: is that right?

6A Pelmanism (adjective + preposition collocations) (p. 178)

Aim

- to recycle adjective + preposition collocations

Rationale

These collocations are often tested in the PET and FCE exams and students find it difficult to remember the prepositions. Worksheets 6A and 6B focus on useful collocations in a way that should make them easier for students to remember.

Time

10 minutes

Preparation

Make one copy of worksheet 6A for each group of four students and cut it into cards. Make sure that your adjective cards are larger than your preposition ones.

Procedure

1 Divide the class into groups of four. Give each group a set of cards. Tell them to lay all the cards out face down on the table at random. Explain that the larger cards are adjectives and the smaller ones prepositions.

2 The students take turns to turn up first an adjective card and then a preposition card. If the two cards do not collocate, then the student simply returns the cards face down in exactly the same place on the table and the next student has a turn. If the cards do collocate, then the student must use them in a sentence. If the others accept the sentence then the student keeps the two cards.

3 The next student then turns up an adjective card and a preposition card and so on, until all the cards have been taken. The winner is the student with the most cards at the end.

ANSWERS

interested in, worried about, good at, wrong with, aware of, afraid of, similar to, different from, typical of, sensitive to

---

6B Bingo (adjective + preposition collocations) (p. 179)

Aim

- to recycle adjective + preposition collocations

Rationale

This activity could be done in the same lesson as worksheet 6A, or it could be kept as a revision activity for a later lesson.

Time

10 minutes

Preparation

Make enough copies of worksheet 6B to provide a bingo card for each pair of students and one copy of the gapped sentences for every student.

Procedure

1 Ask students to work in pairs. Give each pair a bingo card.
2 Read out the adjectives in the list below quickly (don't read out the prepositions). If the collocating preposition is on their card, then they write the adjective next to it. When they have completed their card they shout *Bingo!*

interested	*(in)*
worried	*(about)*
good	*(at)*
wrong	*(with)*
aware	*(of)*
afraid	*(of)*
similar	*(to)*
different	*(from)*
typical	*(of)*
sensitive	*(to)*
bad	*(at)*
keen	*(on)*
frightened	*(of)*

3 Ask the winning pair to read out the adjectives + prepositions together to the rest of the class so that they can check their answers. The first pair to complete a card correctly is the winner. If no student has completed a card when you have finished reading the list, then go back to the beginning and read the adjectives again.
4 Once the activity has been completed, ask students to complete the gapped sentences using an adjective + preposition.

ANSWERS

1 interested in   2 wrong with
3 different from   4 good at   5 worried about   6 frightened of   7 typical of
8 similar to

7A Body parts (p. 180)

Aim

- to revise vocabulary for parts of the body

Rationale

Students often confuse words for different parts of the body, e.g. *wrist* and *ankle*. This activity gives them a quick reference sheet, and the anagrams provide spelling practice.

Time

10 minutes

Preparation

Make a copy of worksheet 7A for every student.

Procedure

1 Ask students to work in pairs. Give each student a worksheet.
2 They should look at the words in the box. The letters are jumbled. Ask them to unjumble the words and then use them to label the parts of the body.
3 Alternatively, copy the diagram on a large sheet of paper and pin it to the board. Ask students to work in teams and come up to label the diagram.

ANSWERS

1 hair   2 forehead   3 nose   4 cheek
5 mouth   6 tongue   7 chest   8 finger
9 wrist   10 knee   11 big toe   12 ankle
13 leg   14 foot   15 heel   16 back
17 hand   18 arm   19 elbow   20 shoulder
21 neck   22 ear

7B Touch your foot with your elbow (p. 181)

Aim

- to help students to remember the words for parts of the body

Rationale

Students find it easier to remember things if they are funny or strange. This activity is a fun way to recycle words for parts of the body and should make the words easier to remember for the students.

Time

5 minutes

Preparation

Make one copy of worksheet 7B for each group of six students and cut it into cards.

Procedure

1 Put students into groups of six around a table. Give each group a set of cards. They spread the cards out face down on the table.
2 Students take turns to pick up two cards. If they think they can touch one part of the body with the other, they say, e.g.
   I can touch my nose with my knee.
   and they do it. If they can do it, they keep the cards. If they can't, they put the cards back on the table and the next student picks up two cards. The winner is the student with the most cards at the end.

7C Dialogues with phrasal verbs (p. 182)

Aim

- to recycle some phrasal verbs taught in the unit
- to introduce new phrasal verbs

Rationale

This provides useful functional language for the Speaking paper of the PET exam, and recycles some phrasal verbs. If students highlight or underline the functions used in the sentences, then they will be able to learn them and use them naturally.

Time

10 minutes

Preparation

Make enough copies of worksheet 7C to provide a copy of activity 1 and one card from activity 2 for each pair of students.

Procedure

1 Ask students to work in pairs and match the two-line dialogues in activity 1.
2 Ask them to read their dialogues aloud to the class to check their answers. Practise the intonation so that they sound happy, interested, etc. when they read the response.
3 Then give each pair one card from activity 2. Each card has a response which uses a phrasal verb. Tell students to write the first line of a two-line dialogue similar to the dialogues they have matched in activity 1, and use the response on their card as the second line. They can use a dictionary to check the meaning of their phrasal verb if they need to.
4 Ask students to read their dialogues to the rest of the class. Make sure that they read them with good intonation – they should sound sorry if their sentence says that they are.
5 As a final stage, ask students to identify useful functional phrases from the cards. Write these functions on the board and ask them to suggest the appropriate phrases. Suggest they make a note of them for use in the PET Speaking paper.
   - showing sympathy (*Oh dear, I'm sorry to hear that*; *Don't worry*)
   - making an apology (*I'm sorry*)
   - giving advice (*You should ...*)
   - giving an opinion (*I think that ...*)

ANSWERS

1

1 e 2 c 3 d 4 a 5 b

8A Where are the cats? (p. 183)

Aim

• to practise describing things in a picture

Rationale

In the PET exam students have to describe a picture, but they are often unsure about how to use prepositions and phrases of place. This activity will develop their confidence in this.

Time

10 minutes

Preparation

Make a copy of worksheet 8A for each pair of students.

Procedure

1 Tell students that they are going to practise prepositions of place, and phrases that describe where things are. Revise these prepositions and phrases by eliciting examples from students and writing them on the board. You could do this by drawing a square on the board and drawing crosses or boxes in the square to elicit: *on, above, behind, in front of, under, in, next to, in the middle, in the corner, on the right/left, at the top/bottom.*

2 Ask students to work in pairs. Give out the worksheets and explain that there are ten cats in the picture. Ask students to look at the picture for a minute and try to find them all. They should not write anything down, but they should try to remember where the cats are.

3 Ask students to turn the picture over and write ten sentences explaining where the cats are. Write the first part of the sentence on the board to help them: *There's a cat ...*
Remind them to use the prepositions and phrases on the board.

4 When they have written ten sentences (or as many as they can remember), they should turn the picture over and check their answers, making any corrections to their sentences.

> **ANSWERS**
> (Other sentences are also possible)
>
> There's a cat behind the TV.
> There's a cat under the lamp.
> There's a cat under the table in the middle of the room.

> There's a cat in front of the table.
> There's a cat next to the armchair, at the bottom of the picture.
> There's a cat in a box, on the right of the picture.
> There's a cat on the bookcase.
> There's a cat in the corner behind the bookcase.
> There's a cat next to the plant pot.
> There's a cat above the curtains, at the top of the picture.

8B Correct the letter (p. 184)

Aim

• to practise error correction

Rationale

Students need to be able to identify and correct mistakes in their own writing. They often find this difficult, and rely on the teacher to correct them. In the FCE exam there is an exercise in the Use of English paper which requires the student to look for mistakes in the text. This activity allows students to look for mistakes and help each other to edit and correct written work without relying on the teacher.

Time

15 minutes

Preparation

Make one copy of worksheet 8B for each pair of students and cut it in half.

Procedure

1 Give the Student A letter to half the class and the Student B letter to the other half.

2 Ask them to work in pairs (AA and BB) to find and correct ten mistakes in their letter.

3 Then regroup them into AB pairs and ask them to compare their letters and explain their corrections. Explain that A has the answers to B's mistakes and vice versa.

ANSWERS

Student A

Dear Jenny

Thank you for your letter. I have <u>never</u> been to Edinburgh, but it sounds a very interesting place to visit! I would like to go there <u>one/some day</u>.

I<u>'ve</u> been quite busy since we last met. I went to visit Michael on Saturday and we <u>went</u> to the cinema. Then we had a meal in that Italian restaurant <u>near</u> the market square. Have you ever eaten there? It was rather <u>crowded</u>, but the food was good and the service was fast. The waitress was very <u>polite</u> and friendly, although she had an Italian accent which was difficult to understand! <u>However</u>, the meal was very enjoyable.

<u>Have</u> you seen the new Spielberg film yet? If you haven't seen it, then we could go together next week. It looks very <u>exciting</u>! That's all for now. Give me a ring next week and we'll arrange to go out together.

All the best

Andy

Student B

Dear Jenny

Thank you for your letter. I have never been to Edinburgh, but it sounds a very <u>interesting</u> place to visit! I would like to go there one day. I've been quite busy since <u>we</u> last met. I went to visit Michael on Saturday and we went to the cinema. Then we <u>had</u> a meal in that Italian restaurant near the market square. Have you ever <u>eaten</u> there? It was rather crowded, but the food was good and the service <u>was</u> fast. The waitress was very polite and friendly, <u>although</u> she had an Italian accent which was difficult to understand! However, the meal was very <u>enjoyable</u>.

Have you seen the new Spielberg film <u>yet</u>? If you haven't seen it, then we <u>could go</u> together next week. It looks very exciting! That's all for now. Give me a ring next week and we'll arrange <u>to go out</u> together.

All the best

Andy

9A Word stress (p. 185)

Aim

- to help students recognise syllables in words
- to help students improve their pronunciation of individual word stress

Rationale

Students often find it difficult to identify where the stressed syllable is in a word. This aspect of pronunciation is extremely important as stressing the wrong syllable can lead to misunderstanding. If students understand how to identify and pronounce word stress, then this will help them to improve their own pronunciation. It will also help their listening, as they will understand how words are pronounced.

Time

15 minutes

Preparation

Make a copy of worksheet 9A for every student.

Procedure

1 Put a word on the board, e.g. *umbrella*. Ask students how many syllables there are. Show them how the word is broken up – *um/brell/a*.

2 Ask students which is the strongest syllable and mark it on the board – *um'brella*. Show them how to find this information in their dictionaries.

3 Give out the worksheet.

4 Ask students to work in pairs and look at activity 1. They should decide how many syllables there are in each word. Make sure that they say the words aloud and help each other with the pronunciation. Check their answers by drawing an empty table on the board and asking students to come and complete the columns. The whole class can then see and correct any mistakes.

5 Ask students to mark the stress on each word in the same way as the dictionary. Practise saying the words aloud.

6 Ask students to look at activity 2. Tell them that all the words in each group have the same number of syllables, but one word out of each four is stressed differently from the others. Ask them to work in pairs to find the word that is different. Make sure that they say the words aloud to each other.

7 As a follow-up, students could make up similar tests for each other using words from the lesson.

ANSWERS

1

One syllable	Two syllables	Three syllables	Four syllables	Five syllables
phrase ways	'teacher 'region re'lax 'whistle 'perfect 'football 'question	com'pletely ex'plosion 'confident maga'zine a'mazing 'adjective 'video 'mountainous	co'mmunicate in'telligent conver'sation ne'gotiate compe'tition pro'fessional	uni'versity exami'nation

2

1 um'brella   2 'January   3 a'mount
4 pro'fessional   5 'language   6 com'puter

9B Dialogue building (p. 186)

Aim
- to provide controlled practice in speaking
- to focus on ways of responding to what people say

Rationale
In the Speaking paper of the PET and FCE exams, students have to work with a partner and talk about their own opinions and ideas. Students often have difficulty in responding to their partner's comments in a natural way. This dialogue building activity will give them practice in making natural responses and in connecting ideas together.

Time
10 minutes

Preparation
Make one copy of worksheet 9B for each pair of students and cut it in half.

Procedure
1 Explain that students are going to build a dialogue together. Give the Student A dialogue to half the class and the Student B dialogue to the other half.
2 Ask them to work in AB pairs and tell them **not** to look at their partner's worksheet. Explain that they each have half of a conversation on their worksheet, and their partner has the other half. Student A should read the first sentence, and B should choose

the best answer from his/her dialogue to respond to it. A should then choose the best response to what B has said, and so on.
3 Remind them that they should try to sound natural, and interested in what their partner has said.
4 When they have completed the dialogue, they should compare their worksheets and tick the responses. To check the answers, you could ask a pair to read their dialogue out to the class. Then ask students to turn the worksheets over and try to recreate the dialogue from memory in pairs.
5 If you have time, you could ask several pairs to read out their dialogues to the class.
6 Ask students to make up their own four-line dialogue about a television programme they have seen, and act it out to the class in their pairs.

ANSWERS

Option 1

A I love going to the cinema, and there are so many good films on at the moment.
B Yes, I agree. I saw a brilliant film last night – that horror film with Matt Damon.
A Really? Why was it so good?
B Well, it had a lot of action ...
A Great! I like films like that.
B The scenery was superb, too. And Matt Damon's such a good actor. Which actors do you like?
A Well, I like lots of people. It really depends on the film.
B Yes, I know what you mean. Let's go together next time – you can choose the film.

Option 2

A I love going to the cinema, and there are so many good films on at the moment.
B That's true, but actually I saw rather a bad film last night – that one with Tom Hanks.
A Really? What was wrong with it?
B Oh, it was too long, and really boring.
A Oh dear! How long was it?
B Oh, I can't remember. It seemed very long. I almost fell asleep in the middle.
A What a pity! But never mind – come with me next time. I'll choose a good film.
B Great idea! Maybe I'll enjoy it more.

10A *If ...* (p. 187)

Aim
- to practise second conditionals

Rationale
Students need a great deal of practice in using conditionals appropriately. This activity gives them an opportunity to use second conditionals in a personal and natural context.

Time
15 minutes

Preparation
Make a copy of worksheet 10A for every student.

Procedure
1 Tell students to complete the sentences with their own ideas. Do the first one with them as an example.
2 Then ask them to find a partner and compare their answers. They should ask questions to find out further information about their partner's answer, and explain their own answers to their partner.
3 Check with the whole class to see if any answers are the same.

10B The canoe trip dilemma
(p. 188)

Aim
- to provide speaking practice using functions of suggesting, agreeing and disagreeing

Rationale
This is a problem-solving task, which should enable students to use all of the functions mentioned. The target language is highlighted in the language box below the text.

Time
10 minutes

Preparation
Make a copy of worksheet 10B for every student.

Procedure
1 Tell students that you are going to describe a difficult situation, and they will have to decide what to do. Give out the worksheet.

2 Read the situation aloud to them. Reading it aloud will help them understand the situation more easily, and will also involve them more immediately in the task.
3 Ask comprehension questions to check their understanding of the situation, e.g.
   1 Where are you? (*on a canoe trip in the mountains*)
   2 How many of you are there, including the leader? (*6*) How many canoes? (*3*)
   3 What is the first problem? (*the leader's mobile phone is broken*)
   4 What is the second problem? (*change in the weather*)
   5 What does this cause? (*loss of tents*)
   6 Why can't you walk along the river? (*too muddy*)
   7 What is the only way to travel? (*by canoe*)
   8 What is the biggest problem? (*hole in canoe/leader's broken arm*)
4 Put the students into groups of four. Tell them that they have to find the best solution to the problem. Point out that the language they will need to use is given in the boxes below the text.
5 When they have reached their decision, ask each group to report back to the whole class. The class can then vote on the best suggestion.

10C Charades (verbs of movement)
(p. 189)

Aim
- to revise vocabulary – ways of moving

Rationale
This is a fun way of making the vocabulary memorable. The vocabulary given here is the sort that students will be able to use in their story writing for the Writing paper of the PET and FCE exams.

Time
5 minutes

Preparation
Make one copy of worksheet 10C and cut it into cards.

Procedure
1 Put the cards into a hat or box.
2 Walk round the room and ask a student to pick a card at random from the hat. The student should then move in the manner of the verb on the card. The other students have to guess the verb.

Alternatives

The student who picks the card could read out the verb and nominate another student to move in the manner of the verb. The teacher could move in the manner of the verb and the students have to guess what the verb is.

11A Survival quiz (p. 190)

Aim

- to practise comparatives and superlatives and ways of giving advice
- to focus students on reading the question properly and help them with multiple-choice questions

Rationale

This activity recycles ideas and words from the unit and promotes discussion. It recycles grammar and should enable students to negotiate and reach decisions. It also makes them read the question carefully: they will have to do multiple-choice questions in the PET and FCE exams.

Time

10 minutes

Preparation

Make one copy of worksheet 11A for each group of four students.

Procedure

1 Ask students to work in groups of four. They decide on the answers to the quiz. They can compare their answers with other groups. Encourage them to use the target language by writing on the board:
The best thing to do isn't ..., it's ...
The worst thing to do is ...
2 Put the answers on the board and discuss them with the whole class. Do they agree with them or not?

ANSWERS

1 B   **2** B   **3** C   **4** B   **5** C

11B What's your advice? (p. 191)

Aim

- to practise giving advice

Rationale

This activity helps students to use the language of giving advice in natural contexts.

Time

10 minutes

Preparation

Make one copy of worksheet 11B for each group of four students and cut it into cards.

Procedure

1 Elicit different ways of giving advice and making decisions. Write them on the board, e.g.

Giving advice	Making a decision
I think you should ...	*I think that the best idea is ...*
Why don't you ...?	*I think that's the right thing to do.*
It's a good idea to ...	*I like the idea of ...ing.*
You could ...	*I think ... is the best.*

2 Tell students that they are going to give each other advice. Give out a set of cards to each group of four students. Tell them to put them face down on the table in a pile.
3 The first student picks up a card and reads the problem to the group. Everyone else in the group offers a different piece of advice, and the group decides which advice is the best. Then the next student picks up a card, and so on.
4 For further practice, students could make their own cards. They could bring these to a later class so that they can revise the language using their own ideas.

12A Memory game (p. 192)

Aim

- to practise memorising techniques

Rationale

This activity recycles vocabulary in a fun way. It also helps students to think about how they remember things and develops study skills.

Time

5 minutes

Preparation

Make one copy of worksheet 12A for each pair of students.

Procedure

1 Ask students to work in pairs. Give out the worksheets.
2 Ask students to look at the words (which all come from the unit) for 15 seconds. Then tell them to turn the page over and work together to try to remember as many words as they can.
3 After two minutes, stop them and tell them to look at the words to check.
4 As a follow-up discussion, ask students why they think they remembered the words they did. Did they use any particular technique to help them remember? Ask them to share these techniques with the class and tell them that they may be useful for remembering new words.
5 Put the following ideas on the board:
   • Group words of similar meaning
   • Group collocations
   • Group opposites
   • Group words that go together in semantic fields (words that are connected in some way, e.g. *hospital* and *doctor*)

12B Compare the pictures (p. 193)

Aim
• to practise comparing and contrasting two pictures

Rationale
In the FCE Speaking paper students have to compare and contrast two pictures. This activity helps them with organising their ideas and linking them in sentences.
Note: In the actual exam, students will compare and contrast photographs, not line drawings.

Time
5 minutes

Preparation
Make a copy of worksheet 12B for every student.

Procedure
1 Ask students to look at both pictures. Tell them that they are going to compare and contrast them. Explain that when they *compare*, they find things that are the same, and when they *contrast*, they find things that are different. Demonstrate by doing one

comparison and one contrast with them, e.g.
Both pictures show a lot of people, but in picture 1 they are wearing casual clothes and in picture 2 they are wearing formal clothes.
2 Ask them to work in pairs and find three things that are the same and three things that are different. They should use the language on the worksheet to help them.

13A Planning a trip (pp. 194–5)

Aim
• to practise speaking: agreeing, disagreeing, giving opinions and suggesting

Rationale
This is a controlled and extended speaking activity which requires students to complete a task. In the Speaking paper of the PET and FCE exams, they will have to complete a task and make a decision. The information about the city is on cards to encourage students to discuss what they read rather than just reading silently to themselves from a worksheet.

Time
25 minutes

Preparation
Make one copy of worksheet 13A (both pages) for each group of six students and cut the first page into cards.

Procedure
1 Tell students that they are going on a day trip to a city together. They have to plan the trip and decide how to spend the time. They must:
   • stay together the whole time
   • visit at least four different places
   • not spend more than £25 each
2 Give each group a set of cards and a 'Plan for the day' worksheet. Explain that the cards contain information about the city. Point out that students will have to fill in a plan, and ask them to fill in the missing information at the top of the plan immediately. Tell them the following:
   • They will arrive in the city at 10 a.m. and leave at 7 p.m.
   • Their return train ticket is paid for, but they must buy their food and drink and pay for any places they visit.

3 The information they will need is on the cards. They should think about:
- what to see
- where to eat
- what to do

Tell students that there is useful language for their discussion at the bottom of the worksheet.

4 When they have planned their day, they fill in their plan. Each group then reports back to the class, describing their plan and explaining their choices.

Note: If time is short, use only half the cards and tell students that they are going on a morning trip, arriving at 10 a.m. and leaving at 1 p.m. Change the number of places visited to two, and the budget to £12.50. Then give them ten minutes to complete the task.

13B The responses game (p. 196)

Aim
- to recycle vocabulary from the unit
- to practise speaking: agreeing and disagreeing, giving opinions and suggesting

Rationale
These functions of language are useful for the Speaking papers of PET and FCE.

Time
10 minutes

Preparation
Make one copy of worksheet 13B for each group of four students and cut it into two sets of cards (A and B).

Procedure
1 Tell students that they are going to practise agreeing, disagreeing, giving opinions and suggesting. Give each group a set of cards with ways of doing this (A), and ask students to divide the cards equally among the group. They should not show each other their cards, but should hold them in their hands.
2 Tell them that the squarer cards (B) have statements on. Give each group a set of these cards and tell them to place them face down in the middle of the table.

3 Students should take turns to pick up a card from the pile in the middle. They read the statement to the group. The others in the group have to try to use one of the cards they are holding to respond to the statement; the first student to find a suitable card should read the response and then add an idea of his/her own, e.g. *Yes, I agree with that because it would reduce pollution.*
4 If the others agree that it is an appropriate response to the statement, the student who gave the response can keep the card from the middle of the table. If not, then another student tries to respond. When an appropriate response has been given, the next student picks up a card and reads it, and so on. The winner is the student with the most cards at the end of the time.
5 It is a good idea to demonstrate this with one group in front of the class before telling the whole class to begin the activity.

14A A jumbled letter (p. 197)

Aim
- to focus on the organisation of an informal letter

Rationale
If students understand the organisation of a letter, then they will be able to complete the exam tasks successfully in PET, FCE and CELS.

Time
10 minutes

Preparation
Make a copy of worksheet 14A for every student.

Procedure
1 Give out the worksheets. Remind students of the work they did on writing a letter in the unit.
2 Tell them that the letter on the worksheet is mixed up. Ask them to work in pairs to number the sentences in the correct order, and then decide how many paragraphs there should be in the letter.
3 Check the answers with the whole class.

ANSWERS

b f i c e a h d k g j

Dear Keith

Thanks for emailing me last week – I was so pleased to hear from you. I'm writing a letter back because I'm having problems with my computer. I'd love to meet you in town next Saturday. You asked me if there was anything special I wanted to do. Well, I've got some ideas.

First of all, it would be great if we could visit the new art gallery. I've heard that there are some really interesting new paintings there. Then, if the weather is good, perhaps we could walk around the park and have a picnic lunch there. If it's raining, then we could eat in a restaurant instead – something cheap like a pizza? Finally, in the evening I'd love to go to the cinema. I haven't seen the new James Bond film yet, and people say it's really good. If you haven't seen it either, then it would be fun to go together.

What do you think? Let me know if you have any better ideas of things to do. I'm really looking forward to seeing you next week.

Best wishes

Georgio

14B That's a terrible idea (p. 198)

Aim
• to practise giving opinions, agreeing and disagreeing

Rationale
In the Speaking papers of the PET and FCE exams students will have to discuss a task and agree or disagree with each other. This activity will help them to express opinions and to practise the required language in a natural context.

Time
10 minutes

Preparation
Make one copy of worksheet 14B for each group of four students and cut up the cards.

Procedure
1 Tell students that they are going to give their opinions on some statements, which they will either have to agree or disagree with. Elicit any ways they can remember of agreeing or disagreeing with someone or something and draw their attention to the language in the speech bubbles.
2 Ask students to work in groups of four and to put the cards face down on the table. The first student should pick up a card and read it to the others in the group. The others should agree or disagree, giving their reasons. Then the next student should pick up a card and read it to the group, and so on.

15 Invent a TV advertisement
(pp. 199–200)

Aim
• to recycle vocabulary and ideas from the unit
• to practise free speaking, including negotiating and making decisions

Rationale
This activity could be used as a single activity, as suggested below, or it could be used as a longer project. In this case, students could plan a detailed TV advertisement over a week, including homework, and could present it to the class in a later lesson.

Time
25 minutes

Preparation
Make a copy of worksheet 15 (both pages) for every student.

Procedure
1 Give out the worksheets. Ask students to do activity 1 in pairs. Check the answers.
2 Ask students to tell you about a television advertisement that they like or don't like. Ask them why they like or dislike it (it's funny, boring, has good music, has a handsome film star in it, etc.).
3 Then tell them that they are going to write their own television advertisement. Ask them to work in groups of four.

4 They should first match the words in the box to the products in activity 2. They can use a dictionary to help them, and they can use the words more than once. The words are all typical of those used in advertisements. Ask them to explain their answers to the rest of the class.

5 Ask students if they can remember the slogans of any current advertisements in their country. Why do they remember them? What makes a good slogan? Then ask them to match the slogans in activity 3 to the products in activity 2.

6 Tell students that before they write their own TV advertisement, you will help them with ideas. Write the word *ice-cream* on the board. Tell them that you are going to write an advertisement for a new ice-cream. Ask the class the questions below and write their answers on the board. (This should stimulate their imagination.) For example:

- It's a new ice-cream. Who buys ice-cream? (*Young people.*)
- What shall we call it? (*Chocobar.*)
- What's special about it? (*It's a bright blue colour; it's crunchy.*)
- Where do people buy ice-cream? Where shall we sell it? (*In street kiosks.*)
- Why is it different? (*It has a joke inside.*)
- Why will people buy it? (*It's cheap, it's fun and it tastes good.*)
- What could the slogan be? (*It's cold – but it's cool!*)
- What will the advertisement show? (*It could have a brightly-coloured van or kiosk with young people wearing brightly-coloured clothes and dancing.*)
- Who will be in it? (*Young dancers of many nationalities. Nobody famous.*)
- Where will it be set? (*In a typical city street.*)
- Will there be any music? (*Yes, a specially written song about the product.*)

7 Ask each group to choose a product to advertise – it could be one from the list in activity 2. They then decide together their own answers to the questions in activity 4.

8 Ask students to plan their own TV advertisement and fill in the form.

9 Each group should then describe their ideas to the class, who can vote on the best one.

ANSWERS

1

1 logo 2 market 3 Consumers 4 brand 5 customers

2

a) value-for-money, fizzy, energy-boosting, refreshing
b) value-for-money, lightweight, state-of-the-art
c) value-for-money, spacious, state-of-the-art, powerful
d) value-for-money, crunchy, energy-boosting

3

1 b 2 c 3 a 4 d

1 Choose the correct words to complete the sentences and give reasons for your choice.

1 I opened the _____ as soon as the postman delivered it. It was from an old friend.

a) letter   b) bag   c) carton

The answer is _____ because _____

_____

2 She felt hungry and went to the _____ to see if there was anything to eat in there.

a) wardrobe   b) fridge   c) desk

The answer is _____ because _____

_____

3 She drove her _____ so fast that the police stopped her and fined her for speeding.

a) bicycle   b) car   c) bus

The answer is _____ because _____

_____

4 My ideal _____ would be in an office as part of a team because I love being with people.

a) holiday   b) hobby   c) job

The answer is _____ because _____

_____

5 It's really important to take some _____ . If you don't, you get fat and unhealthy.

a) food   b) exercise   c) diet

The answer is _____ because _____

_____

2 The words in *italics* are nonsense words. Decide what they mean and write the correct words under the dialogue.

A How many *pobbles* are there in your family?

B Well, I have two brothers and two sisters, so with my mother and father that makes seven of us altogether. What about you?

A Oh, I only have one sister, so there are just four of us.

B Do you get on well with your family?

A Yes, of course – we have a very good *retart*. We like each other a lot. How about you?

B Yes, although I *aggle* with my sister sometimes when we disagree about which television channel to watch!

A Where do you live?

B We live in the middle of the *cuffy*; it's a bit noisy but there are always a lot of interesting things to do. And you?

A We live in the suburbs. I have to catch the *bart* in to school, and it takes a long time because the roads are busy. What kind of place do you live in?

B We live in a big *frudge* in a new apartment block – we're on the tenth floor, so we've got an amazing view!

A Sounds great! I live in a detached *hanter* with a garden.

pobbles = _____

retart = _____

aggle = _____

cuffy = _____

bart = _____

frudge = _____

hanter = _____

wedding	ideal
dictionary	alphabet
uncle	nationality
curtains	pavement
dessert	newspaper
holiday	hobby

Student A My ideal summer job

I am a very lucky person because _____

_____ just _____ _____

_____ _____ an amazing theme

_____ . _____ _____

_____ _____ _____ so I can

go there _____ _____ _____ .

I usually go _____ _____ . I never

get tired of it! _____ _____ always

new _____ _____ _____ and

when I go with friends _____ _____

_____ wonderful time. _____

_____ _____ always more fun

_____ _____ _____

_____ with other people.

_____ _____ _____ too much

homework, _____ _____

_____ , but then _____ _____

_____ ! My brother doesn't enjoy it

_____ _____ _____

_____ – he's usually too busy _____

_____ to come with me. _____

_____ _____ _____

_____ next summer – _____

_____ _____ _____ when

there are _____ _____ _____

_____ visiting the park. _____

_____ _____ _____

_____ and earn money _____

_____ _____ _____ !

Student B My ideal summer job

I am a very lucky person because I live

_____ up the road from _____

_____ _____ park. I have a lifetime

pass _____ _____ _____

_____ _____ whenever I want.

_____ _____ _____ every

weekend. _____ _____ _____

_____ _____ _____ ! There

are _____ _____ things to do

_____ _____ _____

_____ _____ _____ we have

a _____ _____ . I think it's

_____ _____ _____ when

you share things _____ _____

_____ . When I have _____

_____ _____ , I don't go,

_____ _____ I miss it! _____

_____ _____ _____

_____ as much as me – _____

_____ _____ _____ playing

football _____ _____ _____

_____ . I want to work there _____

_____ – there are always jobs _____

_____ _____ a lot of people

_____ _____ _____ . Then I

can enjoy myself _____ _____

_____ at the same time!

A cruise	A holiday on a ship	A travel agent's	A place where you can book a holiday
An off-peak ticket	A ticket for travel at an unpopular time	A return trip	A journey to a place and back again
A racket	Something used to play tennis	Hand luggage	Bags you can take on to a plane with you
A package holiday	A holiday where the travel and accommodation are sold together	Chess	A game played on a board
Camping	Staying in a tent	Jogging	Running to keep fit
A theme park	A place for having fun, with rides and activities	A court	A place to play tennis
A pitch	A place to play football	A hobby	Something to do in your free time
A bat	Something used to play baseball and table tennis	A track	A place to do athletics

1 Complete this table with the correct form of the words.

Noun	Verb	Adjective
apology		
	smoke	
		exciting
impression		
	manage	
description		
		improved
		informative
enjoyment		
	waste	

2 Correct the mistakes in form in these sentences.

1 It is very unhealthy to sit for a long time in smoke rooms.

_____

2 I thought the way he won the race was very impression.

_____

3 He wrote a wonderful describe of the view from the window of the hotel.

_____

4 The dictionary is very information about the use of new words.

_____

5 If you study hard then your English will improvement.

_____

6 We really enjoyable playing chess.

_____

3 Find three nouns, three verbs and three adjectives in the wordsquare.

c	f	g	h	l	m	g	k	v	c	b
s	u	c	c	e	s	s	f	u	l	f
t	p	a	c	h	m	l	d	t	e	p
a	j	r	e	p	e	a	t	b	s	a
t	s	e	n	d	x	s	s	d	s	i
i	n	f	o	r	m	a	t	i	o	n
o	s	u	k	i	y	p	r	o	n	f
n	f	l	j	t	i	k	q	g	v	u
z	g	f	m	e	x	c	i	t	e	l

4 Use the words you found in the wordsquare to complete these sentences.
You may need to change the form of the verbs.

1 He's such a famous director. I think he's one of the most _____ film-makers in the world.

2 The idea of being a film star really _____ me. I think it must be a wonderful job.

3 You can get a lot of _____ about absolutely everything on the Internet nowadays.

4 I'll meet you at the _____ , then we can get on the train together.

5 Why don't you _____ me an email – we can keep in touch easily that way.

6 You must be very _____ to save your work on the computer. You don't want to lose it by mistake!

7 I'm sorry, I didn't hear what you said. Could you _____ it, please?

8 I fell over last week and bruised my leg. It was _____ for days!

9 I really enjoy my weekly English _____ . I learn a lot of new words and I love speaking another language in the classroom.

Look at the picture and decide how you can use the words in the box to describe it.
Then complete the sentences below.

behind them	in the city	talking together	shops on each side	a woman
two people	a lot of bags	hot and sunny	relaxed and happy	stressed
in a hurry	a summer dress	a skirt and a short-sleeved blouse		jeans and a T-shirt

1　The picture is _____ .

There are lots of _____ of the street.

In the middle of the picture there are _____ .

On the right I can see _____ .

The weather is _____ .

2　The two people in the middle of the picture are _____ .

The man is wearing _____ and the woman is

wearing _____ .

The woman _____ is wearing _____ .

She is carrying _____ .

3　The two people in the middle of the picture look _____

but the other woman looks _____ because she

is _____ .

Complete this version of the story with the correct form of the verbs in brackets.
Use past tenses.

The Jones family (1) _____ (drive) to their campsite. There (2) _____ (be)

a lot of luggage in the car, and they (3) _____ (feel) very excited. While they

(4) _____ (drive) along they (5) _____ (sing) songs and (6) _____

(laugh). They (7) _____ (look) forward to a wonderful holiday. They

(8) _____ (arrive) at the campsite and (9) _____ (put up) their tent. Next

they (10) _____ (go) to a nearby restaurant and (11) _____ (have) a meal,

and then they (12) _____ (go) to bed because they (13) _____ (feel) very

tired. When they (14) _____ (wake) up the next morning it (15) _____

(rain). They (16) _____ (try) to play tennis, but it (17) _____ (rain) too

hard so they had to go back into the tents. After three days of rain they (18) _____

(decide) to go home, but as soon as they (19) _____ (arrive) at their house the

sun (20) _____ (come) out!

1 Find words in the wordsquare to complete these phrasal verbs.

get *about*

get _____

get _____

get _____ _____

get _____ _____

get _____ _____

u	p	o	a	e
a	w	t	b	o
a	h	g	u	r
y	t	r	u	e
i	w	n	o	v

2 Complete the sentences with a phrasal verb from activity 1. You may have to change the form of the verb.

1 It can be difficult for old people to ___*get about*___ when they can't walk very well.

2 I never seem to _____ anything – I always get caught!

3 So many companies nowadays use automatic answering systems – it takes ages to _____ to a real person.

4 It's easy to _____ an illness if you have a positive attitude.

5 What are you children _____ ? You look very guilty!

6 I _____ all the other students in my class. We've become really good friends.

1 The conversation below is mixed up. Work with a partner to number the lines in the correct order. The first line has been done for you. Then practise reading it aloud with your partner.

[1] A Let's go out tonight – we could go bowling.

[ ] B What did she say?

[ ] A Oh, I phoned her last night and I think she's already doing something else.

[ ] B That's a good idea – but what about Sue? Do you think we should invite her?

[ ] A Oh, well, maybe I misunderstood her.

[ ] B Right. We can go out with Sue another day.

[ ] A That's right. So I think we should go bowling without her.

[ ] B Anyway – you think she doesn't want to come with us, is that right?

[ ] A I think she said last night that she planned to go to the cinema with some friends.

[ ] B Really? She told me last week that she wanted to go out with us tonight.

2 Look at the conversation again and underline two ways of making a suggestion, three ways of agreeing, one way of giving your opinion and one way of checking if you understand something.

3 Now work with a partner. Make up your own conversation, following the ideas in the chart. Practise your conversation with your partner. Then act it out to the rest of the class.

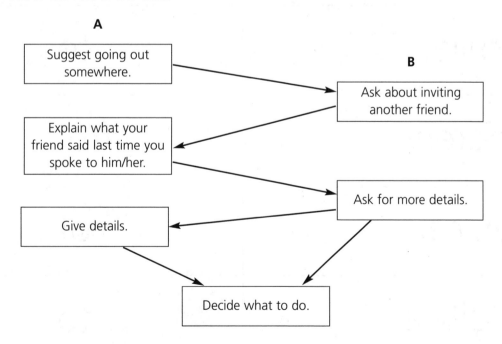

interested	in
worried	about
good	at
wrong	with
aware	of
afraid	of
similar	to
different	from
typical	of
sensitive	to

in	from
of	to

of	to
about	in

with	to
at	of

about	to
of	in

with	from
about	to

of	at
from	to

in	to
with	of

about	in
on	at

Complete these sentences using an adjective + preposition.

1 I love finding out about old things – I'm really i_____ history.

2 You look ill – what's w_____ _____ you?

3 Life in the country is very d_____ _____ life in the town.

4 He won lots of tournaments last year – he's really g _____ _____ tennis.

5 I'm not sure what to do about that new job – I'm really w_____ _____ it.

6 I can't go up tall buildings – I'm really f_____ _____ heights.

7 What kind of food do you think is t_____ _____ your country?

8 I usually like the same things as my sister – her interests are very s_____ _____ mine.

Label the picture. Use the jumbled words in the box to help you.

1 _____

2 _____

3 _____

4 _____

5 _____

6 _____

7 _____

8 _____

9 _____

10 _____

11 _____

13 _____

12 _____

22 _____

21 _____

20 _____

19 _____

18 _____

17 _____

16 _____

15 _____

14 _____

ram	gel	thecs	heldrous	striw	nalke	cenk	neek
are	horeefad	toof	blewo	sone	ginefr	nahd	
guntoe	kabc	eleh	eckhe	ibg eto	thumo	arhi	

arm	knee
ear	forehead
foot	elbow
wrist	nose
finger	ankle
hand	back
heel	cheek
tongue	shoulder
big toe	mouth
hair	leg

1 Match 1–5 with a–e to make dialogues.

1 I just can't do any more now. I'm so tired. I need a rest.

2 It's great news that you passed your exam with such a high grade!

3 I don't know what time he's arriving. Can you please watch for his taxi so that we don't miss him?

4 I feel so fed up. This rainy weather is really depressing!

5 I'm so happy. I've just discovered that I've won the competition and I'm going on a holiday to the USA!

a) Yes, it's really getting me down too. Maybe we need a holiday!

b) Well done. When do you set off? Can I come with you?

c) Yes, I hoped that I'd get through it with a good mark. I'm really pleased.

d) No problem. I'll certainly look out for him.

e) Me too. Let's sit down. I'm completely worn out!

2

Don't worry, it won't take you long to *get over* it. It's only a cold.	I'm sorry, I'm not sure what the answer is. Can I *look into* it and call you back?
No, I'm sorry, I can't. I want to *look over* my notes before I go to bed.	You should *take up* a hobby. That would give you something to do at weekends.
I think that you always *take on* too much work. You should try to relax more!	I think you should buy a newer car. That one looks as if it might *break down*!
I can't tell you what it means. Why don't you *look* it *up* in the dictionary?	If the noise is very bad then you should complain. Don't *put up with* it.
You should *put on* some warm clothes if you're going out. It's cold today!	Oh dear, I'm sorry to hear that. It's always difficult when you *break up with* a girlfriend.

There are ten cats in this picture. Where are they? Can you find them all?

Student A

Find and correct
ten mistakes in
Andy's letter.

Dear Jenny

Thank you for your letter. I have ever been to Edinburgh, but it sounds
a very interesting place to visit! I would like to go there some days.

I'd been quite busy since we last met. I went to visit Michael on
Saturday and we have been to the cinema. Then we had a meal in that
Italian restaurant nearby the market square. Have you ever eaten
there? It was rather crowding, but the food was good and the service
was fast. The waitress was very politeness and friendly, although she
had an Italian accent which was difficult to understand! And, the
meal was very enjoyable.

Did you seen the new Spielberg film yet? If you haven't seen it, then
we could go together next week. It looks very excited!

That's all for now. Give me a ring next week and we'll arrange to go out
together.

All the best

Andy

Student B

Find and correct ten
mistakes in Andy's
letter.

Dear Jenny

Thank you for your letter. I have never been to Edinburgh, but it sounds
a very interested place to visit! I would like to go there one day.

I've been quite busy since we've last met. I went to visit Michael on
Saturday and we went to the cinema. Then we have had a meal in that
Italian restaurant near the market square. Have you ever eat there? It
was rather crowded, but the food was good and the service has been
fast. The waitress was very polite and friendly, so she had an Italian
accent which was difficult to understand! However, the meal was very
enjoying.

Have you seen the new Spielberg film just? If you haven't seen it, then
we could to go together next week. It looks very exciting!

That's all for now. Give me a ring next week and we'll arrange going out
together.

All the best

Andy

1   How many syllables? Put the words in the box into the correct column. The
first one has been done for you.

| teacher   communicate   university   completely   region   explosion |
| confident   magazine   intelligent   conversation   amazing   adjective |
| relax   whistle   negotiate   video   perfect   mountainous   examination |
| phrase   competition   professional   football   question   ways |

One syllable	Two syllables	Three syllables	Four syllables	Five syllables
	teacher			

2   Say all the words aloud and underline the word that has a different stress
from the pattern at the start of the line.

e.g. ●●	teacher	<u>hotel</u>	table	tennis
1 ●●●	chemistry	umbrella	probably	animal
2 ●●●	September	October	January	November
3 ●●	lesson	spider	challenge	amount
4 ●●●●	independent	professional	information	disadvantage
5 ●●	language	enough	forget	correct
6 ●●●	incomplete	cigarette	Portuguese	computer

Mark the stress on all the words. Then practise saying them with your partner.

Student A

A   I love going to the cinema, and there are so many good films on at the moment.

B   _____

A   ☐ Really? Why was it so good?

    ☐ Really? What was wrong with it?

B   _____

A   ☐ Oh dear! How long was it?

    ☐ Great! I like films like that.

B   _____

A   ☐ Well, I like lots of people. It really depends on the film.

    ☐ What a pity! But never mind – come with me next time. I'll choose a good film.

B   _____

✂ -

Student B

A   _____

B   ☐ Yes, I agree. I saw a brilliant film last night – that horror film with Matt Damon.

    ☐ That's true, but actually I saw rather a bad film last night – that one with Tom Hanks.

A   _____

B   ☐ Oh, it was too long, and really boring.

    ☐ Well, it had a lot of action ...

A   _____

B   ☐ The scenery was superb, too. And Matt Damon's such a good actor. Which actors do you like?

    ☐ Oh, I can't remember. It seemed very long. I almost fell asleep in the middle.

A   _____

B   ☐ Yes, I know what you mean. Let's go together next time – you can choose the film.

    ☐ Great idea! Maybe I'll enjoy it more.

Complete the sentences with your own ideas.

1 If I won a lot of money, I _____
   _____ because _____
   ._____ .

2 If I could do anything I wanted, I _____
   _____ because _____
   _____ .

3 If I could meet one famous person, I _____
   _____ because _____
   _____ .

4 If I had to live in another country, I _____
   _____ because _____
   _____ .

5 If I could have any pet I wanted, I _____
   _____ because _____
   _____ .

6 If I could be good at one sport, I _____
   _____ because _____
   _____ .

7 If I could eat a special meal, I _____
   _____ because _____
   _____ .

8 If I could go to a special place, I _____
   _____ because _____
   _____ .

You are on holiday at an adventure school in the mountains. You have gone on a five-day white-water canoeing trip. Apart from the trip leader, none of you have ever done this before, and you are not very good at it. You need a lot of help. You have three canoes, with two people in each. On the first day, your leader finds that his mobile phone is broken and you can't make contact with your school. You decide to continue with the trip because you are expected to arrive at a meeting point down the river in four days' time. Suddenly, the weather changes and you have to put up your tents and take shelter from torrential rain. Overnight the weather gets worse and two of the tents are washed away down the river. Everyone has to share the other two tents. The path beside the river is so muddy that you can't walk along it, so you can only travel by canoe. The water in the river is moving very fast because of the heavy rain. You have enough food, and so you decide to continue down the river in the canoes to the meeting point, which is three days away. That day one of the canoes hits a rock and the leader breaks his arm. The canoe has a big hole in it. You all sit down and decide what to do.

You can:
• wait for someone to come and find you.
• send some people ahead to canoe for three days to the meeting point.
• try to send someone back up the river to the adventure school, two days away.
• Anything else?

Discuss what to do, giving good reasons for your ideas. As a group, decide what is the best thing to do. Use the expressions below.

Asking for ideas	Suggesting ideas	Disagreeing with ideas	Agreeing with ideas	Deciding what to do
OK, so what do you think we should do? Has anyone got any ideas? What do you think?	If we ... then we ... I think we should ... Why don't we ...? We could ...	That's a good idea, but ... I don't think that's a good idea because ... I don't really agree with that because ...	That's a good idea because ... Yes, I agree with you.	So we're going to ... So we all agree that the best thing to do is ...

Explain your ideas to the rest of the class.

run

limp

stagger

walk

jump

crawl

hop

slide

skip

dance

jog

stroll

In groups, decide on the best answer to the following questions.

 1 What is the worst thing to do if you are bitten by a poisonous snake?

    A wash the bite with water

    B suck out the poison

    C kill the snake

 2 What is the best way to survive an attack by a shark?

    A try to swim away

    B hit the shark back

    C shout loudly

 3 What is the most difficult thing to do in an earthquake?

    A stay indoors

    B put out fires

    C avoid things falling on you

 4 What is the worst thing to do if you are attacked by a bear?

    A stay still

    B climb a tree

    C hit the bear back

 5 Which is the most sensible advice if you have frostbite?

    A warm up as quickly as possible using hot water

    B rub the skin quickly

    C take painkillers

Which group got the most answers right?

Which group got the most answers wrong?

My friends want me to go out with them tonight but I don't want to go.

I have to buy a present for my brother's birthday but I don't have much money.

I should visit my grandmother this weekend but I want to play football.

I have a new friend, but my parents don't like her.

I have an exam next week and I feel really nervous about it – I can't sleep.

I want some new clothes but I don't have enough money to buy any.

I'm going for an interview for a job but I don't know what I should wear.

I want a new hairstyle but I don't know what hairstyles suit me.

I want to learn how to cook.

I want to get fit.

I want to write to a penfriend in England but I don't know how to arrange it.

I want to learn another language but I don't know what the best way to learn is.

games

party   food

computer

experience

machinery

photographic

famous   unforgettable

pack

reminder

suitcase   person

memory

friend

technique   school

touch

in

Compare and contrast these two pictures.

Restaurants in the city are expensive. A meal costs about £15.	There are a lot of cheap takeaway restaurants where you can get a meal for about £3.	The Museum of History is free. It is open until 5 p.m.	There is a sightseeing tour of the city by bus. It takes two hours and costs £5.
The Art Gallery has a special exhibition. It costs £7, but students can get in for £5.	There is a street market which sells cheap souvenirs.	There is a zoo. It costs £10 and has a lot of unusual animals.	There is a wonderful park, which is free. It has a special picnic area.
There is a castle just outside the city which you can reach by bus in 30 minutes. The single bus fare is £1. Entrance to the castle is £5 and £3.50 for students.	You can buy a special ticket for £5 which you can use on all buses and trains for the whole day.	You can hire bicycles for the day, which cost £5.	There is a swimming pool and leisure centre with a gym. A day ticket costs £5.
You can take a boat trip on the river. It takes three hours and costs £10, including lunch on the boat.	There is an afternoon concert of classical music in the park, which is free.	There is a football match in the afternoon in a magnificent new stadium. Tickets cost £15.	There is a special cinema with a huge screen showing the newest films. Tickets cost £6.

In groups, look at the cards and make your plan for a day trip in a city.
Remember you must:

• visit at least _____ places

• not spend more than £ _____

• stay together

Plan for the day

Time	Activity	Reason	Cost £
Start time: _____ _____ _____ _____ _____ Finish time: _____	*Arrive in city*	*Start of trip*	 Total cost: _____

Agreeing

Yes, I agree with that.

That's a good idea.

Why not?

Disagreeing

No, I don't like that idea.

I'm sorry, I can't agree.

Making suggestions

Why don't we ...?

What do you think about ...?

Shall we ...?

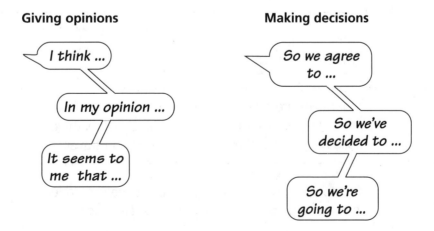

Giving opinions

I think ...

In my opinion ...

It seems to me that ...

Making decisions

So we agree to ...

So we've decided to ...

So we're going to ...

A

Yes, I agree with that because …	No, I don't like that idea because …
Why don't we …?	That's a good idea because …
It seems to me that …	OK, but what do you think about …?
I'm sorry, I can't agree as …	That's a shame because …
Well, in my opinion …	That's a good point, but …
Why not? I think that …	It's difficult to say, because …
I can't agree with that because …	Really? I think that …
What a good idea! We could …	That's a problem because …

B

No one should be allowed to smoke in public.	There are too many cars on the road.	People shouldn't get married until they are over thirty.	Football is a dangerous game.
Children shouldn't have to go to school if they don't want to.	Chocolate is bad for you.	Travelling to other countries is a bad thing.	There are no classes today.
CDs are too expensive.	Everyone should be given a computer.	Travelling to other countries is a waste of time.	Everyone should have two holidays a year.
We should learn about other countries in the world at school.	Mountains are more interesting places for holidays than beaches.	It is vital to have a guidebook with you when you travel.	Souvenirs are a waste of money.
Sport is bad for you.	This town is an interesting place.	Everyone should learn to speak English.	Speaking English is easy.

The lines in this letter are mixed up. Number them in the correct order, and then decide how many paragraphs there should be.

Dear Keith

☐ a) *Then, if the weather is good, perhaps we could walk around the park and have a picnic lunch there.*

☐ b) *Thanks for emailing me last week – I was so pleased to hear from you. I'm writing a letter back because I'm having problems with my computer.*

☐ c) *First of all, it would be great if we could visit the new art gallery.*

☐ d) *Finally, in the evening I'd love to go to the cinema.*

☐ e) *I've heard that there are some really interesting new paintings there.*

☐ f) *I'd love to meet you in town next Saturday.*

☐ g) *If you haven't seen it either, then it would be fun to go together.*

☐ h) *If it's raining, then we could eat in a restaurant instead – something cheap like a pizza?*

☐ i) *You asked me if there was anything special I wanted to do. Well, I've got some ideas.*

☐ j) *What do you think? Let me know if you have any better ideas of things to do. I'm really looking forward to seeing you next week.*

☐ k) *I haven't seen the new James Bond film yet, and people say it's really good.*

Best wishes

Georgio

I think that everyone should have at least ten weeks' holiday a year.

There should be a computer on every child's desk in every school.

We should all recycle paper and cans and if we don't we should go to prison.

No one should be allowed to drive their own car. We should all use public buses.

No one should smoke until they are 25.

All children should wear school uniform.

Everyone should take up a new hobby every year.

There are too many tourists everywhere.

Music nowadays is very bad.

Everyone should leave their parents' home when they are 18 and live independently.

Violent films should not be shown on television or in the cinemas.

The government should pay parents of young children to stay at home and look after them.

Agreeing

I think that's right because …

I agree with that because …

I like that idea because …

That's an excellent idea because …

Disagreeing

I think that's wrong because …

I don't agree with that because …

I don't like that idea because …

That's a terrible idea because …

1   <u>Underline</u> the best word to complete these sentences.

1 I love the new *logo/mark* on the Nike T-shirts.

2 Companies always do *market/shop* research before they launch a new product.

3 *Consumers/Clients* have spent more money in general this year – in the shops, on holidays, and on entertainment.

4 People often choose to buy a particular *mark/brand* because it is famous.

5 Shop assistants should always be polite to their *consumers/customers*.

2   Which words in the box can you use to describe products a–d? Which adjective can be used with all four products?

a) a new soft drink

b) a new mobile phone

c) a new car

d) a new type of biscuit

```
fizzy   spacious   lightweight   crunchy
state-of-the-art   energy-boosting
value-for-money   refreshing   powerful
```

3   Now match the slogans to the products in activity 2.

1 Keep in touch.

2 You'll never be left behind.

3 It's the fizz that you'll remember.

4 Your coffee will be lonely without them.

4   You are going to plan your own TV advertisement. Choose a product from activity 2, or an idea of your own. First think about the product:

• Who is it for?

• What is its name?

• What's special about it?

• Where will people buy it?

• Why is it different from other products?

• Why do you think people will buy it?

• What could the slogan be?

Now think about the advertisement.

• What will it show? (The product in use? A funny story?)

• Who will be in it? (Anyone famous?)

• Where will it be set?

• Will there be any music?

TV advertisement proposal

Our product is a type of ....

It's for ....

It's called ....

It's special because ....

People will buy it (*say where*) ....

It's different because ....

....

People will buy it because ....

....

Our slogan is ....

....

Our TV advertisement will show ....

....

....

The people in it will be ....

It will be set in ....

The music will be ....